THE HOLLYWOOD SEQUEL

THE HOLLYWOOD SEQUEL

HISTORY & FORM, 1911–2010

STUART HENDERSON

A BFI book published by Palgrave Macmillan

First published in 2014 by
PALGRAVE MACMILLAN

on behalf of the
BRITISH FILM INSTITUTE
21 Stephen Street, London W1T 1LN
www.bfi.org.uk

There's more to discover about film and television through the BFI.
Our world-renowned archive, cinemas, festivals, films, publications and learning resources are
here to inspire you.

Palgrave Macmillan in the UK is an imprint of Macmillan Publishers Limited, registered in
England, company number 785998, of Houndmills, Basingstoke, Hampshire RG21 6XS. Palgrave
Macmillan in the US is a division of St Martin's Press LLC, 175 Fifth Avenue, New York, NY
10010. Palgrave Macmillan is the global academic imprint of the above companies and has
companies and representatives throughout the world. Palgrave® and Macmillan® are
registered trademarks in the United States, the United Kingdom, Europe and other countries.

Front cover design: Paul Johnstone
Designed by couch

Set by Cambrian Typesetters, Camberley, Surrey
Printed in China

This book is printed on paper suitable for recycling and made from fully managed and sustained
forest sources. Logging, pulping and manufacturing processes are expected to conform to the
environmental regulations of the country of origin.

British Library Cataloguing-in-Publication Data
A catalogue record for this book is available from the British Library
A catalog record for this book is available from the Library of Congress

ISBN 978–1–84457–651–7 (pb)
ISBN 978–1–84457–652–4 (hb)

CONTENTS

Acknowledgments

First, I must thank the University of Warwick, whose postgraduate scholarship provided the funding which made possible my undertaking of the PhD thesis on which this book is based. The thesis may never have come into being without Jon Burrows, who expertly guided me through the project from the beginning, even before I quite realised what it would be about. Jon asked all the right questions, offered expert advice and an unflagging engagement with every aspect of my research, and also gifted me with the phrase the 'McClane Principle', which became the structuring device for Chapter 6: for all of which, I am very grateful.

My historical research was hugely aided by the staff and curators at various libraries and archives, in particular: Sandra Joy Lee and Jonathan Auxier at the Warner Bros. Archive at USC; Barbara Hall at the Margaret Herrick Library; Ned Comstock at the Cinematic Arts Library at USC; Julie Graham and Simon Elliott at the UCLA Performing Arts Library; Mahnaz Gaznavi at the AFI's Louis B. Mayer Library; Clay Stalls at the William H. Hannon Library at Loyola Marymount University; and all of the staff at the BFI Library, an essential resource for any film scholar. Wes Craven, Joe Dante and Jay Baker at CAA were each very generous in giving me interview time and an insider's view of sequel production. Thanks must also go to Shannon Fifer at Warner Bros. and David F. Miller at Fox, who kindly granted permission for me to access and quote from their respective studio archives.

Facilitating my time in the archives were Ian Newman, Kate Marshall, Jules Claassen, Carla Henderson and T. W. Leshner, all of whom generously accommodated me during my time in Los Angeles; and Lorsen and Susan Camps, who kindly provided a home from home in Earlsdon.

Will Clarke and Danny Perkins offered invaluable support, and generously allowed me to keep my hand in the professional world of film distribution while I re-engaged with academia. Nizam Ali kindly gave over a huge amount of free time, typesetting the original text and making everything look considerably smarter. When it came to cover design for the book itself, both Ben Parker and Paul Johnstone were instrumental in achieving the right look and feel. Both Jon Ashton and James Zborowski read drafts of the thesis, and provided excellent critical commentary and insight. Jon and James are among the many friends and colleagues (both at the University of Warwick and Studiocanal) who have kindly discussed sequels with me, offering up much food for thought along the way, in particular: Hannah Andrews, Bea Appleby, Emilie Barra, J. Blakeson, Charlotte Brunsdon, Catherine Constable, Paul Cuff, Jon Davenport, Giles Hanson, Cynthia Rice Hanson, Tom Hughes, Paul Johnstone, Benjamin Lee, James MacDowell, Nick McKay, Richard Nowell, Richard Overall, Ben Parker, Michael Piggott, Mike Riding, John Rodden, Anna Sloan, Hugh Spearing, Tom Steward, Emily Want and James Whitfield.

When it came to turning the thesis into a book, José Arroyo, Jon Burrows, Peter Krämer, Steve Neale, Peter Stanfield and James Whitfield all offered invaluable advice and support. At BFI Publishing/Palgrave, thanks must go to Rebecca Barden for seeing the project's initial potential and to Jenni Burnell for expertly (and patiently) guiding me through the process.

I am eternally grateful to my parents, Cliff and Jenny Henderson, who encouraged my rampant cinephilia from the beginning, and indulged my no doubt exhausting excitement over the release of *Return of the Jedi* (1983), the first sequel I saw at the cinema. Finally, I must thank Eric Anderson, whose unflagging love and support, and willingness to sit with me through the lousy films as well as the good ones, has made it all far more enjoyable than it might have been.

'Here we go again … again': Introducing the Hollywood sequel

One of the three fictional trailers which begin the Hollywood satire *Tropic Thunder* (2008) advertises *Scorcher VI: Global Meltdown*, starring Tugg Speedman (Ben Stiller). Accompanied by apocalyptic images of Earth engulfed in flames, a stereotypically gruff male voiceover reminds us that 'one man' saved the world from annihilation not only in *Scorcher*, but also in *Scorcher II*, *III*, *IV* and *V* – the camera zooming in to reveal Speedman standing heroically atop some burning rock, holding a huge gun in one hand and a baby in the other. 'Now,' the voiceover continues, 'the one man who made a difference five times before, is about to make a difference, again. Only this time, it's different.' The trailer proceeds to reveal the world encased in ice, with the camera again zooming in to show Speedman atop a rock, this time in arctic gear, with not one but two guns in his hands and two babies strapped to his chest. As the trailer cuts to reveal the title of the film, we hear Speedman wearily intone: 'Here we go again … again.'

It may exaggerate certain movie marketing tropes for comedic purposes, but this trailer also encapsulates much of what is fascinating about the nature of the sequel – for while it satirises the formulaic nature of some Hollywood follow-ups, it also tacitly acknowledges our own appetite, as audiences, to come back for more. And, while we are often led to believe this is a contemporary phenomenon, the commercial impulse the *Scorcher VI* trailer sends up has in fact been a fixture in Hollywood for nearly 100 years, with the first feature-length sequels emerging in the 1910s. Yet, despite its enduring popularity with both producers and audiences, the sequel has been given remarkably short shrift by academic film studies.

Intended as a corrective to this oversight, this book will provide both a chronological account of the sequel's persistent presence in American cinema over the past century, and a consideration of its recurrent identifying features as a narrative art-form. Underlying this book as a whole are three key questions:

1. What are the recurring formal characteristics of the sequel in all its variations in North American cinema?
2. To what extent have these characteristics changed over time?
3. How are these changes related to the shifts in the economic and industrial structures of the American film industry?

As both the phrasing of these questions and the title of this book suggest, I intend here to pay attention to matters of both history and form. Striking this balance is crucial because scholars have tended to forgo detailed discussion of the sequel's form, in favour of making under-researched statements about its ideological implications and its place in film history. This ahistoricism arguably stems from the sequel's role in the debate about what constitutes con-temporary, 'postclassical' Hollywood cinema and, more broadly, from the problem of definition, of answering the question: 'What is a sequel?'

A critical absence: history and form

Although the sequel has, until recent years, been given little dedicated attention, this is not to say that the films themselves have been ignored – as the voluminous material on *Aliens* (1986), *Terminator 2: Judgment Day* (1991), and *The Matrix* films (1999–2003) and *The Lord of the Rings* (2001–3) trilogies attests – but the bulk of this criticism takes little interest in their status *as* sequels, choosing instead to focus on their place within a director's body of work, their repre-sentations of gender and so on. In the 1990s, the sequel became more visible in relation to debates around what constituted the 'new' or 'post classical' Hollywood, with scholars such as Thomas Schatz and Timothy Corrigan invoking the form as symptomatic of industrial and aes-thetic shifts within the industry after 1975. For Schatz, sequels and series were a clear sign of 'an upswing in defensive market tactics', part of a larger 'conservative turn' in the industry, which saw a reduction in the number of 'innovative and offbeat films' being produced.[1] For Corrigan, they represented a more fundamental formal shift, being indicators of a 'wasting and evacua-tion of contemporary narrative', which tailor themselves to 'a distracted and interrupted view-ing'.[2] Needless to say, in linking the rise of the sequel to an ideological shift, writers such as Corrigan have not usefully contributed to an understanding of the sequel's longstanding role in Hollywood history. In this respect the academy has marched in step with popular criticism of the sequel, which has been widespread and persistent since the late 1970s and has mani-fested itself in writing by – among many others – Vincent Canby, Stephen M. Silverman, James Monaco, Janet Maslin, Peter Rainer, Richard Corliss, Julie Salamon and J. Hoberman, whose oft-quoted review of Hollywood from 1975 to 1985 decried the bout of 'sequelitis' which had sup-posedly afflicted the industry in that decade.[3]

Too often, it seems, the history of the sequel has been subsumed or obscured by other histories. Even Roger Hagedorn's otherwise insightful essay on the history of the serial form cites films we might otherwise understand to be sequels (*Aliens, The Jewel of the Nile* [1985]) in order to make the point that 'contemporary cinema has also returned to the serial'.[4] Given that the literary sequel predates or is at least contemporaneous with the serial in fiction, one could argue that the films Hagedorn quotes are drawing as much on a tradition dating back to *Don Quixote: Part II* (1615) as they are on the serials from early cinema or the serialised fiction of Dickens and Balzac which helped drive newspaper sales in the nineteenth century.

More recently, Peter Krämer, Steve Neale and Sheldon Hall have all made efforts to cor-rect such ahistorical assumptions about sequelisation, but these are brief comments within studies whose objects of study are broader than the sequel itself.[5] Both Neale and Krämer quote Thomas Simonet's survey of what he terms 'recycled-script films' between 1940 and 1979,[6] in which he concludes that 'there were approximately six times as many recycled-script films in the 1940s as in the 1970s'.[7] Due to its 1979 end-point, this otherwise invaluable research is of limited use in dispelling assumptions about the intensification of sequel produc-tion from the 1980s onwards. Assumptions about the contemporaneous nature of the sequel have thus persisted in subsequent criticism, whether it be in the general historical thrust of writing by Justin Wyatt or Winston Wheeler Dixon, who stress Hollywood's increased reliance on 'pre-sold' properties, or in specific references to the sequel by Kristin Thompson and Michael Allen.[3]

To be or not to be continued: the question of definition

If accounts of the sequel's history in film studies are flawed, discussion of its form was practically nonexistent until around 2008. Kristin Thompson, Michael Allen and Thomas Simonet have each offered definitions of the sequel in relation to the series and the serial, but all are forced to concede that these are largely speculative or cursory. More recently, Carolyn Jess-Cooke has provided a definition which arguably mystifies more than it clarifies: 'whereas seriality and series defy change, the sequel champions difference, progress and excess'.[9] Jess-Cooke quotes examples such as the James Bond films (1962–) and *The Perils of Pauline* (August–November 1914) in which 'the protagonists never age, never (re)marry, never switch jobs', subsequently adding that 'genre-driven series' such as *Star Wars* (1977) and *Star Trek: The Motion Picture* (1979) are 'strictly devoted to the playing out of a "narrative scheme that remains constant"'. These statements, in tandem with these examples, do little but muddy the semantic water. The series in cinema might well be described as defying change, but can we really apply the same logic to the serial, with *Pauline*'s 'cliffhanger' device clearly setting it apart from the series format?[10] Similarly, if the *Star Wars* and *Star Trek* sequels are in *some* respects committed to reiterating a particular narrative scheme, we cannot ignore that they also have storylines which develop from one film to the next.[11] More nuanced definitions have begun to emerge in recent years, from writers such as Jennifer Forrest and Constantine Verevis, but again these have usually been in service of discussions centring around other, related forms such as the film trilogy and the series film.[12]

In order to get more fully to grips with the slippery nature of the cinematic sequel, it is worth briefly considering writing about its literary counterpart. As with film, most accounts of these literary sequels take little interest in their status *as* sequels,[13] but there are a handful of exceptions to this general drift – in particular the work of Gérard Genette, Christopher Paul Richards and Umberto Eco.[14] Although he never uses the term 'sequel', instead choosing to dub it the 'retake', Eco's essay entitled 'Innovation and Repetition: Between Modern and Post-Modern Aesthetics', nonetheless takes us to the heart of the matter. In the retake, he proposes, 'one recycles the characters of a previous successful story in order to exploit them, by telling what happened to them after the end of their first adventure'.[15] This, in basic terms, is what distinguishes the sequel from other, similar narrative forms – and yet it is not quite sufficient. Providing a working, workable definition of the sequel, I would suggest, requires looking at both textual and extratextual factors, primarily in terms of the context and patterns of a film's distribution and exhibition. It also requires that we clear away some of the semantic clutter surrounding the term 'sequel', specifically by distinguishing it from the other terminology with which it is often either used in conjunction or deemed to be interchangeable: the *series*, the *serial*, the *franchise*, the *saga*, the *trilogy* and indeed, on occasion, the *remake*.

In short, the defining characteristic of the sequel is its acknowledgment of a chronological narrative relationship with a prior instalment. This 'acknowledged chronology' is what distinguishes the sequel from the 'series film', which was particularly prevalent in the 1930s and 1940s, and was exemplified by the B-grade detective series featuring characters such as Charlie Chan, Mr Moto and Sherlock Holmes, and which has historically been the formal template for the James Bond films. The dividing line between the sequel and the series film is this: while both forms revisit characters from an earlier episode, the latter can be identified primarily by its general lack of commitment to maintaining narrative continuity from one instalment to the next. As Jennifer Forrest has observed, 'the series ostensibly belongs to an eternal present'[16] – and yet, as will become clear in Chapter 2, there are certain series films, particularly those dealing with the vagaries of family life, which in fact display a level of commitment to episode-to-episode continuity. By the same token, some films commonly understood as sequels demonstrate a disregard for continuity which aligns them more clearly with the series format. In the Heat of the Night (1967), for example, tells us that its protagonist, police detective Virgil Tibbs (Sidney Poitier), works for the Philadelphia force and that he is unmarried. In the sequel, They Call Me MISTER Tibbs! (1970), however, Tibbs is working for the San Francisco force ('We've got twelve good years invested in you', notes his police chief boss) and is married with two children, one of whom, his wayward son Andy (George Spell), appears close to adolescence.

The distinction between the sequel and the serial is more overtly marked, although the difference here is less one of narrative form than it is of the context of distribution and consumption. Like the sequel, an individual episode within a serial tends to explicitly follow or build from events in previous episodes. Unlike the sequel, however, whether printed in a newspaper, shown at a cinema, or broadcast on radio or television, the serial format is defined by its regular and relatively frequent supply of short episodes. Now, of course, we have a far greater degree of control over when and how many episodes of a serial we consume in one sitting, and Netflix's recent innovation with series such as House of Cards (2013) takes that approach one step further,[17] but the format remains primarily identifiable on those terms, and it has had little or no place on the big screen since the arrival of television in the early 1950s. Sequels, conversely, are feature length and appear months or years rather than days or weeks apart, and so tend to carry with them a greater importance than any single episode of a series or serial.

As for the trilogy, the franchise, the saga and indeed the spin-off, while each of these terms is frequently used to collectively describe a group of films rather than an individual work, this does not negate the fact that in most cases that group of films contains one or more sequels. It seems appropriate to describe the Twilight films (2008–12) as a saga, for example, because it consists of a predetermined number of episodes, thus distinguishing it from the ongoing Fast and Furious series (2001–) or the Pirates of the Caribbean franchise (2003–). This does not undermine the fact that the second episode is the sequel to that first film, and the third episode is the sequel to both of those preceding instalments. Similarly, while I agree to some extent with Claire Perkins and Constantine Verevis's statement that the 'film trilogy is a form that is practiced and perceived as distinct', I will also go on to argue that, while it is important to distinguish between a preconceived trilogy such as The Lord of the Rings and one which was created ad hoc, the manner in which the narratives of The Two Towers (2002) and The Return of the King (2003) are interlinked is not fundamentally different from the manner in which Spider-Man 2 (2004) and Spider-Man 3 (2007) function in relation to Spider-Man (2002).[18] In other words, the second and third, or indeed fourth and fifth, instalments in a numerically determinate group of films – a quadrilogy, quintology, septology and so on – are as legitimately labelled sequels as a standalone follow-up such as *The Son of Kong* (1933) or *Sister Act 2: Back in the Habit* (1993).

At the most basic level, then, the cinematic sequel is a film which is defined by a dual form of temporal relationship. The first part of that relationship exists at the formal, or textual, level: the events a sequel portrays occur *after* the events of a previous film and, even if there is little causal connection between these two sets of events, it is made clear that there is a chrono-logical relationship between them. The second part of that relationship is extratextual. As in the fictional world, the sequel as a film, as an event in the real world, occurs after the original. More to the point, the relative infrequency and feature-length narrative format which are com-monly associated with the sequel (as opposed to episodes within a serial) mean that the form has historically had to succeed on its own terms, both as a narrative artwork and a commer-cial enterprise. The prequel is so called precisely because it inverts only the former part of this temporal relationship: in extratextual terms it is a sequel to a previous film, but at a textual level it tells a story which precedes that of the original. The term 'spin-off' is perhaps the most prob-lematic, because it is commonly used to describe the follow-up to a successful film in another medium (particularly in the form of a television show based on a film, or vice versa), and because it might well tell a story which takes place after the events of the original, thus fulfill-ing my dual criteria of a fictional world and real-world chronology. The core distinctions here are that the spin-off tends to follow characters which were either previously subsidiary or parts of an ensemble (*Ma and Pa Kettle* [1949], *X-Men Origins: Wolverine* [2009]), and that it has the (often unfulfilled) potential to depict events which are happening in parallel to the ongoing story of the central protagonist.[19]

If this definition seems to state the obvious, that is because of the prevalence of confused, imprecise writing about the sequel both in academic film studies and elsewhere. This situa-tion has no doubt been exacerbated because exceptions to any rule governing the form of the sequel are very easy to come by. *The Godfather: Part II* (1974) is both a sequel and a pre-quel to its predecessor. *Halloween III: Season of the Witch* (1983) bears no narrative relation to the first two films, carrying over only the basic premise, as is the case with *Final Destination 3* (2006). Are the movie versions of *McHale's Navy* (1964) and *Sex and the City* (2008–) sequels to the TV series which spawned them? Should we class the two adaptations of Louisa May Alcott's *Little Men* (1934 and 1997) as sequels, to the 1933 and 1994 versions of *Little Women*, despite there being no connection between the talent involved in either? And if a film with no narrative or character-based connection to an earlier film is marketed as its sequel, as *Adrift* (2005) was to *Open Water* (2003) in some countries, does that mean it is a sequel, despite all of the textual evidence to the contrary? Faced with such multifarious problem cases, we have to accept that sequel status is a historically dynamic designation, and that the boundaries of any definition between the sequel, the series, the serial and the saga will always be highly porous. There *are* boundaries, nonetheless; working definitions which producers and audiences jointly recognise and which have in fact changed very little in the past century. The definition I have advanced, therefore, is neither absolute nor free of histor-ical specificities, but it does provide a working base from which to consider the particulari-ties of the sequel form over time.

One thing after another: history and form

In approaching the sequel, I have sought to produce a history which remains attentive to questions of form, and a poetics of the form which is consistently grounded in the material, historical reality of the industrial context in which these films were produced and distributed.[20] The first half of this book is dedicated to a chronological account of sequel production in North America (which from hereon in will be referred to as 'Hollywood')[21] from 1911–2010, the intention being not only to offer a more nuanced picture of the many and varied ways in which sequelisation has been deployed by the industry over the past century, but also to establish a foundation for some of the broader formal and aesthetic issues which I address thereafter. Chapter 1 begins with an account of some of early American cinema's recurring characters, before considering the growth of the sequel in tandem with that of the feature film. Picking up after the synch-sound revolution, Chapter 2 considers the multifarious roles of the sequel within a vertically integrated studio system whose contractual hold over creative talent offered a broad range of options for capitalising on a prior success. Chapter 3 notes that the period from 1955 through to 1975 saw a brief decline in all forms of cinematic seriality, and seeks to explain why this might have been so in relation to the rise of television. Last, Chapter 4 considers the sequel's shifting role as the major studios became part of multimedia conglomerates in the 1980s, tracing a haphazard progression towards the franchise-orientated landscape of 2010, driven in no small part by the impact of home video. Drawing on interviews, studio records, trade journals and fan magazines, each chapter balances an overview of the trends in sequelisation with individual case studies, the latter including the Thin Man series (1934–47), *The Bells of St. Mary's* (1945), *Planet of the Apes* and its sequels (1968–73), and the *A Nightmare on Elm Street* series (1984–94), situating the films discussed within the broader contexts of both industrial change and other contemporaneous forms of seriality, from silent serials in the 1910s through to the increase in direct-to-video sequels that accompanied the DVD boom at the turn of the millennium. In order to add further ballast to this section, I have undertaken a survey of all sequel and series film production in Hollywood from 1911–2009, groundwork which allows me to make relatively informed statistical observations about sequel production trends over the past century.[22]

Building upon the historical context provided by the opening chapters, the second part of the book is dedicated to an examination of the Hollywood sequel's formal characteristics. Chapter 5 is primarily concerned with the manner in which the sequel form differs from and implicitly challenges the notions of closure and the unitary work of art which inform the classical Hollywood paradigm. Chapter 6 addresses the pleasures a sequel might offer which are not specifically related to narrative continuation, in particular the interaction between star persona and character, and the prevalence of a knowing self-referentiality. Finally, Chapter 7 examines the form's repetitious tendencies, interrogating the relationship between genre and the sequel in relation to convention, expectation and formula.

In placing equal emphasis on history and aesthetics, I aim both to develop a typology of the sequel form, and to build a more complete picture of the many ways in which Hollywood has sought to repeat its previous successes, the historically specific conditions which have governed these repetitions, and the compositional norms which have resulted. One of the reasons that such ground has yet to be covered, I would suggest, is that film scholars – whether inclined towards the study of film as an art, a business or both – have tended to assume that a seemingly unitary cause, the commercial success of a film, leads to a similarly unitary effect: a sequel to that film. We know that sequel production (in Hollywood at least) is all about following the money, and that the films themselves tend towards the formulaic, offering audiences more of the same. The reality is that the measures of a film's success are specific to the organisation of the industry at any given time, and that the manner in which one might capitalise on such a success has varied accordingly. In the account which follows, therefore, it is my intention to demonstrate that one cause can have many effects; that, in terms of both the sequel's history and its form, there is more than one answer to the question: 'What happened next?'

PART I | *HISTORY*

1 | Early sequels, 1911–28

Before movies told coherent stories with recognisable characters, they could not present the sequels to those stories. From this basic but fundamental assumption, it follows that the early history of the sequel in American cinema necessarily intertwines with the history of narrative's role in the medium. Just when fictional narrative became the dominant impulse remains a matter of considerable debate, with Charles Musser arguing that 'story films' had become the central product of the American film industry by the summer of 1904; a periodisation which conflicts with Tom Gunning's influential notion that a 'cinema of attractions', concerned less with telling stories than 'presenting a series of views to an audience', dominated until around 1906–7.[1] Either way, the primacy of narrative form was not the sole precondition for the emergence of the cinematic sequel. Rather, the sequel in its fullest sense could not come into being until there was an incentive for both producers and exhibitors to differentiate their product, and an environment in which each individual film emerged as an autonomous cultural and commercial commodity.

Effective product differentiation could only be achieved if producers had at least a modicum of control over the exhibition of their films and, if a film's sequel status is established in part via what Gérard Genette would call paratextual markers (title, advertising and publicity), then early film manufacturers were at a considerable disadvantage.[2] Until around 1906, films in the United States were exhibited in a broad range of venues, none of which were dedicated to the screening of motion pictures.[3] Often, film was part of a larger programme of entertainment, meaning both that audiences were unlikely to be paying solely to see moving pictures, and that producers had very little control over the context in which they were presented. With few permanent, dedicated venues, the notion of a repeat audience for moving pictures was yet to take hold, meaning that exhibitors could make no firm assumptions about what their audience had or hadn't previously seen. The Nickelodeon boom between 1905 and 1908[4] may have solved some of these issues, and encouraged the growth of the story film,[5] but it also continued the vaudeville traditions of showmanship and variety, with the theatre manager free to create a programme of entertainment and provide contextual information as he wished. There was, in other words, only limited economic value in producing a sequel when there was still no guarantee that it would either be advertised or presented as such. Until it became standard practice for audiences to pay to see specific narrative films starring particular performers, or at least until it became clear to exhibitors and producers that this is what audiences were doing, there would be little impetus to directly capitalise on the popularity of any one film with a direct follow-up. This is not to suggest that manufacturers were disinclined to exploit successes where possible, as the race between Vitagraph and Edison to dupe films by Méliès,[6] alongside Edwin S. Porter's remakes of competitors' hits,[7] make clear. Nonetheless, there could be little in the way of systematic exploitation until the pattern of supply and demand – and the relationship between audiences, exhibitors, distributors and producers – was more formally regulated.

It is perhaps unnecessary to point out that the early history of the sequel involves exhibition and distribution practices as much as it does production trends, but it is only because of the creeping standardisation in all three areas at this time, leading up to and then on from the incorporation of the Motion Picture Patents Company in 1908, that the sequel as we now understand it came to be a valuable commodity. There is evidently a complex interaction between these forces and the demands of the audiences they jointly sought, and I do not want to imply that any one set of interests carried the day in the cultivation of the form. Nor should we assume some kind of teleological march towards the emergence of the sequel. What follows will briefly survey the period prior to 1912, stressing that both the notion of protracted storytelling and recurring characters (or something resembling them) are evident from the outset: an indication that the constituent parts of the sequel as we now understand it were in existence some time before the rise of the standalone feature film facilitated their coalescence.

Before 1912: character and story

Whereas the default explanation for contemporary Hollywood's reliance on the adaptation of popular existing material is that it guarantees audiences will turn up, Charles Musser identifies the pre-1908 reliance on popular stories, songs and comic strips as one of three means by which manufacturers sought to make their films comprehensible to audiences, suggesting that 'most films worked within a highly specific, well-known cultural framework'.[8] In Musser's account, the reliance on pre-existing source material was, of course, just as commercially motivated as it is today (audiences weren't likely to think favourably of movies they found incomprehensible), but it represents a means to a subtly different end. Still, it seems unlikely that audience comprehension was the sole driving force behind the trend for adapting existing material, as evidenced by the numerous movies drawing on comic strips, which represent some of the earliest examples of recurring characters (as opposed to *character types*) in cinema.

Among these were the *Happy Hooligan* films, twenty-five of which were released between 1900 and 1903, the first eight of which starred J. Stuart Blackton and were produced by Vitagraph;[9] Biograph's three *Alphonse and Gaston* pictures from 1903, both based on comic strips of the same name by Frederick Opper; the five-scene adaptation of Carl E. Schultze's *Foxy Grandpa* strip (and subsequent musical revue) into five scenes starring Joseph Hart, produced by American Mutoscope and Biograph in 1902;[10] and the five *Buster Brown* scenes shot for Edison in 1904 by Edwin S. Porter, taken from the strip by Richard Felton Outcault.

There were, however, some crucial distinctions between, for example, Blackton's role as Happy Hooligan and the star–character pairings that came later. First, it is arguable that Happy Hooligan on film was less a straightforward adaptation of the titular comic strip, and more an amalgam of similar characters borrowing that name. Second, there was only a slim chance the audience would be aware of any casting consistency. Blackton probably never received a credit on screen or off, and the action was staged sufficiently far from the camera that positively identifying him as the figure in the Hooligan costume, and as the same figure seen in said costume in previous *Hooligan* entries, would have been extremely difficult. This latter issue was the result of a practice which was relatively standard until around the middle of 1909,[11] whereby such credits were rarely supplied by manufacturers or distributors, either on the film itself or in advertising, leaving the paying public in the dark about who they were watching in the fiction films of the period. It was not until the 1909–10 season that Edison, Vitagraph and other producers began regularly advertising their stars as such, with Biograph, home of the biggest names of the era, resisting until 1913.[12] If stars were credited, this was usually motivated by their association with either the legitimate theatre or, as was the case for Joseph Hart in the *Foxy Grandpa* films, with the specific production being reproduced for the camera. It was only after 1910, therefore, that audiences could routinely expect to be provided with *both* the names of the characters and the actors who played them.

This sporadic, uneven development of a star system was in some instances replicated when it came to notions of character consistency – even after the standardisation of on-screen credits. Perhaps the most famous example of this inconsistency is that of 'Broncho Billy', created by Gilbert M. Anderson, co-founder, with George K. Spoor, of the Essanay production company. Anderson wrote, directed and starred in numerous Essanay Westerns before appearing for the first time as the title character in *Broncho Billy's Redemption* (1910), an outlaw who redeems himself in the act of saving a father and daughter from dying on the prairie. He went on to appear as Broncho Billy in more than 100 films, becoming synonymous with the character. Only a handful of these films survive, but from the synopses collated by Anderson's biographer David Kiehn it is evident that little more than the character name was carried over from film to film.[13] Sometimes Billy is not an outlaw but a sheriff (*Broncho Billy's Christmas Deed* [1913]; *Broncho Billy Misled* [both 1915]), a ranger (*Broncho Billy and the Lumber King* [1915]), or a gold miner (*Broncho Billy and the Claim Jumpers* [1914]); sometimes he is settled (*Broncho Billy's Mistake* [1913]; *Broncho Billy's Mexican Wife* [1915]), while on other occasions he is a wandering drunk, or courting a girl played by Marguerite Clayton – who also on occasions played his wife.

Unlike the Essanay Westerns, Biograph's *Jones* series, directed by D. W. Griffith and released between December 1908 and August 1909, did maintain a level of consistency. Tom Gunning has suggested that the series 'signalled Biograph's wooing of middle class family audiences with a form of comedy unlikely to offend their sensibilities with slapstick rowdiness',[14] and we might further speculate that one of the features distinguishing these films from more 'disreputable' forms of comedy is the lip-service they paid to psychological realism in the form of character consistency. As played by John R. Cumpson and Florence Lawrence (both unbilled, although the latter become known as 'the Biograph Girl' shortly thereafter), the Joneses were also original creations, making this possibly the first film series to revisit characters over a series of episodes without recourse to pre-existing source material. There was nothing in the way of sequential development evident within the films themselves, each being a pretext for Mr Jones to comically upset (sometimes, but not always, intentionally) the equilibrium strived for by his wife, but they were consistent in situation, with their marriage always *in media res*. Despite the narrative stasis, the Biograph Bulletin entry for the last in the series, *Mrs Jones' Lover; or, 'I Want My Hat'*

(1909), reveals an assumed familiarity between the audience and the characters: 'We are all cognizant of the fact that our friend Jones is of a jealous disposition, for the little episode at the rehearsal of the Amateur Dramatic Club is still fresh in our minds.'[15] The colloquial, almost conspiratorial tone of this entry, referring back to the plot of *The Joneses' Have Theatricals* (1909), suggests that, while there is no explicit narrative continuation, the information regular viewers have retained about Mr Jones, accreted over the course of multiple films, will aid their comprehension and enhance their enjoyment of this latest entry. By striking this balance, in which characters do not develop but nonetheless become known quantities with associated traits, Griffith's films are absolutely typical of the series format which was quickly becoming a staple of film production in North America. And the Joneses were not alone: Kalem launched the *Girl Spy* series (devised by and starring Gene Gauntier) in 1909, which in turn encouraged Yankee to launch a series centring on a 'girl detective', commencing with *The Monogrammed Cigarette* in 1910. In both cases, each standalone film featured recurring, consistent characters in unconnected stories.

Although the evidence of recurring characters in early cinema underlines its reliance on other artworks, the practice of storytelling in instalments owes as much to technological and logistical restrictions unique to the form as it does to cultural and industrial norms. Predictable as it may be to attribute film-making innovations to D. W. Griffith, he would seem to be responsible for one of the first films billed as a sequel: *His Trust Fulfilled* (1911). A direct continuation of *His Trust*, released one week earlier, Griffith's film was in fact the second part of what the director intended to be a two-reeler running to nearly twenty minutes (or nearly 2,000 feet) in length. The two films follow the travails of George (Wilfred Lucas), a loyal slave whose Confederate colonel master is killed in the Civil War, leaving him to look after the master's widow and orphan daughter. The first culminates with George saving the two from a house fire started by Union soldiers and taking them, along with the colonel's sword, to shelter at his cabin. The second picks up four years later and concerns George's attempts to look after the now-adult daughter (Dorothy West) as she seeks an education and a husband, thus 'fulfilling his master's trust'. That Biograph was unwilling to take the risk of releasing such an unconventionally long film is not surprising, given that the whole industry was organised around the one-reel format until the middle of 1912.[16] Biograph therefore insisted that Griffith split the two reels and add explanatory subtitles at the beginning of each.[17] *His Trust*'s title frame is thus followed with a subtitle explaining that the film 'is the first part of a life story, the second part being "His Trust Fulfilled," and while the second is the sequel to the first, each part is a complete story in itself'. This attempt to acknowledge the films' interconnected nature while downplaying any interdependence was reiterated by the trade reviews, with *Moving Picture World* stating that *Fulfilled* was a 'story complete in itself yet really a continuation of the earlier release',[18] and *Motion Picture News* running reviews of both under an article entitled 'Two Notable Films'.[19] Regardless of Griffith's original intentions, these comments are more than publicity bluff, as the stories told in each reel can function independently of each other, especially given the four-year ellipsis between the end of the first and beginning of the second. At the same time, the fact that it was originally shot as a single piece indicates that, while *His Trust Fulfilled* did function as a sequel of sorts, its status is not uncomplicated. Aesthetically, the acknowledgment of the two-part structure at the beginning of *His Trust* alters the manner in which it is understood, and makes it the forefather to a contemporary saga such as *Kill Bill* (2003–4), which makes explicit its multi-part intentions from the outset, rather than after the fact.

Writing on the sequel in this period, Carolyn Jess-Cooke has suggested that film 'did not usually continue one text, as is common in the blockbuster era, but was commonly defined by its "promiscuous intermingling" and continuing of many source texts'.[20] What the *Jones* and *Girl Spy* series and the comic-strip adaptations indicate, however, is that manufacturers were, in fact, appealing directly to specific audience knowledge from very early on. But while recurring characters were a commonplace, attenuated narratives were not. *His Trust* was at least partially the result of Griffith's desire to tell a longer, more complex story; telling it in two parts was a commercial necessity rather than an artistic preference. From the outset, then, the sequel was both a tool for extended storytelling and a means of reducing a perceived commercial risk. Of course the nature of that risk in 1911 stemmed not from the pressures of saturation release patterns and ever-spiralling production costs we associate with contemporary Hollywood, but from justifiable concerns over the commercial viability of a longer film. The commingling of narrative concerns and commercial imperatives means that we might understand these early instances of attenuated storytelling as a single seed, out of which grew not one but two of the most important cinematic forms of the following decade: the feature film and the serial.

The serial and the feature: two impulses, one aim

While it is a common assumption that the serial paved the way for the feature film in the 1910s, schooling audiences in the consumption of long-form narratives, the causal relationship between the two forms is rather more complicated. When the first episode of Edison's *What Happened to Mary* debuted in cinemas in July 1912, simultaneous to the publication of the story in *Ladies World*, it marked less a break from earlier practice than the refinement of a strategy which had been in place in publishing since the 1840s. Movie audiences were already well versed in the episodic narrative format from the serialisation of novels in newspapers and 'story papers', the pervasiveness of which, Ben Singer argues, 'served as both a precondition and an incentive for the creation of film equivalents'.[21] They may have also previously seen Victorin Hippolyte-Jasset's *Nick Carter, le roi des detectives* (1908), one of a handful of serials the director made for Studio Eclair which were imported into the States.[22] Bringing the two media together, *The Motion Picture Story Magazine* had subsisted since its debut in early 1911 on the publication of the stories found in films on release (including *His Trust*, in April of that year), but it had not engaged in the systematic, synchronised approach taken by Edison and Hearst and it is this element of co-ordinated cross-media synergy, rather than its episodic narrative structure, which marks out *Mary* as a genuine turning point.[23]

Mary and the serials which immediately followed did not deploy the device that has now come to symbolise the genre, the cliffhanger at the end of each episode. Instead, as Singer points out,

> the earliest serials … tended to present a self-contained narrative in each episode, although an overarching premise established in the first episode (such as a conflict over the heroine's inheritance) carried over from episode to episode to motivate a series of separate adventures.[24]

There is some disagreement as to when the cliffhanger ending became standard: Singer posits Pathé's hugely successful *The Perils of Pauline*, which ended some but not all episodes with cliffhangers, as the turning point, whereas Eileen Bowser points to Louis Feuillade's *Fantomas*, and Kalton C. Lahue and Anthony Slide to *The Adventures of Kathlyn*, both of which appeared in 1913.[25] Regardless of who set the precedent, the early serials attempt a similar balancing act to that performed by *His Trust* and *His Trust Fulfilled*, delivering a story 'complete in itself' while also continuing a larger narrative thread. This balancing act, which foregrounds standalone qualities over continuation and connectedness, arguably stemmed from a model of exhibition and distribution orientated around casual and sporadic 'drop-ins' rather than the regular attendance required for comprehension of a multi-part narrative, alongside a well-founded lack of confidence in exhibitors' commitment to screen all of the episodes in the correct order.[26] The desire to make longer films had already been demonstrated by Griffith among others, but it was the serial which revealed the commercial potential of extended narratives to exhibitors and producers alike. Nor did they necessarily revolutionise what Singer terms the 'entrenched system of short-reel distribution'.[27] In some respects the serial offered manufacturers a compromise position; allowing them to produce long-form narrative works in single-reel instalments, as evidenced by Edison's announcement, early in 1914, that it would not increase production of multiple-reel features, but would instead produce more serials.[28]

Furthermore, by the time of *What Happened to Mary*, the feature film, as we now understand it, had already begun to develop. The concept of the 'headline' attraction had been around since the early 1900s, informing, among others, Edison's production of multi-scene series such as *Buster Brown*. It was only later in the decade, however, that the term became systematically associated with a film's duration. In 1909 the 'feature' was a relatively malleable concept, referring to any film consisting of more than one reel; a definition confused still further by the fact that the earliest instances of feature-film distribution, pioneered by Vitagraph throughout 1909, occurred in weekly single-reel instalments.[29] Even though some exhibitors ignored the prescribed pattern and screened multiple reels in a single performance,[30] in the case of a Vitagraph feature from this period such as *Napoleon, The Man of Destiny* (1909), Eileen Bowser has observed that 'there was no imperative to run both reels together, because they were not treated as modern story films, with a continuous narrative'.[31] There is little, therefore, to distinguish these early features as first exhibited from the series films which were already becoming a part of the industry's output in 1909.

As it grew through the mid-1910s, however, and as the cliffhanger ending became standard, the serial trend did assist in bringing about certain shifts in industry practice. Inscribing a correct and autonomous narrative order within the text, the serial reduced the programming input of exhibitors, while its popularity demonstrated regular and systematic audience attendance was not only possible but commercially preferable. And, at a time when programmes were changed every few days, the serial was ensured an extended run over the course of several months at any given venue, which in turn meant more money could be dedicated to marketing and publicity.[32] So, while it was evidently not responsible for giving birth to long-form film narratives, the serial did in some respects prefigure the rise of the feature film in that it helped shift the cinemagoing focus away from the variety model, and towards the idea of the standalone attraction.

Where, then, is the sequel in all of this? If I have devoted considerable space to the emergence of the series film and the serial, it is because we need to understand that these two storytelling techniques – representing two equivalent but nonetheless subtly distinct commercial and narrative approaches – were already in place by the time the feature film became a regular fixture between 1914 and 1915. I have already suggested that most Hollywood sequels tend to hybridise the self-contained episodic structure of the series film with the continuing narrative strands one finds in the serial; a combination we can now understand as drawing on what were already well-established cinematic traditions. The serial is particularly key in the history of the sequel, because it was hugely instructive from a commercial standpoint. Not only did it inaugurate integrated, synergistic marketing strategies, the serial also demonstrated that, when blessed with a phenomenally successful cinematic product, producing a sequel was a perfectly valid response. Eager to capitalise on the success of *What Happened to Mary*, and with that now drawing to a close, Edison released a follow-up, *Who Will Marry Mary?*, in the summer of 1913,[33] thus establishing a template whereby *The Exploits of Elaine* (1914) could be followed by *The New Exploits of Elaine* (1915) and *The Romance of Elaine* (1915), both featuring Pearl White as 'Elaine Dodge'; and *The Diamond from the Sky* (1915) followed by *The Sequel to Diamond from the Sky* (1916), although it should be noted in the case of the latter that Lottie Pickford and Irving Cummings, the two original leads, did not reprise their roles in the sequel. Despite these examples, the sequel was not necessarily the default response to a successful serial. That Helen Holmes followed *The Hazards of Helen* (1914) with *The Girl and the Game* (1915), in which she appeared as another character named Helen that we may or may not associate with the earlier role, indicates the manner in which the burgeoning star system created opportunities to associate one product with another without making an explicit narrative connection. The first feature-length films to be billed as sequels did not begin to appear until after 1915, and exhibit that same casual opportunism; suggesting the extent to which the term represented first and foremost a commercial strategy more than it did a cluster of formal norms.

Relative values: the first sequels

Perhaps the most blatant misuse of the sequel classification in this period is also one of the very first such designations for a feature film in Hollywood history: *The Fall of a Nation* (1916), dubbed by writer-director Thomas Dixon as 'The Sequel to *Birth of a Nation*'. Author of *The Clansman*, the novel on which Griffith's hugely successful 1914 feature was based, Dixon was reportedly unimpressed that Griffith had received all of the credit for that venture, and set out to redirect that attention (and its attendant commercial rewards) by embarking on an ambitious plan to produce and direct a series of features under his own steam, even going so far as building his own studio in Hollywood. *The Fall of a Nation* was to be the first of many productions from Dixon's National Drama Company, incorporated in July of 1915. Thereafter he wrote both the film's screenplay and a novelisation bearing the subtitle *A Sequel to 'The Birth of a Nation'*, which was published in June 1916, to coincide with the premiere of the film.[34] Despite its derivative title and marketing campaign, the film was not narratively connected to either *The Clansman* or *Birth of a Nation*. Although the film itself is now lost, the novelisation survives and from it (and its press reviews), we are able to establish that *The Fall of a Nation* begins with the surprise invasion of the United States by the 'European Confederated Army', led by the Germans, and follows the attempts of US citizens (including the intriguing combination of the Loyal Legion of American Women and the Ku Klux Klan) to overthrow the newly installed emperor and claim back their country.

In aspiring to the epic status of *Birth of a Nation*, and in again staging a battle for freedom on home soil, Dixon's film has obvious thematic similarities to that earlier work, but there is no continuity of either character or narrative, problematising its claims to sequel status. Perhaps in recognition of this, the reviews categorise it as generically related to a cycle of films contributing to the then-prevalent debates around preparedness and the United States' involvement in (or abstinence from) the war then raging in Europe; a cycle which also included *The Battle Cry of Peace* (1915) and *Civilisation* (1916). This stance is encapsulated by the rather weary headline accompanying the *New York Times* review: 'America Is Invaded Again in the Films'.[35] That review, along with those in trade magazines *Moving Picture World*, *Wids* and *Motion Picture News*, makes direct comparisons with Griffith's film, primarily in relation to the staging of the battle scenes, but none attempts to reinforce the sequel claim. The *Variety* reviewer does introduce the film as 'Thomas Dixon's sequel to his "Birth of a Nation"', but makes no other attempt to connect the two films.[36]

Although an extreme case, Dixon's efforts to capitalise on the success of *Birth of a Nation*, and his evident belief that he had every right to designate *The Fall of a Nation* a sequel, given its shared connection with his other work, are indicative of the prominent role that literary sequels were playing at this point. Away from the serial, producers had yet to generate sequels independent of existing source material. The understanding of what constituted a sequel would in the 1910s have derived largely from literary examples of the form, so it is understandable that features contemporaneous to *The Fall of a Nation*, such as *Secret of Storm Country* (1917) and *The Squaw Man's Son* (1917), functioned as adaptations of legitimate literary sequels, having little if any direct connection to their cinematic predecessors, *Tess of Storm Country* (1914) and *The Squaw Man* (1914) respectively. Perhaps not coincidentally, the novel *Secret of Storm Country* by Grace Miller White was published in 1917, suggesting that White may have been prompted to write a sequel to *Tess* by the considerable success of the 1914 movie version starring Mary Pickford.

The source material for *The Squaw Man's Son*, on the other hand, was already in existence, with Edwin Milton Royle having published *The Silent Call*, a follow-up to his hugely successful 1905 play *The Squaw Man*, back in 1910. The original film was among the first American feature films to achieve considerable box-office success, and was the first to be produced by the newly formed Jesse L. Lasky Feature Play Company, founded by Lasky, Samuel Goldwyn and Cecil B. DeMille, who made his directorial debut transferring the play to the screen. Broadway star Dustin Farnum took the lead role of Captain James Wynnegate, a British officer who comes to America and falls for Nat-U-Rich (a role credited to Red Wing), a Native American princess, who saves his life.[37] They marry and have a son together, thus providing the inspiration for the sequel. Produced again by Lasky, who had by this time merged with Adolph Zukor's Famous Players and taken a stake in Paramount, *The Squaw Man's Son* was released in August 1917 and explicitly advertised as a sequel to *The Squaw Man*. Ignoring the existence of *The Silent Call*, on which the film is directly based, many reviewers seem to assume that the sequel was an original commission by Lasky and Co: 'the logical thing to do', suggested *Variety*, 'after the original proved so great a success'.[38] Unlike *The Fall of a Nation*, the film's connection with its predecessor was deemed its primary attraction, with *Wids* advising exhibitors: 'If, for any reason, you have to play this, I would concentrate all my advertising on the fact that this is a sequel to "The Squaw Man".'[39] Other than Royle and Lasky, there is no consistency of creative personnel across the two films, with DeMille replaced by Edward LeSaint and none of the original cast members present.

In the three years which elapsed between the release of *The Squaw Man* and its sequel, major changes in distribution practices for feature films had begun to occur. The state rights system through which that film had been sold had been replaced by 'a national enterprise dominated by about ten big companies', while Paramount had introduced a 'full-service program package' in which exhibitors were contracted to take only its product, on the basis that they would receive two features per week.[40] This arrangement meant that Famous Players–Lasky were committed to delivering more feature films than ever before, a development which inevitably placed greater pressure on the search for source material, and might therefore explain the increasing frequency with which producers revisited previous successes.

The burgeoning star system was of course another factor in the drive to standardise supply and demand, with Paramount offering exhibitors a 'star series booking' option, in which they were committed to taking a package of films containing a particular star.[41] Accordingly, *The Squaw Man's Son* was advertised not only on its own merits but also as part of a Wallace Reid package. Having signed a contract with Lasky in 1915, Reid was at this point developing into a major star, and was committed to headlining several films a year. Thus in the case of *The Squaw Man's Son*, the sequel served a programming function in this early incarnation of the studio system; filling a gap in the production schedule and providing an appropriate role for a contracted player, while minimising financial risk by drawing on a literary property which had built-in awareness.

Sequels continued to serve a similar function in Reid's career as his star rose, as evidenced by the cycle of films which followed the release of *The Roaring Road* (1919). Directed by James Cruze, who made seventeen films with Reid, *Road* centres on 'Toodles' Walden (Reid), a car salesman who is drafted in by his boss to win a road race on behalf of their company. Despite being an amateur, Walden overcomes the odds and eventually emerges triumphant. Box-office figures are unavailable but, according to Lasky, 'audiences couldn't get enough of him behind a steering wheel',[42] and he worked Reid accordingly, churning out a series of racing pictures with Reid at the helm. *The Roaring Road* was based on three short stories by Byron Morgan, 'Junkpile Sweepstakes', 'Undertaker's Handicap' and 'Roaring Road', which had appeared in the *Saturday Evening Post* in autumn 1918. Following the success of the first film, Morgan's stories formed the basis for six more Reid-starrers, of which two were direct sequels: *Excuse My Dust* (1920) following *The Roaring Road* and *Too Much Speed* (1921), following *What's Your Hurry?* (1920). The latter pair see Reid as 'Dusty' Rhoades, a truck driver undertaking daring road journeys to save lives. In *Excuse My Dust*, Reid returns as 'Toodles' Walden, who has forsaken racing to settle down with his new wife (again played by Ann Little) and baby son (played by Reid's own son, Wallace Reid Jr), but is tempted out of retirement when his speed record comes under threat.

Neither Cruze nor *Roaring Road* screenwriter Marion Fairfax were involved, but the returning cast, characters, narrative continuity and involvement of Byron (whose source story sequel, 'The Bear Trap', was published in July 1919, after *The Roaring Road* had proven successful) mean that *Excuse My Dust* is one of the few films of the period whose sequel status is unambiguous. That was not necessarily the manner in which *Dust* or *Too Much Speed* were critically received, however. Typical is the *New York Times* review of *Too Much Speed*: "'Won by a Race" might be the standing title of all of the Wallace Reid–lovely-girl–grumpy-father pictures which have been coming out regularly for the last year or more.'[43] *Variety* describes *Excuse My Dust* not as the sequel to *The Roaring Road* but instead as 'the third of a series of stories of the roaring road that have appeared in "The Saturday Evening Post"',[44] while *Motion Picture News* advised exhibitors to inform their patrons that *Too Much Speed* 'is a fitting sequel to "Excuse My Dust," "The Roaring Road" and "What's Your Hurry?"'.[45] Only *Photoplay* indicated the direct narrative connection between *Excuse My Dust* and an earlier film, recalling that Walden is the 'erstwhile demon driver of the good old Darco bus that won the Los Angeles–San Francisco road race', but in their account this took place not in *The Roaring Road* but in a non-existent film entitled *Speed Up*.[46] Perhaps reviewers were simply unable to keep up with Reid's output, but either way it seems clear that, despite their direct and explicit narrative connections, these sequels were classified less as direct descendants to their predecessors, than as further additions to the broader Reid racing picture cycle.

Famous Players–Lasky did little to clarify the situation, with advertisements for *Too Much Speed* and *Excuse My Dust* making no reference to their antecedents. The absence of an 'A Sequel to …' subheading suggests the extent to which Reid's star persona had converged with a particular character type and set of genre conventions: the successful formula was larger than any one film. Despite the connections between the films themselves, Famous Players–Lasky was treating them much as it would any successful star–genre combination. We have already seen this in operation with *Broncho Billy*, and it was standard practice for comedic actors of the time, such as Charlie Chaplin and Marie Dressler, to blur the lines between character and star persona from film to film, but to ignore actual narrative connections seems completely alien from a contemporary vantage point. It seems characteristic of the nascent studio system that the sequel might serve as fodder, feeding a production line for a vertically integrated business model in which the star was the central commodity: an attitude which persisted to some degree until the system was dismantled in the 1950s.

In the independent sector things were different. Starved for the most part of stars, producers would have to find other ways to attract capital investment and audiences, as evidenced by National Film Corporation's response to the success of *Tarzan of the Apes* (1918). Established by William Parsons in 1915, National Film Corp. was an independent production company which survived for less than ten years. Its biggest success came after Parsons secured the rights to Edgar Rice Burroughs's novel *Tarzan of the Apes*, which had first appeared in 1912 and had already spawned several sequels. This acquisition was evidently a major financial investment for an independent company, with Parsons claiming in interview that he had 'set a new record with respect to price for film rights on any story, the consideration being $50,000' [47] – although Robert Fenton and Gabe Essoe indicate that there was a certain amount of publicity bluff in Parsons's declaration. In the contract signed by Burroughs, the author was promised a $5,000 advance on royalties; the $50,000 in fact took the form of capital stock in Parsons's fledgling company.[48] Still, *Tarzan* was not simply the National Film Corporation's biggest invest-ment, it was the reason for its existence, with Parsons having reportedly purchased and remod-elled the Oz Film Company's old Hollywood studio 'to suit the special requirements of the company's coming productions'.[49] Starring Elmo Lincoln in the title role, *Tarzan of the Apes* was soon acquired for distribution by the First National Exhibitors Circuit.

Officially formed in April 1917, First National consisted of a broad base of state's rights franchisees. Together they would acquire films, and distribute them to the venues under their control, thus creating a national circuit designed to rival that of Paramount.[50] Although it planned to move into production, in the meantime First National needed to acquire product from elsewhere; films that were strong enough to bring audiences to theatres no longer per-mitted to exhibit Famous Players–Lasky's star-studded output. Given the phenomenal success of Burroughs's character in print, *Tarzan of the Apes* was just such a property, and had already enjoyed a healthy four-week run at the Broadway in New York when it was announced in March 1918 that First National had picked up distribution rights and would take it nationwide with sixty prints on 2 April.[51] With an extensive exploitation campaign, which reportedly included the publication of 'Tarzan' stories in 5,000 newspapers and magazines, and 'several live apes' under contract to appear in the lobbies of key theatres,[52] First National and National Film Corp. were attempting to position *Tarzan* as a major event: with many exhibitors reporting house records in the film's first run, and with an eventual gross of reportedly more than $1 mil-lion, it was a strategy which paid off.

Reviewing *Tarzan of the Apes*, *Variety* suggested that, 'After looking at the screen production and noting its ending, it looks as though the producers are prepared to shoot the sequel to this story, providing the initial release "gets over".'[53] This hunch proved correct: *The Romance of Tarzan* was ready to be screened and introduced by Parsons at a meeting of the First National directors on 18 July 1918, just a few months after the first film's release. First National acquired it for exclusive distribution that same day.[54] Exactly when Parsons made the decision to pro-duce a sequel is unclear. No production announcements appear in any of the key trade mag-azines between April and June of 1918, perhaps in part because Parsons was attempting to keep his plans from Burroughs. Rather than base the new film on one of the published sequels, Parsons and his team were purportedly adapting 'the concluding chapters' of *Tarzan of the Apes*, thus supposedly avoiding the need to license new material from Burroughs, or pay him any additional advance. The author was incensed and immediately commenced legal action against Parsons, claiming that he had yet to receive any royalties from the first film. It has previously been suggested that the contract was weighted in Parsons's favour and there was nothing Burroughs could do, but the First National files contain a letter from the author confirming that he had received payment from Parsons of $2,500, in exchange for use of 'The Romance of Tarzan' title – a move which suggests that Parsons wanted to avoid further legal action, or indeed any danger to the valuable distribution pact with First National.[55]

As the story in this case dealt with Tarzan's (Elmo Lincoln) attempts to assimilate into 'civilised' society and win the love of Jane (Enid Markey), the majority of scenes could be shot on interior sets, rather than requiring an exterior simulation of the apeman's jungle habitat: a move which meant the shoot for *The Romance of Tarzan* would be both quicker and cheaper than *Tarzan of the Apes*. Opening in October 1918, the sequel opened wider and faded sooner than its predecessor. Rather than allow a lengthy exclusive engagement in one venue, First National in this instance rushed the film into wide release, giving the Strand Theatre in Manhattan a one-week window from 13 October before opening it at several of the other circuits in the New York area. First National claimed that this unusual move had been taken because of the 'extremely heavy' amount of advance booking applications from exhibitors across the country.[56] Reviewers were rather less enthusiastic, with the *New York Times* concluding: 'As the uncivilized Tarzan, Elmo Lincoln is splendid, but as Tarzan in a dress suit – that is different.'[57] Of course, even if the film's critical and commercial fortunes had been brighter, it is unlikely National Film Corporation would have been able to produce a further sequel, given Burroughs's recent dealings with Parsons.

Although quite different in nature to the Reid vehicles, *Tarzan*'s production history exemplifies certain continuing threads in the history of the sequel. First, Parsons's relatively economical circumnavigation of the legal challenge from Burroughs suggests the ambiguity surrounding the use of original source material for sequelisation. With motion pictures added to the list of works protected by copyright in 1912,[58] producers could no longer freely adapt material – but the release of *The Romance of Tarzan* suggested that they might legally generate more than one film property from a single story acquisition – a practice which, as we shall see, remained a grey area until around 1940, and which indicated that most authors were still learning about the potential fate of their intellectual property in the hands of the film industry.[59] Second, the connection between the speed at which *Romance* was produced and Parsons's purported right to produce a sequel using already licensed material, with the latter clearly facilitating the former, points to what will become a recurrent trend in this account – a trend whereby sequel producers will attempt to utilise those elements over which they already have a proprietary hold (be that stars or story material) in order to save both time and money.

Thus far I have counterposed the approach taken by independent producers with that of the star-driven studios. But as *The Romance of Tarzan* was finishing its run at the end of 1918, an accumulation of factors meant that this division was soon to be blurred. Some of the biggest stars were about to become their own producers, and in their hands the sequel was to take on a new commercial significance.

Poor relations? *Don Q, Son of Zorro* and *The Son of the Sheik*

If the film-making landscape described thus far feels unlike that of contemporary Hollywood, I shall conclude this chapter with a consideration of two films whose production contexts prefigure a trend in sequelisation which would only return to prominence after the dismantling of the studio system some twenty-five years later. The impetus behind both *Don Q, Son of Zorro* (1925) and *The Son of the Sheik* (1926) feels oddly contemporary, and it is no coincidence that both are from United Artists, a studio created and organised in explicit opposition to its competitors, at which stars and directors had far greater creative and commercial autonomy. Incorporated in April 1919 as a production and distribution organisation owned by Charles Chaplin, Mary Pickford, Douglas Fairbanks and D. W. Griffith, United Artists Corporation had exclusive rights to handle its owners' pictures for the next five years, taking a relatively small distribution fee of 20 per cent of the gross in the United States and 30 per cent in other territories. Although each of the four owners were committed to contributing nine pictures to the company over the following five years, they were otherwise at far greater liberty than they would have been under contract at another studio.[60] Unlike Wallace Reid at Paramount or Theda Bara at Fox, Chaplin, Pickford, Fairbanks and Griffith would not be held to punishing work schedules for a weekly salary. Heading up their own independent production companies, they had genuine creative control and, as Tino Balio points out, in creating a distribution company 'they could oversee, in addition, the crucial functions of sales, advertising, and publicity'.[61] More pertinently, the distribution contracts did not allow block-booking, meaning that each United Artists release had to be sold individually and that, in theory at least, 'merit alone would determine a picture's success or failure'.[62]

We can begin to see, therefore, how each United Artists film effectively had event status, with greater emphasis on its success as an individual enterprise; conditions of release very similar to those of the two *Tarzan* films, and conditions which would become the norm only after the impact of the *Paramount* decree in 1948.[63] Under these circumstances, the dynamic between a star's persona and their commercial viability was intensified: Fairbanks and Pickford may have enjoyed their freedom, but they were also only as good as the box-office returns for their last film. Out of this context, *Don Q, Son of Zorro* and *The Son of the Sheik* emerge as responses by Fairbanks and Rudolph Valentino to what they believed audiences wanted, responses which both involved the invocation of earlier, more successful incarnations of their respective personas.

This is not to suggest there were no broader organisational concerns at play, at least in the case of Fairbanks. By the latter half of 1924, United Artists and its founding principles were under serious threat: Griffith, having delivered his ninth contracted picture, was on the verge of splitting from his co-owners; the company deficit had grown to $500,000; and, having decided to discontinue distributing films made by outside producers, there continued to be a shortage of product.[64] As a shareholder, there was more at stake for Fairbanks than his career as an actor, but his ongoing individual contribution to the success of United Artists was certainly a factor, and in 1924 that contribution had faltered somewhat. Premiering in March of 1924, *The Thief of Bagdad* was certainly a hit but not the success Fairbanks had evidently anticipated when he invested some $2 million into its production, meaning that its contribution to the United Artists bottom line was probably minimal at best.[65] This relative underperformance, particularly in light of it being his first release (and contribution to the UA coffers) since *Robin Hood* in 1922, was decisive when it came to Fairbanks's selection of his next project. If it was indeed the case that he wanted a sure-fire hit, then his decision to produce a sequel to *The Mark of Zorro* (1920) becomes explicable both in terms of his star persona and his role as producer.[66] Not only would a new Zorro film return him to the role which had been instrumental in setting the template for his subsequent career, it would also allow him to keep production costs down, with its Spanish and Californian settings being rather easier and cheaper to evoke using Hollywood locales than the fantastical Arabia of *Bagdad*. Despite these economies, *Don Q*'s budget was a still sizeable $496,958, a fair portion of which went towards the construction of thirty-five sets, including 'a faithful re-creation of Don Diego Vega's California home as it appeared in *The Mark of Zorro*'.[67]

The scale of the sequel underlines the growth of Fairbanks's ambitions since its rather more modest predecessor. Produced for around $169,000, *The Mark of Zorro* had been Fairbanks's fourth film for United Artists and his first foray into a genre with which he would come to be forever associated: the swashbuckler. Hitherto best known for his contemporary-set comedies, many populated with self-performed stunts, the star's move towards something both more serious and romantic which would appeal to both men and women was, according to biographer Jeffrey Vance, a reaction to negative feedback from exhibitors.[68] Whatever the original motivation, it became a huge success, grossing more than three times its production cost and delineating a new version of the Fairbanks persona which he would inhabit for the remainder of his career.

As a further result of its box-office success, and as further indication of the cross-pollination between movies and popular fiction at the time, Zorro's creator Johnston McCulley was inspired to revive the character after the movie's release, much as Byron Morgan and Grace Miller White had done after *The Roaring Road* and *Tess of Storm Country*. Starting in 1922, 'The Further Adventures of Zorro' was published in *Argosy All-Story Weekly* and incorporated the 'Z' motif which derived not from the original story, 'The Curse of Capistrano', but instead from Fairbanks's movie adaptation. As if completing the cycle of influence, it was McCulley's literary response to *The Mark of Zorro*'s popularity which helped sow the seeds for a cinematic sequel, with Fairbanks purchasing the rights to 'The Further Adventures' in 1922 on the basis that he would at some point return to the character.[69] By the time Fairbanks chose to move ahead with the sequel, however, he instead favoured Kate and Hesketh Prichard's novel *Don Q's Love Story* as a primary source, with McCulley receiving no credit on the finished film, again suggesting the rudimentary state of author's rights in relation to movie adaptations at this time.

Aside from the reference to *Zorro* in its title, the advertising material did little to clarify *Don Q*'s status as a sequel to *The Mark of Zorro*, with no use of the term nor any overt reference to the earlier film in its poster or other artwork. No-one aware of *The Mark of Zorro*'s existence, however, could fail to make the connection upon seeing the new film, as suggested by the reviews in both trade and consumer press. *Variety* praised the return of 'the same old Doug that made "The Mark of Zorro" a real picture', in what it described as 'in a measure a sequel to that screen masterpiece'. It was, the reviewer suggested, 'Fairbanks as the public wants Fairbanks',[70] an observation supported not least by the audience applause which reportedly greeted the flashbacks to the earlier film which are incorporated into *Don Q*. *Photoplay*, meanwhile, concluded its equally glowing review with this request for another instalment: 'And now, Mr. Fairbanks, won't you tell us the adventures of old man *Zorro*'s grandson?'[71]

Don Q was a considerable success, ranking among the highest grossers of 1925,[72] more than recouping its production costs and solidifying its star's commercial reputation. It was not the last time Fairbanks would return to a character for a sequel – that came with *The Iron Mask* (1929), in which he reassembled several of the original cast members from *The Three Musketeers* (1921) – suggesting that the success of *Don Q* was some influence on the manner in which Fairbanks would conduct the remainder of his career. That both of these sequels were considerably more lavish and expensively produced than their predecessors illustrates

Poster for *Don Q, Son of Zorro* (1925)

one tendency of sequel production which we will see recurring throughout Hollywood history. Although there were alternative choices at hand, as epitomised by the quick and cheap approach taken by Parsons for *The Romance of Tarzan*, it is clear that Fairbanks, competing primarily with himself in both commercial and artistic terms, was operating with the confidence of a producer who believes there is a built-in audience for a sequel to a prior success.

As its title suggests, *The Son of the Sheik* is evidence that Fairbanks was not the only star whose subsequent career choices show the influence of *Don Q*. But this was no straightforward repeat of that scenario: Rudolph Valentino's standing was rather more precarious, the box-office success of *The Son of the Sheik* more vital to his ongoing career than *Don Q* was to that of Fairbanks, and his relationship to the character somewhat more complicated. Fairbanks was coming off the back of a hit, albeit an unprofitable one, whereas Valentino was one film (*The Eagle* [1925]) into what was effectively a second comeback,[73] this time supported by United Artists. As a man who had publicly fallen out with Famous Players–Lasky and Adolph Zukor, disillusioned by the constricted working conditions of his contract, Valentino was the perfect addition to the United Artists roster, signing with them in May 1925.[74] Unlike his earlier contracts with Metro and Famous Players, Valentino now had a modicum of input into the projects he would undertake.[75] Joseph M. Schenck, recently appointed chairman of United Artists, signed Valentino to his newly created Feature Productions label on the condition that Natacha Rambova, Valentino's wife and hitherto a major influence, withdraw from direct involvement in his career choices.[76] As biographer Emily Leider suggests, 'Everyone agreed that his next picture had to be a success, and that Natacha's unpopularity, combined with his record of quarrelling with producers, had weakened his hand.'[77]

Rushed into production and hurriedly released in November, *The Eagle* was a return to commercial form of sorts, but this was soon undermined by the poor performance of *Cobra* (1925), the last picture made under his previous contract with producer J. D. Williams, released three weeks later.[78] Such mixed messages at the box office only served to increase the pressure on his next move. In light of Fairbanks's successful re-engagement with the Zorro character, it makes sense that Schenck would see fit to do the same for Valentino, but, unlike *Don Q*, this was as much a capitulation to the perceived wishes of the moviegoing public, as it was a choice driven by the star himself. The Sheik had become the touchstone role of Valentino's career, with the press regularly referring to him as such. Based on the hugely popular romantic novel from 1919 by Edith Maude Hull, *The Sheik* (1921) was such a phenomenal commercial success that, as Leider puts it, 'Valentino the man became permanently melded to his desert Sheik persona.'[79]

Schenck was therefore merely responding to this continued intermingling of star and character, in making as blatant an appeal as possible to the audience who had made *The Sheik* such a resounding success. His task was made easier by Hull herself who, as with Johnston McCulley, must have been responding in part to the success of the film when she wrote a sequel, *The Sons of the Sheik*, published in 1925. Hull signed over the film rights to Schenck on 7 December 1925, just a few weeks after *The Eagle*'s appearance in cinemas, for a sum of $21,000.[80] If Valentino was not thrilled about reverting to type, there were nonetheless some rewards for

Poster for *The Son of the Sheik* (1926)

him in terms of the nature of the production itself: he would have a chance to work with acclaimed director George Fitzmaurice; he could indulge his passion for horse riding; and he could demonstrate his range by playing both the wise old Sheik of the original film and his impetuous offspring. He could, in short, 'correct some of the flaws in The Sheik'[81] by playing a character of strength and authority, answering those critics who had brought his masculinity into question, while also stretching himself as an artist.

In case the film's title was not sufficient, its marketing stressed the connection to the original film, with posters and other advertising bearing the subtitle 'A Sequel to "The Sheik"'. Redundant as it may now seem, there was some necessity for this designation at the time, given the manner in which Valentino's original embodiment of Sheik Ahmed Ben Hassan had mutated into a more amorphous concept, serving to inform not only his own persona and future performances but also a series of 'copycat pictures' such as Burning Sands (1922) and The Arab (1924).[82] The 'Sheik' was now as much a stock character type as the vamp and the tenderfoot, but Valentino was the original and the United Artists campaign sought to exploit this at every turn.

Now widely understood as a posthumous release, The Son of the Sheik was in fact premiered a good six weeks before Valentino's death, a result of peritonitis, in August 1926. United Artists' preview strategy, meaning an engagement in one venue exclusive to that locality with premium ticket prices, was roadshowing by another name, a tactic originally rejected by Fairbanks, Pickford and Chaplin but subsequently adopted for Robin Hood (1922) and Rosita (1923) among others.[83] Such were the arrangements with the Grauman's Million Dollar Theater in Los Angeles and the Strand in New York, where The Son of the Sheik opened on 8 and 25 July respectively.[84] Not only was Valentino very much alive at this point, he was actively engaged in promoting the film and made public appearances in both cities, meaning that the huge audiences who initially flocked to the see the film were paying to see a living star, possibly even in the flesh.[85]

Despite the phenomenal initial response, the houses in Los Angeles and San Francisco were both reporting significant drop-offs in their second and third weeks, leading some to express concern that the previews had all but absorbed the demand in these cities, making prospects for a longer run elsewhere seem limited.[86] Unfortunately, as far as the film's box-office performance was concerned, Valentino's death could not have been better timed. While in past years, the death of a star such as Wallace Reid had led to the withdrawal of his films from cinemas, the extraordinary public response to Valentino's passing (and the evident financial rewards of catering to it) prompted exhibitors to break with precedent and instead book not only The Son of the Sheik but also earlier works, including The Sheik itself.[87]

An epitaph as much as it was a film, it is perhaps no surprise that the grosses for The Son of the Sheik exceeded those of the original, passing the $1 million mark at the worldwide box office within a year.[88] Gaylyn Studlar has argued that the film is 'structured more on the order of a Fairbanks film', and that, in its attempts to 'recuperate Valentino into normative cult-of-the-body, character-building masculinity', it is atypical of the star's oeuvre.[89] Given the extent to which the film was promoted and received as Valentino's return to the role which made him famous, and given that Schenck invested in the property precisely because of this connection, this seems to rather overstate the film's revisionism. The influence of Fairbanks, and of the negative press centring on Valentino's masculinity, on the film's content is clear, but it is precisely this incorporation of new elements within an existing formula which means the film sits comfortably alongside more contemporary sequels such as *Terminator 2: Judgment Day*, *Rocky Balboa* (2007) and *Die Hard 4.0* (2006), in which a star revisits a defining role after a lengthy interval, and in which the character (and in turn the persona) is subtly adjusted to suit the tenor of the times and reflect popular trends. I will return to this tendency in Chapter 7, but for now it need only be said that it was the unique situation of United Artists at this time which led to star-orientated sequel production being approached on such an atypically grand scale, carrying with it the air of a major event.

2 | Sequels in the factory, 1929–54

The 31 May 1936 edition of the *New York Times* included three articles which explained much about where Hollywood was going and where it had been. In 'Consider the Sequel', the *Times*' then-regular film critic Frank S. Nugent considered 'the growing tendency of the infant motion picture industry to indulge in the venerable practice of Shintoism'. He explained:

> We refer of course to that form of ancestor-worship tinged with honest reverence for the dollar, which deifies past cinema successes and urges producers to bullwhip their writing staffs into the creation of a sequel, companion-piece or postscript, bearing a reminiscent title and having – they devoutly hope – all the heroic qualities of the inspired originals.[1]

On the same day, Nugent's colleague John T. McManus reported on the results of a recent Warner Bros. poll, headed 'Thumbs Down on Doubles', which claimed that the feedback proved 'what folks have thought all along, that the double-feature system of cinema exhibition is almost universally unpopular'.[2] Elsewhere, an article entitled 'Small Profits Feed Poverty Row' gives an overview of independent studios such as Chesterfield and Invincible, which were surviving, just, despite the majors' move into B-film production.[3]

The very existence of Nugent's piece, almost fifty years before J. Hoberman diagnosed himself with a case of sequelitis, is further evidence of the oft-overlooked role of the sequel in what is commonly understood to be Hollywood's 'Golden Age'. The two other pieces, meanwhile, give some indication of the industrial environment which fostered the appetite for sequelisation as described by Nugent. The 'B-movie' and the double bill are central to an understanding of the sequel in this period, not least because their existence as exhibition and production categories led to a boom in the series film. Although the boom was over by the mid-1940s, by which time the majors were scaling back or halting their B-movie output, series film production persisted until television took off in the early 1950s. The series film was the most prevalent form of cinematic seriality in this period, much as the serial had been in the 1910s.[4] As a result, it is the series film against which any sequel of the period must be defined, both in terms of its narrative strategy and its production and exhibition contexts.

While the series film as a mode would not have been viable without the studio system, there is no monolithic explanation for the numerous and varied instances of cinematic seriality during the quarter-century under scrutiny in this chapter. The umbrella terms commonly used to characterise Hollywood history in the two decades between the synch-sound revolution in 1927 and the *Paramount* decree in 1948 – the studio era, the classical era or the Golden

Age – imply a coherence and stability which disintegrates upon closer inspection. True, the pace of change was in some respects slower in the 1930s and 1940s than it had been in American cinema's first three decades, but, given the year-on-year tumult of that earlier period, this is a modest claim indeed. By 1930 the industry had settled into a relatively stable oligopoly of eight key studios (the 'Big Five' of Warners, MGM, Paramount, RKO and Fox, so named because they each owned cinema chains, unlike the 'Little Three', consisting of Columbia, Universal and United Artists, whose operations were restricted to production and distribution), but this status quo was under constant threat: from the huge debts amassed in the conversion to sound in the late 1920s; the financial fallout of the Depression; the Justice Department's antitrust drive against the vertical integration of production, distribution and exhibition practised by the Big Five; disputes with independent exhibitors and with key stars such as James Cagney and Olivia de Havilland; World War II, with its attendant government strictures and drain on human and material resources; the post-war migration to the suburbs; and ultimately the rise of television. The industry successfully rose to many of these challenges, but they were challenges nonetheless. So while the collapse of the studio system is generally seen as a post-1949, post-*Paramount* decree phenomenon, the cracks in that system, and the accompanying shifts in production practice, were evident as early as 1940. Crucially for this history of the sequel, we can already see in the 1940s the signs of a nascent blockbuster mentality that would become standard issue after the divorcement of the major studios' from their theatre holdings in the 1950s, and intensify over the following decades.

We begin in 1929, when the dust kicked up by the introduction of synchronised sound had largely settled, and conclude in 1954, by which time all of the studios bar MGM had divested themselves of their exhibition interests,[5] placing the final nail in the coffin of an industrial model which had cohered in the 1920s, and, despite the aforementioned tumult, survived for the best part of twenty-five years. This mode of organisation, I will argue, both facilitated sequel production, allowing producers to react to a hit film with a speed that would become rare in subsequent decades, while simultaneously rendering it less necessary, as evidenced by the numerous star/genre/studio combinations which eschewed any explicit continuation of narrative or character. That hundreds of sequels and series films were produced in this period, despite this broad range of available options for capitalising on a prior success, is an indication of just how integral cinematic seriality was to the studios. While this suggests a line of continuity between Hollywood practice then and now, the majority of sequels in this period could not have been made without the infrastructure of the studio system. Before we look at certain case studies which bear this out, we must first address two key industry events which determined the role of the sequel in this period: the rise of the double bill and subsequent institutionalisation of the B-movie; and, concomitantly, the increase in series film production.

One of the challenges in historicising the Hollywood sequel is that so many examples from this era have fallen from view, with only a few noteworthy exceptions (the Thin Man series, *The Bells of St. Mary's*, *Bride of Frankenstein* [1935] and, perhaps, *Love Finds Andy Hardy* [1938]) now considered canonical works. Many of the films discussed here are mentioned fleetingly if at all in the numerous popular and academic histories of Hollywood, but, as vital evidence of Hollywood's longstanding commitment to financially motivated Shintoism, they are nonetheless worthy of study.

To 'B' or not to be in business: filling the double bill

The incredible rise of the double bill is generally understood – as are so many aspects of movie history from this period – to be an indirect result of the Depression. The impact of the Wall Street crash of October 1929 reached Hollywood rather late, with movie attendance reaching a new high of 80 million patrons per week in 1930. But by 1932, with weekly attendance having steadily fallen to 55 million and ticket prices slashed, the illusion that the industry was recession-proof had evaporated, and exhibitors were taking desperate measures to convince audiences to spend what little money they had on a picture show.[6] Incentives included free matinees for women, half-price student tickets, two-for-one tickets and even food, silverware, cars or cash as prizes in competitions such as Bank Night.[7] The double bill was the most reliable of these enticements, offering two pictures for the price of a single ticket, and emphasising quantity regardless of quality. Although not a new practice, having initially been deployed in the late teens and 20s throughout New England, it only really took hold after 1930, becoming a staple part of the programme at 40 per cent of the operating theatres by 1932.[8] Initially opposed to the practice on the assumption that it would 'break open the market for independent producers',[9] the major studios (as represented by the Motion Picture Producers and Distributors of America) attempted to make it illegal, but by 1934 even their own affiliated theatres were getting in on the act, and in August the government's National Recovery Administration officially legalised the double bill. By October 1935, when Loew's and RKO announced they would be adopting a double-bill policy at their first-run theatres, the 'two-for-one' offering had become a national institution, albeit one that would remain more popular in certain regions than others, and contentious throughout the decade ahead.[10]

For the studios, the proliferation and valorisation of double billing meant a huge increase in demand for product. Although they had hitherto stratified their production rosters, distinguishing between high-budget 'specials' and mid-range or low-budget movies, now those distinctions calcified into a more rigid caste system, defined by the needs of exhibitors. As Brian Taves and Don Miller have explained, this did not mean a simple division between A- and B-pictures, with the studios also producing 'programmers', films with more elaborate sets, better-known stars and budgets from $100,000 up to $500,000, which could play at either end of the programme, dependent on the theatre.[11] This flexibility in terms of their billing status meant they also had the potential to become surprise successes, a point worth highlighting because several of the key films to spawn sequels discussed later in this chapter – including *Four Daughters* (1938) and *The Thin Man* – fall into this category. Whereas for A-pictures exhibitors paid the distributor a percentage of the net profits, for Bs (or any programmer playing primarily as a B) they paid a relatively low flat fee. On the downside this put a cap on potential earnings, but the upside was a relatively predictable rate of return, allowing producers to budget their B-level titles according to the number of theatres at which they were likely to play – a calculation that was particularly predictable for those studios who owned the theatres in which said movie would be playing.[12] As Richard Jewell has pointed out in relation to RKO, films falling somewhere between the A/B divide may have had the benefit of flexibility, but they were also a source of disagreement between exhibitors and studios, with the former often arguing that they should play them for a flat rental.[13] Furthermore, Ulf Jonas Bjork's study of exhibition practices in Seattle in spring of 1938 makes clear that there was considerable flexibility when it came to billing, meaning that 'a film that was the main feature at one neighbourhood house could be the second film at another'.[14]

Despite these complicating factors, it is nonetheless clear that the rise of the double bill, in tandem with the practice of block-booking (which assured the majors that exhibitors would have to take their B-product along with their As) allowed them to produce high volumes of low-budget fare at minimal risk. Had those conditions not existed, it seems unlikely that the Big Five would have set up dedicated B production units – as Warner, Fox, Paramount and MGM had all done by 1935 – whose work would account for around 50 per cent of total output for the second half of the decade. As Tino Balio explains, these were not the only benefits to the studios, with B-movies enabling them 'to operate at optimum capacity and to provide a training ground for young actors and actresses on their way up and a resting place for performers on their way down'.[15]

In the studio era, then, the term 'B-movie' had little to do with a film's artistic merit (even if it came loaded with those implications), but rather was a designation based on the circumstances of its production, distribution and exhibition. Like their counterparts on Poverty Row,[16] the B-movie producers at the majors tended to meet their production quotas by remaking or recycling plots, repeating and returning to certain characters and situations. As we shall see with the rise of television, and later with video and DVD in subsequent chapters, cinematic seriality has tended to flourish at times when demand for product (usually driven by the arrival of a new exhibition platform) outweighs supply. It was this which saw the series film assume a new prominence from the mid-1930s onwards.

The first franchises: series film production in the 1930s

Led by recurring characters, almost always derived from presold properties that were themselves serial in nature – comic strips, radio shows, dime-store fiction – it is tempting to pigeonhole the series films of this period as precursors of today's contemporary franchises. There are some stark differences, however, both in terms of their formal characteristics and the economic rationale behind their production, which make this comparison only partially appropriate.

Before examining these specifics, however, I must put my introductory comments on the distinction between the series film and the sequel into context. To recap, while both forms revisit characters from an earlier episode, the latter can be identified primarily by its lack of commitment to maintaining narrative continuity from episode to episode. Thus each of Fox's eight *Mr. Moto* movies (1937–9) proceed as largely discrete narrative units, with no carryover from case to case, and so Warner's 'Torchy Blane' (Glenda Farrell) is engaged to her boyfriend Detective McBride (Barton MacLane) in the first film, *Smart Blonde* (1936), but five films later, in *Torchy Gets Her Man* (1938), they are only dating, with no mention of their earlier marital commitment. Just as there is no absolute dividing line between the sequel and the series-film format, there is likewise little evidence to suggest that the studios made any clear distinction between these two formats on aesthetic grounds: films such as *Four Wives* (1939) and *The Miniver Story* (1950) were most certainly referred to as sequels or follow-ups by those producing them, but so too, on occasion, were the second or third films in a series that had no continuing narrative thread. The fuzzy nature of the terminology is equally evident in Frank Nugent's aforementioned article, in which he brackets the series films featuring the Charlie Chan and Philo Vance characters with sequels-proper such as *Bride of Frankenstein* and *Dracula's Daughter* (1936).

During the studio era three types of series were in evidence, distinguishable primarily by the varying levels of interconnection between their individual episodes. The most loosely bound type might be described as thematic or, better yet, 'conceptual'. The 'conceptual series' is exemplified by Warner's *Gold Diggers* (1933–8) and MGM's *Broadway Melody* (1935–40) movies, both of which repeat basic narrative situations and reassemble certain key talent (including Busby Berkeley, Dick Powell and Joan Blondell in the former and Eleanor Powell and Robert Taylor in the latter) but never carry over characters or continue narrative strands from previous films. This strategy had already been deployed by MGM in response to the success of *Our Dancing Daughters* (1928), following this with *Our Modern Maidens* (1929) and *Our Blushing Brides* (1930), all three starring Joan Crawford and Anita Page as friends struggling to land a man, but never as the same characters. Perhaps the most famous example came later, with Paramount's teaming of Bob Hope and Bing Crosby, first in *Road to Singapore* (1940) and then in a further six Road movies in which they reiterated a particular dynamic, without ever playing the same pair of friends.

The second type is the 'series film' proper, in which characters are carried over, often into similar, repetitive situations, but within discrete narrative units. This is not to say that they make no use of their audience's potential knowledge of the overall series – latter episodes in the Sherlock Holmes series (1939–46), for example, might allow the audience to enjoy the familiarity of interplay between Basil Rathbone as Holmes and Nigel Bruce as Watson – but there is little or no specific reference to events in previous episodes and no acknowledgment of a chronological narrative relationship between one film and the next.

The third, least prevalent type is what I would term the 'series with continuity'. Here, to a greater or lesser extent, there will be an acknowledged chronology: overt reference might be made to events, relationships or characters' from earlier films; and characters' lives will in some sense develop, be it through education, marriage, parenthood or the ageing process. Prior events may have little direct bearing on the events of the new episode, but their passing will not be forgotten or go entirely unmentioned. In the opening scene of *You're Only Young Once* (1937), the second film in the Hardy family series (1937–58), we see Judge Hardy retiring from the bench to his chamber and talking with Frank Redmond, the local newspaper owner with whom he clashed in the first film, *A Family Affair* (1937), over the building of an aqueduct. Their conversation makes direct reference to this earlier disagreement and to the outcome of *A Family Affair*, in which the judge triumphed over the big business interests behind the aqueduct. Furthermore, Frank's visit to the judge is a direct result of this resolution: he unwisely invested in the aqueduct, is out of credit and so needs the judge to act as his guarantor on a loan. That the judge and Frank are now played by Lewis Stone and Frank Craven, replacing Lionel Barrymore and Charley Grapewin from the previous film, might somewhat confuse matters, but it does not negate the fact that the film-makers are making some effort to pick up where the first film left off.

Elsewhere in *You're Only Young Once*, another form of continuity is demonstrated in the presentation of Mickey Rooney's Andy Hardy character. Much is made of Andy's progression to adulthood: his relationship with girl-next-door Polly (Margaret Marquis in *A Family Affair*, replaced here and for the remainder of the series by Ann Rutherford) has blossomed from the embarrassed first kiss in the final moments of *A Family Affair*, into a 'steady', but of course still chaste, relationship; and, when his mother refers to his 'little friends' over dinner, Andy rages back 'Little friends? When is this family going to treat me as though I'm grown up?!' Most of *You're Only Young Once* follows the Hardys' vacation to Catalina Island, and presents a largely self-contained set of events that have little if anything to do with the action from *A Family Affair*. Nonetheless, I would argue that even this modest continuity is sufficient to suggest that it, and other similar films within such a series, can legitimately be understood as sequels – much like *Bad Boys II* (2003) or *Home Alone 2: Lost in New York* (1992), where new narrative developments have an equally limited causal connection to their antecedents.

Clearly such distinctions, though tangible, were not standardised across the industry, nor were they necessarily applied consistently throughout a series. Rather, I would propose that they are largely the result of the material involved. The Hardys' appeal relates at some level to their representation of an average family and it therefore makes sense that one source of drama for new episodes would be the process of change that any family might experience as children grow up and parents age. Even Columbia's longrunning Blondie series (1938–49), otherwise largely unconcerned with narrative continuity, acknowledges the passage of time via the maturation of Blondie's (Penny Singleton) two children: Cookie (Marjorie Ann Mutchie), whose birth is documented in *Blondie's Blessed Event* (1942); and Alexander (Larry Simm), who is eventually allowed to drop the moniker 'Baby Dumpling' as he becomes a teenager in later films.

Most of the series from this period, however, are centred around detectives such as Charlie Chan, Mr Moto, Sherlock Holmes, Boston Blackie, the Saint, the Lone Wolf and the Falcon; lonesome adventurers such as the Cisco Kid and Red Ryder; or comic figures such as Glenda Farrell's Torchy Blane, Lupe Velez's 'Mexican Spitfire' and George Sidney and Charles Murray's Cohen and Kelly. Most of these characters arrive on screen fully developed and remain largely unchanged from one film to the next. Novelty is primarily generated not through developments in the character's lives, but through a new case or adventure which introduces some combination of new supporting characters, new locations and a new narrative enigma, all of which are specific to that film and do not recur in future episodes.

There are other considerations here, considerations which extend beyond a set of shared formal characteristics and call for an examination of the production and exhibition context. It seems no coincidence, for example, that those series which maintain a higher level of continuity – the Hardy family and Dr Kildare films being exemplars – are from MGM, the company which spent as much on its B-grade product as Universal might budget for something it classed an A. It should also be noted that the increased focus on Andy in the Hardy series had a commercial imperative: the huge success of *Love Finds Andy Hardy* clearly indicated to MGM that this character would draw the largest audience.

Issues of continuity aside, the Hardy films were typical in terms of production rate: most series in the 1930s and 40s averaged two releases per year, sometimes up to three or four from smaller studios, such as Republic's Red Ryder films featuring Bill Elliott. One implication of this approach is that a second or third film would often have to be pushed into production before its predecessor had been released. Thus in August 1937, before screenwriter Kay Van Riper had even finished the screenplay for *You're Only Young Once* (at that point titled *Another Family Affair*), producer Lou Ostrow wrote to scenario department chief Edwin H. Knopf, asking him to 'tie her up for another screenplay along the lines of the one she is just completing'.[17] And, before the completed *You're Only Young Once* was released in December of 1937, Van Riper was putting the finishing touches to her third Hardy family screenplay, in time for it to begin shooting at the beginning of February 1938. That the third Hardy picture was a certainty before the second was completed is borne out by an address to camera by Lewis Stone, appearing after the film's end credits. 'Ladies and Gentleman,' begins Stone, still in costume, 'I hope you've enjoyed the adventures of my, I mean Judge Hardy's family, because Metro Goldwyn Mayer has in preparation further revelations of the loves and hopes and fears of Marian, Andy, Aunt Milly, Mother and incidentally myself.' This postscript indicates not only the extent to which MGM was intent on creating a successful series, but also the level of integrated production planning that was required to make it so.

Of course, given the system of exhibition into which these films were being fed, the financial risks involved were relatively modest. According to the Eddie Mannix Ledger,[18] *A Family Affair* earned $502,000 in rentals (of which the vast majority, $373,000, were from the US) against a production cost of $178,000, returning a profit of $153,000. Costs for *You're Only Young Once* were slightly higher at $202,000, in part due to the second-unit location shooting required on Catalina, while costs for *Judge Hardy's Children* (1938) were pared back to $182,000, effectively matching those of the first film. Even if their respective box-office takings had been only half that of *A Family Affair*, they would still have turned a small profit, but in reality both films' total earnings exceeded that of the first film.[19] Had this not occurred, a drastic drop-off in earnings was still unlikely, given that these films would be booked into the same theatres as their predecessor, often as the bottom half of a double bill, and presumably for similar flat rental fees. This is underlined by the fact that MGM proceeded with *You're Only Young Once* despite having only limited economic encouragement from *A Family Affair* itself: a review of box-office reports from its first three weeks on release indicates little audience enthusiasm, with the only positive word coming from Chicago's Oriental Theatre, where trade had been 'excellent' – which may in fact have been attributable to the unusual inclusion of a band and 'Amateur Hour' tie-in with WENR radio which accompanied each show.[20] Had *A Family Affair* been produced at either mid-range or top-level costs, and had it been positioned as an A-grade release, it seems unlikely that the Hardys would have continued their cinematic life. But, playing it (unofficially) as a B, it was feasible for MGM to recoup and turn a profit on its modest production investment. For a vertically integrated major studio, then, once a B-level series had been established, production could be maintained on a rolling basis with only minimal exposure.

Although MGM moved quickly to establish a series after the release of *A Family Affair*, there is no evidence to suggest this had been planned when it acquired the rights to *Skidding*, the play by Aurania Rouverol on which it was based. Nonetheless, such foresight was valuable when it came to potential story acquisitions, and can be seen elsewhere in the industry in the mid-1930s. One such example is Warner Bros.' deal with author Erle Stanley Gardner for his story 'The Case of the Howling Dog', featuring the character of Perry Mason. The initial agreement is dated 9 April 1934, but Walter MacEwen had been tracking the story since January of that same year, when it began to appear in serial form in *Liberty* magazine. Mason had first appeared the year before in three serialised stories – 'The Case of the Velvet Claws', 'The Case of the Sulky Girl' and 'The Case of the Lucky Legs' – so its series potential was already clear. Accordingly, the 9 April agreement included not only a holdback on Gardner selling the motion-picture rights to the three pre-existing works, but also an option for the next five Mason stories, with purchase prices increasing to $15,000 for the first two options, $20,000 for the following two options and $25,000 for the fifth.[21] The initial 'consideration' for 'Howling Dog' was $10,000, slightly above the $8,400 average Warner paid for B-picture source material in 1934, but below the $12,000 average it paid for potential A-picture properties.[22] One might assume that the taking of additional options was purely strategic, allowing Warner to test Perry Mason's popularity with one film while precluding the possibility of any direct competition from other bidders. Nonetheless, the studio's intent to create a series is evidenced by another agreement with Gardner, dated 10 May, in which it exercises its first option for an as-yet-unpublished Mason novel, *The Case of the Curious Bride*. This came more than a month before *The Case of the Howling Dog* went before the cameras in June and four months before its release in September of that same year. Warner waited until after that release before picking up any further options, presumably limiting its risk to the story acquisition and screenplay costs, but did so very quickly thereafter, buying 'The Case of the Lucky Legs' and 'The Case of the Velvet Claws' in an agreement dated 10 October. The marketing for *The Case of the Howling Dog* reflects Warner Bros.' commitment to making Perry Mason a long-term fixture in cinemas: 'MEET PERRY MASON', reads the front page of the sales brochure, 'You'll be seeing lots of him – so get acquainted now – in THE CASE OF THE HOWLING DOG.'[23]

Warner's approach to the Perry Mason properties was not unusual. The company would later replicate it in its acquisition of Carolyn Keene's 'Nancy Drew' stories in May of 1938. Similarly, a precedent had been set earlier in the decade by Fox in its acquisition of Earl Derr Biggers's Charlie Chan novels and subsequent creation of a movie series beginning in earnest with *Charlie Chan Carries On* (1931).[24] Nonetheless, it is a useful indication of the speed at which decisions had to be made in order to establish and maintain a series at this time. A counterpoint can be found in the case of Philo Vance, a character whose creator, S. S. Van Dine, would only sell rights on a single-novel basis. Accordingly, although thirteen Philo Vance movies appeared between 1929 and 1940, they were released only sporadically, were produced variously by Paramount, MGM and Warners and saw Van Dine's gentlemanly detective played by eight different actors.

As we shall see in Chapter 4, the manner in which the studios in the 1930s set about establishing series from the first film onwards bears some resemblance to the more contemporary practice of franchise building from the 1990s onwards. It is important to note, however, that the speed and relatively low budgets with which these films were produced set them clearly apart from what came later. Questions of budget in particular are key, because the peak of series film production in the 1930s and early 40s coincided with the major studios' peak investment in low-cost movies. With the 1940 consent decree restricting block-booking to blocks of no more than five, and the first-run market proving increasingly profitable, the major studios would gradually reduce their low-budget production, so that this had virtually ceased by 1945.[25] MGM was still releasing Andy Hardy and Dr Kildare pictures after the war, but otherwise series production was relegated to Columbia, Universal and minors such as Monogram. By the early 1950s, Columbia and Universal were also abandoning the traditional series model. The latter established the Ma and Pa Kettle and the Francis series in 1949 and 1950 respectively but released only one entry per year, instead of the traditional two or three, abandoning both by 1955.

Of course, while series production was in many respects the dominant mode of movie seriality in the studio era, numerous examples from this period – both during and after the series boom – illustrate a broad spectrum of approaches to the sequel. So how did Hollywood's unique organisation during this period affect the production of sequels? As we shall see, this in part depends upon the studio involved.

MGM and the A-grade series

Although MGM denied any involvement in B- movie production, A Family Affair had clearly not been conceived to exist at the same level as the studio's A-grade releases. Even after the break-out success of Love Finds Andy Hardy, which earned more than $1.6 million in the United States alone (nearly eight times its production cost, and four times as much as A Family Affair), budgets for the subsequent Hardy films were not hugely increased, remaining below $500,000 until 1944's Andy Hardy's Blonde Trouble, which cost $723,000. Until this point, the series had delivered incredibly consistent returns for the studio, with each of the nine films between Love Finds and Blonde Trouble making between $1.1 million and $1.5 million in profits across domestic and foreign markets. They were produced like clockwork by the Seitz Unit, named after director George B. Seitz, who was responsible for all but the last two of the Hardy movies, which were made after his death in 1944. Alongside Mickey Rooney and Lewis Stone, other regulars included Kay Van Riper, who was involved in six of the screenplays, and cinematographer Lester White, who shot eleven of the movies for Seitz. As for their exhibition context, from Love Finds Andy Hardy onwards the Hardy films were top of the bill in most situations – and even then their costs remained at the lowest end of MGM's budget range until the mid-1940s and their production circumstances were equivalent to that of B-grade series films from other studios.[26] A similar observation can be made of the Dr Kildare films, which again remained consistently profitable propositions for first-run theatres, but which the studio churned out at the rate of two or three per year between 1939 and 1943.

There was, however, another approach to series development at the studio, more in keeping with its official stance against B-movie production, and exemplified by its response to the respective successes of Tarzan the Ape Man (1932), which uses the characters created by Edgar Rice Burroughs in an original story, and The Thin Man, based on a Dashiell Hammett novel recommended to the studio by director W. S. Van Dyke.[27] In both cases, MGM was quick to move a sequel into development, but took the time to ensure that these were A-grade productions in all respects rather than quick cash-ins.

Although there has been some debate over the exact status of The Thin Man because of its B-level $231,000 production costs, and incredibly short shooting schedule of just eighteen days,[28] it was clearly exhibited like an A-picture: at the top of the bill at both the MGM-owned Capitol Theatre in New York and the Loew's State in Los Angeles, and at the Chicago Theatre, part of the Paramount-owned Balaban & Katz chain. Furthermore, despite the low budget and the detective-fiction source material, the film bears little resemblance to B-movies from other studios, in that it uses both location shooting and already established names, with William Powell as retired private detective Nick Charles and Myrna Loy as his wealthy wife Nora. Loy was not quite A-list material when *The Thin Man* went into production in April 1934,[29] while Powell was already deemed a star – but both actors' stock rose following the film's May 1934 release.[30] *The Thin Man* went on to become both MGM's tenth-highest earner and its fifth most profitable release of the season.[31]

There was no pre-existing source material for a sequel to Hammett's novel, but by 29 August 1934 the producer Hunt Stromberg (who would go on to oversee the next three films in the series) had submitted six pages of notes on how a follow-up should play out. These notes describe the sequel's opening scenes much as they would eventually appear in the released version of *After the Thin Man* (1936), and also indicate that Stromberg was at pains to stress the need for the kind of narrative continuation largely absent from series films, stating that he wanted 'to give some idea of how this sequel should start and be presented as a follow-up'. His suggestions include the return of Joe Morelli (Edward Brophy), a suspect from *The Thin Man* who, it transpires, is once again under suspicion for a crime he didn't commit, and a new mystery revolving around Dorothy Wynant (Maureen O'Sullivan), daughter of the original 'Thin Man', and her husband Tommy (Henry Wadsworth): 'Wynant did have enemies', Stromberg explains, 'We planted that in the first picture.' These plot points ultimately failed to survive the drafting process, perhaps in part because, as Stromberg himself admits, 'the millions of people who have seen THE THIN MAN will be smarter now in spotting suspects or guilty ones than they were in the first picture', and that 'In a sequel such as this, the audience would make up its mind instantly that a character like Joe Morelli is not guilty [Stromberg's emphasis]'.[32] Nonetheless, *After the Thin Man* does indeed pick up directly where its predecessor left off, with Nick and Nora on a train home to San Francisco, and, as Stromberg's notes propose, sees them arrive at the station only to be collared by reporters eager to talk to the famous Mr Charles, before proceeding to Nora's opulent home for peace and quiet, only to find that their friends have organised a surprise party to celebrate their return.

Even with these opening moments in place, there was evidently considerable work to do before a sequel would be ready to go before the cameras, with Hammett commissioned to write a full treatment that autumn. Stromberg dictated notes for this treatment on 26 March 1935, but it was more than a year before Frances Goodrich and Albert Hackett, the husband-and-wife team credited for the first film's screenplay, delivered a finished draft. Given the success of *The Thin Man*, there was some pressure to ensure that its sequel would be a worthy successor, as W. S. Van Dyke explained in an interview: 'This time it must be an original story written solely for the screen, yet it must retain an interest equal to, if not greater than, that of the first story.'[33]

The leisurely pace at which development proceeded can be explained in part because MGM had little need to hurry through another Thin Man film. They were able to capitalise on the chemistry between Powell and Loy, established first by *Manhattan Melodrama* (1934)[34]and then *The Thin Man*, by setting up further Powell–Loy pairings. As a result, *Evelyn Prentice* went into production in August 1934, and was followed by *Libelled Lady* (1936) and *The Great Ziegfield*

(1936). All three were completed before *After the Thin Man* began shooting in September 1936, with the last two becoming major hits. *Ziegfeld*, in fact, was the highest earner of MGM's 1936–7 season, but it was not the studio's most profitable release; that honour belonged to *After the Thin Man*, which made the studio more than $1.5 million in the same period.[35]

That the sequel's commercial success vastly outstripped that of the original was an indication of both Powell and Loy's increased star-power and also the broader trend of improving admissions and box office as the industry recovered from the Depression. There was little doubt that there would be further sequels, although again these appeared only at two- or three-year intervals. Because they were central to its success, production could not proceed without Loy and Powell, with the lapse between sequels sometimes due to exterior forces affecting their availability. Powell's struggle with cancer kept him away from work for much of 1938 and 1939, while Loy's commitment to her work with the Red Cross during the war meant she made no other films between *Shadow of the Thin Man* in 1941 and *The Thin Man Goes Home* in 1944.[36] These intervals did little harm to the box-office returns, with each sequel notching up domestic earnings of between $1.4 million and $1.9 million. Of course, by the time *Song of the Thin Man* earned $1.4 million domestically in 1947, increased admission prices meant that attendance for the series was actually dwindling. More crucially, although each of the sequels was made at what H. Mark Glancy has identified as 'average' production costs for MGM,[37] those average costs had increased dramatically over the series' thirteen-year lifespan. *Song of the Thin Man*'s production costs exceeded $1.6 million, ultimately resulting in a loss of $128,000, and signalling the end of what had been a remarkable run.[38]

Partially because of the intervals between episodes, and partially because of their high production values and commercial resilience, the Thin Man series has more in common with today's franchises than most of its contemporaries. Nonetheless, MGM's repeated pairing of Loy and Powell in other films, facilitated by their long-term contracts, meant that it was able to exploit the Thin Man's popularity across a broad spectrum of releases with an ease that would be unthinkable after the collapse of the studio system.

If it could rely on the pairing of Loy and Powell to attract audiences even outside the Thin Man series, MGM had greater reason to rush into a sequel to *Tarzan the Ape Man*. It faced direct competition from Sol Lesser, whose pre-existing agreement with Edgar Rice Burroughs gave him the right to produce and release one serial and, cut from it, one feature film based on Burroughs stories.[39] The serial itself was not a major threat, but the feature would be more problematic, so MGM moved quickly to forge another agreement with Burroughs, in this case giving the studio not only the rights to make another film based on the Tarzan character but also additional options to produce a further two sequels. That agreement was finalised in April 1932, just a few weeks after the premiere of *Tarzan the Ape Man*, but it was a full year before the studio had a script near completion, and not until August of 1933 that shooting on *Tarzan and His Mate* (1934) began.

According to Thomas Schatz, while Louis B. Mayer was keen to cash in on *Tarzan*'s success, production head Irving Thalberg 'convinced him to limit production to one Tarzan movie every two years, hoping to keep the premise fresh and to maximize profits'.[40] It is certainly true that the first four MGM Tarzan sequels – *Tarzan and His Mate*, *Tarzan Escapes* (1936), *Tarzan Finds a Son!* (1939) and *Tarzan's Secret Treasure* (1941) – appeared at two- or three-year intervals,

Two of MGM's A-grade series: Johnny Weissmuller, Maureen O'Sullivan and Johnny Sheffield in *Tarzan Finds a Son!* (1939); Myrna Loy, William Powell, Dickie Hall and Asta, the dog in *Shadow of the Thin Man* (1941)

but it is hard to ascertain to what extent this was strictly the result of a co-ordinated strategy as opposed to the demands of production. In the two years that elapsed between *Tarzan the Ape Man* and *Tarzan and His Mate*, the studio was not quietly biding its time in order to create pent-up demand, but was instead dedicating many months and nearly double the original's production cost to mounting an even more ambitious film that involved multiple locations, an underwater sequence, rear projection, real and model elephants and even a newly trained rhino. With a change of director and minor cast members, retakes of the underwater sequence demanded by the Production Code office, and Maureen O'Sullivan (as Jane) out of action for forty-five days because of an appendectomy, the shoot ran on for a full eight months.[41] Although the delays and personnel changes were unfortunate, the scale of the production was probably seen as necessary in order to ensure that MGM bested the competition. This now came not only from Lesser's *Tarzan* serial and feature, but also from other studios who had ventured into similar territory since MGM had released the jungle-set *Trader Horn* (its highest earner of the 1930–1 season) and announced its plans for *Tarzan the Ape Man*. While *Tarzan and His Mate* was in production, Paramount had released *King of the Jungle* (1933) and RKO had launched the box-office phenomenon *King Kong* (1933) and its sequel *Son of Kong* (1933).

While it proved as much of a draw overseas as the first film, *Tarzan and His Mate*'s domestic earnings were slightly lower ($811,000 versus $1.1 million for the original) and the vast increase in production costs meant that it made a relatively modest profit of $161,000.[42] This may in part explain why MGM waited until January 1935 before announcing a third Tarzan adventure which, after a very troubled production process, was finally released two and a half years after its predecessor in November 1936.[43] *Tarzan Escapes* had originally been due for release at the end of 1935, so it appears that here again the interval between sequels was as much down to the logistical demands of the production as it was to careful scheduling – and this in turn was the result of MGM's need to position its series as a first-run attraction, dedicating considerable time and money to each sequel. This pattern was broken only for the studio's sixth and final film, *Tarzan's New York Adventure* (1942), which was put before the cameras just four months after the completion of *Tarzan's Secret Treasure*, in order to make use of the character one last time before Lesser took over all rights. It was shot quickly and budgeted at a relatively modest $707,000, but was still intended to play as an A-picture – which it did, becoming MGM's fifth highest earner of the season.

Alongside their A-grade exhibition and production contexts, the Tarzan and Thin Man films both exhibit an intention to maintain narrative continuity and develop their characters across the series. In both cases, this largely takes the form of advancing the personal lives of Tarzan and Jane and Nick and Nora, specifically by introducing a child into their respective relationships: Boy (Johnny Sheffield), the orphaned survivor of a plane crash who becomes the subject of *Tarzan Finds a Son!*; and Nick Jr, the offspring whose imminent arrival Nora announces at the end of *After the Thin Man* and who is introduced as a baby in *Another Thin Man* (1939). In this respect, then, while we may colloquially refer to these as 'series', both sets of films represent collections of sequels, as opposed to the true series films which helped fill out double bills during the same period. This is not to imply that financial largesse was what separated series films from sequels: MGM was proving as much with its Hardy films and so, in rather more straitened circumstances, was Universal Pictures.

Counting on Dracula (and Deanna): Universal and sequelisation

While MGM cultivated and maintained its image as the Tiffany's of the movie industry, Universal spent the best part of the studio era operating on a very different level. Chapter 1 demonstrated how the organisation of United Artists created an environment in which a star such as Valentino or Fairbanks, as producer and master of his own fate, might be encouraged to opt for the safety of a sequel to an earlier hit in order to stabilise or resurrect a faltering career. We can see echoes of this strategy, adopted not by a star in this case but by a studio, when we consider the output of Universal in the 1930s and two varying instances in which it used sequelisation, first with its horror output and later with films starring Deanna Durbin.

Run by Carl Laemmle, Universal was neither solely a distribution outlet in the manner of United Artists, nor a vertically integrated giant like MGM. While it had maintained a studio (on the 230-acre site known as Universal City) since 1915 and employed a large number of contract staff to oversee its production and distribution operations, Universal had only ever had a fleeting stake in exhibition (from 1926, when Laemmle set up Universal Chain Theaters, Inc., until the coming of sound in 1927), and so lacked the automatic access to the first-run market enjoyed by the Big Five. Under Laemmle, the company had been slow to move fully into feature production (specialising in cheaply made shorts, serials and two-reelers until the early 1920s), less aggressive than its competitors in the bid to acquire theatres and somewhat tardy in fully converting to sound.[44]

As the effects of the Depression finally impacted the industry in 1931, the fact that Universal owned no theatres and none of the associated debt became its saving grace, meaning that the company turned a modest profit of $400,000 that year, while its competitors (aside from the mighty MGM) made losses – and this despite a programme of costly productions instigated by Laemmle's son, Carl Laemmle, Jr, who had become head of production in 1928. And yet, while advantageous in the short term, it was the Laemmles' lack of exhibition real estate which ultimately dictated their production roster and laid the foundations for the demise of their regime.[45] Universal still needed to ensure access to the lucrative first-run theatres owned by the Big Five. This meant both that it needed to produce features suitable for that market and, arguably, that the studio was therefore more likely to doggedly emulate any of its own first-run successes than its competitors, as was the case with the series of films following the premiere of Tod Browning's *Dracula* (1931) on 14 February 1931.

Often considered a *sui generis* hit, *Dracula* was in reality a belated continuation of an earlier cycle of spectacular horror films from the silent era, notably *The Hunchback of Notre Dame* (1923) and *The Phantom of the Opera* (1925), two of Universal's biggest hits of the decade, both starring Lon Chaney – who Universal would have cast as Dracula were it not for his untimely death.[46] The production history of the Universal horror films of this period is well documented and need not be recounted in detail.[47] What is noteworthy, however, is the relatively limited role sequels played in the early stages of this particular cycle. When *Dracula* became an unequivocal success early in 1931, one might have assumed a direct sequel to be Junior Laemmle's logical next step. Instead, in May 1931, the studio purchased Peggy Webling's stage adaptation of Mary Shelley's *Frankenstein*. Laemmle therefore opted not for another *Dracula* but instead for a comparable combination of genre and talent, as evidenced by the

announcement that Bela Lugosi, 'Dracula himself', would star as the monster in this new production, to be directed by James Whale.[48]

In retrospect, it seems self-evident that Lugosi was a poor fit for the role, but Universal was
acting as any studio would have done at that time, pairing a contracted star with a film in the
genre for which he was famous. Accounts vary as to how Lugosi came to be replaced,[49] but
the casting of the relatively unknown Boris Karloff ultimately provided Universal with a new
star around which to build subsequent horror productions. Negative reactions at preview
screenings led the studio to alter the ending to Frankenstein (1931), adding an epilogue in which
it is revealed that Dr Henry Frankenstein (Colin Clive) has in fact survived the fire which appar-
ently destroyed his creation,[50] although it has also been suggested that Laemmle wanted these
changes so as to leave the door open for sequels.[51]

Frankenstein opened at the end of 1931 to enthusiastic reviews and strong box office, joining Dracula as one of the studio's biggest hits of the period. Why, then, were sequels to both of
these productions so slow to appear, particularly when other studios had begun to release
competing horror movies? In the case of Dracula, we might assume that Junior Laemmle was
in part discouraged by the obstacles to narrative continuation presented by the film's denoue-
ment, in which Van Helsing (Edward Van Sloan) kills the count by driving a stake through his
heart. Even if this were surmountable, there remained issues of timing and talent availability.
There was no sequel to Dracula in development so, with Frankenstein no longer an option, the
best way to capitalise on Lugosi's sudden commercial value was to assign him to another horrific tale already in the works: Murders in the Rue Morgue (1932).

With its central protagonist still alive at its conclusion, the interval between Frankenstein
and Bride of Frankenstein in 1935 is less explicable in terms of narrative restrictions, so here
again talent considerations come to the fore. According to James Whale's biographer, the director had no immediate interest in making a sequel, feeling he had 'squeezed the idea dry'.[52]
Meanwhile, despite having entered into bitter dispute with the Laemmles over his credit for
the original film, writer Robert Florey submitted a short treatment for a sequel, entitled The
New Adventures of Frankenstein – The Monster Lives!, early in 1932. Whether unenthused by the
treatment or disinclined to hire Florey again after his dispute over the Frankenstein credit, the
studio returned it to him within a few weeks.

It was not until the following year that Laemmle commissioned staff writer Tom Reed to
write a treatment for the sequel, tentatively titled The Return of Frankenstein, which Reed duly
submitted in June 1933.[53] Universal announced the project in July, as part of a two-picture deal
with Boris Karloff, whose contract had been allowed to lapse earlier that same year.[54] That the
project failed to move forward until the following year appears to be largely due to James
Whale. The director's biographer has suggested that the success of his The Invisible Man (1933)
in November 1933 led Junior Laemmle to believe that Whale was the only man who could
deliver an effective Frankenstein sequel. Given his aforementioned lack of interest, Whale had
to be convinced. This meant Laemmle agreeing to finance One More River (1934), an adaptation of a John Galsworthy novel which had become a pet project for Whale. It was only in June
1934 that Whale officially began preparatory work on the Frankenstein sequel.[55] That Universal
honoured Whale's wishes rather than pushing ahead without him is some measure of the
respect he commanded, or rather a sign of the studio's faith in his ability to deliver commercial

results: it would have been unwise to gamble such a commercially important production on an untested director.

Originally budgeted at $293,750, *Bride of Frankenstein*, as it was finally named, ended up costing nearly $400,000 by the time shooting finished in March 1935. Debuting at the Fox chain's landmark New York theatre, the Roxy, in May of that year, it went on to become another major success for Universal. This was just as well, given the investment and Universal's precarious position within the industry. Its success also encouraged the Laemmles to continue with their recently announced development of six 'super-features' to be produced by Junior, who had by then handed back the reins of the studio to his father: *Bride* had been the first and there were five more to come.[56] Such a strategy was not sustainable, however, and by the end of the year Carl Laemmle, Sr had taken out a loan for $750,000 with J. Cheever Cowdin's Standard Capital Company. As was his right according to the terms of the loan, Cowdin purchased a majority interest in the studio when the loan was not repaid in March 1936, forcing the Laemmles out and bringing in Charles Rogers to oversee production.[57]

Just as Laemmle Senior was losing grip on his empire, shooting on *Dracula's Daughter* (1936), a much delayed sequel to the Tod Browning original, was coming to a close. The protracted history of that production stemmed largely from an absence of easily adaptable material, caused in part by the intervention of David O. Selznick. Then based at MGM, Selznick had cannily purchased 'Dracula's Guest', a short story by Bram Stoker, from his widow Florence in September 1933. The purchase was officially made on behalf of MGM, but the studio's concerns about potential legal action from Universal over the use of the word 'Dracula' in the title eventually led it to pass on its option. That left Selznick free to sell on the rights to the story and a finished screenplay by John L. Balderston (adapter of both *Dracula* and *Frankenstein*) to Universal in September 1934, an outcome which David J. Skal has suggested Selznick anticipated from the outset.[58] Quite why a full year then elapsed before Universal submitted a new treatment to the Production Code office in September 1935 is unclear, but the timing suggests that it was *Bride of Frankenstein*'s successful launch in May of that same year which encouraged Junior Laemmle to push ahead with another horror sequel.

Regardless, by the time it was released in May 1936, the self-styled 'New Universal' regime had turned away from horror. It was only when a double-bill reissue of *Frankenstein* and *Dracula* in the summer of 1938 proved a success that the studio – which had undergone a further regime change earlier that year when Nate Blumberg and Cliff Work had taken over from Robert Cochrane and Charles Rogers respectively – returned to the genre with *Son of Frankenstein* (1939).[59] Produced and directed by Rowland V. Lee, that film went vastly over both schedule and budget, but was sufficiently successful to encourage further forays into the genre. Thereafter, as the number of Universal horror sequels proliferated, so the characters were gradually untethered from both their literary and cinematic origins. Although only Karloff returns in *Son*, this time accompanied by Lugosi as Ygor, its plot nonetheless concerns the effects of Dr Frankenstein's legacy on his descendant, played by Basil Rathbone. By the time of *Frankenstein Meets the Wolf Man* (1943), however, any connection became increasingly tenuous, with Lugosi now playing the Monster, a shift explained by the fact that Ygor's brain had been implanted into the Monster's body at the end of the previous film, *Ghost of Frankenstein* (1942). This gradual move away from carefully constructed sequels towards more cursory attempts at narrative continuation reflects not only the exhaustion of the source material but also the limited amount of time and money the studio was then willing to dedicate to these productions. With only occasional exceptions, the studio's horror sequels in the early 1940s were an important part of its high-volume, low-cost strategy at that time, just as the success of their predecessors in the early 1930s had led the Laemmles away from that very business model and towards a precipitous quest for A-grade prestige.[60]

Although Karloff and Lugosi were valuable commodities within the horror genre, and were for this reason treated as stars within the gates of Universal City, their fame and commercial value was modest compared to that of the stars under contract at the majors. Although she rose to fame only after he and his son had been forced out, Deanna Durbin's star-making film *Three Smart Girls* (1937) was an indirect result of Laemmle Senior's commitment to European production. A lighthearted family musical following the exploits of the Craig sisters – Joan (Nan Grey), Kay (Barbara Read) and Penny (Durbin) – *Three Smart Girls* was the result of a collaboration between producer Joe Pasternak and director Henry Koster, both of whom had been employed in Berlin by Laemmle's German subsidiary, Deutsche Universal GmbH. As Helmut G. Asper and Jan-Christopher Horak have documented, Pasternak and Koster were seen as remnants of the Laemmles' regime and, having left Germany as the extent of the Reich's anti-Semitism became clear, had to fight for work under Charles Rogers when they arrived at the studio in March 1936. Nonetheless, they convinced him to allow them to make *Three Smart Girls* and coached Durbin through her first starring role as Penny Craig. Produced for $326,000, the film earned a phenomenal $1,635,800 following its release in December 1936, establishing Durbin as box-office gold and elevating Pasternak and Koster to premium status at the studio.[61]

Whereas the success of *Dracula* had to some extent been foreseen by Junior Laemmle, it appears that the popularity of *Three Smart Girls* took Charles Rogers by surprise: not only because the budget he granted Pasternak and Koster was relatively modest, but also because no other Durbin project had been scheduled prior to its release.[62] Despite this blank slate, a sequel was not the studio's automatic response to the film's success. Instead, Rogers gave Pasternak and Koster the go-ahead for *One Hundred Men and a Girl* (1937), which centred on the attempts of young Patricia (Durbin) to organise her own orchestra. There followed two further Durbin films produced by Pasternak and directed by Koster, *Mad about Music* (1938) and *That Certain Age* (1938), before a sequel to *Three Smart Girls* went into production.

By the time *Three Smart Girls Grow Up* went before the cameras in December 1938, nearly two years after the release of its progenitor, Durbin was Universal's most consistently successful star. *Three Smart Girls* had been produced at the upper end of the budgetary scale imposed at the post-Laemmle Universal in 1936, but its success had prompted a steady escalation in costs for Durbin films which led to the sequel being produced for $810,000, more than double the cost of the original. This vast increase in budget is more an indication of the studio's confidence in Durbin's bankability at that time than a belief that a sequel to her first hit was a sure thing, an impression reinforced by the film's marketing materials. Of the multiple display advertisements in the press book for *Three Smart Girls Grow Up*, only two versions make any explicit reference to the earlier film, with the first bearing the headline 'THEY WERE "SMART" BEFORE … BUT WAIT'LL YOU SEE 'EM NOW!' and the second headed 'THE WORLD HAS EAGERLY WAITED FOR THEM TO GROW UP!' The latter is also the only advert to give equal prominence to the three leads, with equally scaled close-ups of Nan Grey and Helen Parrish (replacing Barbara Read as Kay) flanking that of Durbin. With the recurring hook in most of the copy being 'She Sings the Songs You Asked to Have Her Sing!', it is evident that the film is being sold less on its direct connection to *Three Smart Girls* than on its place within the larger Durbin canon, a continuum orientated not around narrative elements but instead around facets specific to her broader star persona. This is not to suggest the film itself ignores its sequel status, for while its central plotline (Penny's attempts to assist in her older sisters' romantic entanglements) has no direct connection with that of its predecessor, it must nonetheless acknowledge, as its title makes explicit, that the Craig sisters are indeed growing up.

With Durbin's stock at its peak in 1938–9, *Three Smart Girls Grow Up* was evidently not an attempt to restore lustre to a fading star – and the same was true of *Hers to Hold* (1943), the third and final film to feature Durbin as Penny Craig.[63] Although Pasternak and Koster had left Universal in 1941 and 1943 respectively, and although she was no longer a child-star phenomenon, Durbin was still a valuable commodity in the early 1940s, and the two films which preceded *Hers to Hold*, *It Started with Eve* (1941) and *The Amazing Mrs. Holliday* (1943), were hugely profitable.[64] News of the sequel emerged early in 1942, when it was announced as *Three Smart Girls Join Up*,[65] but production was postponed until January of the following year, by which time it had been renamed – presumably because the final script, centring on Penny's wartime romance with an air force flyer, featured neither of the other two Smart Girls. Once again, the advertising for *Hers to Hold* makes only casual reference to its sequel status, indicating that this was deemed to be of minimal commercial import relative to its place within the Durbin filmography.

Unlike Universal's early horror sequels, in which the talent involved was relevant only insofar as it reinforced those films' generic credentials, the *Three Smart Girls* series suggests a studio operating more like one of the Big Five; a studio whose central commodity is a star, rather than a character or narrative property. This was not, as such, a sign of things to come. Although it did cultivate and utilise other major stars throughout the 1940s, including Donald O'Connor and the comedy team of Abbott and Costello, Universal also remained committed (unlike its vertically integrated competitors) to producing modestly budgeted films such as those in the Sherlock Holmes and Inner Sanctum (1943–5) series. Universal deployed *Three Smart Girls Grow Up* and *Hers to Hold* to feed the Deanna Durbin production line, much as Famous Players had once done with the Wallace Reid racing cycle; a move which indicates that when key talent were under long-term contract, sequels were more useful than they were essential, regardless of the studio involved.

Turning point: independent production

Although the years from 1939 through to 1946 were the best of times for the Hollywood studios, there were already signs that the worst of times may lie just around the corner.[66] The year 1946 marked a high-point in cinema admissions in the United States, but shortly thereafter the studios became embroiled in a trade war with Great Britain (at that point still the most valuable foreign market); were subject to a congressional investigation into Communist sympathies within the industry; and were delivered a crushing blow when the Supreme Court ruled that they must divest themselves of their theatre holdings as part of the *Paramount* antitrust decree. By 1950, other aspects of post-war American life were also taking their toll, specifically an increased migration from the cities (which contained the biggest theatres) into the suburbs, and increased competition for the population's leisure time, which came from a variety of areas, but most notably from television. These events had little immediate bearing on sequel production, but the *Paramount* decree and the rise of television do explain the shifting status of the sequel after the divorcement. Most of these changes would not be evident until the latter half of the 1950s, but Leo McCarey's *The Bells of St. Mary's* in 1945 does point towards the dynamics of sequel production in the later decades – albeit in ways which are still ultimately rooted in the studio system.

Among the many changes wrought by the *Paramount* decree, perhaps the most significant for the history of the sequel is the industry's subsequent move away from the production line, producer-unit approach, towards what Janet Staiger has termed the 'package-unit system', in which long-term studio contracts were replaced by an 'industry-wide pooling of materials ... and the transitory combination of labor-force and means of production'.[67] There had always been an element of independent production within the industry, but the notable increase in such productions within the studio gates in the 1940s can be seen as the beginning of a gradual move towards a model closer to that long championed by United Artists, in which each film was individually planned, financed and sold to exhibitors on its own merits. This shift was encouraged by changes that were taking place both within and outside the industry. First, a change to the laws governing capital gains tax meant that an individual could set up a 'single picture corporation'; an entity designed to produce just one picture before being dissolved, leaving its profits to be taxed at the capital gains rate of 25 per cent, rather than the far higher rate of income tax for top earners. Second, with the box office booming and loans rarely returning losses, many major banks relaxed their lending policies and actively competed to provide film financing.[68]

While it would not become standard practice until after the studios had sold off their theatres, certain key stars and directors (including Katharine Hepburn, James Cagney, John Ford and Frank Capra) had already adopted this approach in the early 1940s.[69] Leo McCarey was one of the most successful of this wave of producer–director hyphenates, due in no small part to the enormous popularity of *Going My Way* (1944) and its sequel, *The Bells of St. Mary's*. Starring Bing Crosby as the musically inclined Father O'Malley, these films were the highest-grossing hits of their respective release years, with the former winning multiple Academy Awards and the latter achieving the then-rare feat of outgrossing its predecessor.[70] McCarey had worked at Paramount during the mid-1930s, but had not made a film there since *Make Way for Tomorrow* (1937). Although the studio had fostered some inhouse independent units in the early 1930s, these had always been subject to similar levels of oversight and studio approval as their contracted producers, meaning that independence was very much a relative term.[71] In 1943, however, they entered into a deal which involved not only McCarey and Crosby but also RKO; a deal which hinted at the extent to which creative talent would increasingly be able to leverage their perceived commercial value to exert some control over the projects they made.

McCarey and Crosby had long been friends and were keen to work together on a project then called *The Padre*, which the director had been developing at RKO with screenwriter Frank

Cavett. Both had prior contractual obligations, however, which would have to be overcome: Crosby was in the middle of an eleven-picture deal with Paramount which had commenced in 1941, while McCarey was one picture into a four-picture deal with RKO.[72] To work around these commitments, in early May 1943 they made reciprocal deals via each other's home studios which would enable them to work together on two separate projects. The first of these would be *The Padre*, the screenplay for which McCarey purchased from RKO and brought with him to Paramount, where he signed on to produce and direct a feature based on Cavett's work for that studio. Simultaneously, Crosby signed with RKO for one yet-to-be-specified picture which was to be directed and produced by McCarey subsequent to *The Padre*.[73]

Although McCarey sold his rights in *The Padre* screenplay to Paramount, he would, in exchange for his services, be given a percentage share of all gross receipts in excess of 1.6 times the film's budgeted production cost of $1 million, with this percentage escalating should the gross exceed $2 million.[74] Lavished with critical praise upon its release as *Going My Way* the following May – 'What you're going to like best about this picture is – everything!' cheered the *Chicago Tribune* – the film's enormous commercial success validated McCarey's decision to take a percentage deal, reportedly delivering him royalties in excess of $1 million.[75]

When McCarey and Crosby committed to working together on two projects, these were not intended to be an original and its sequel – prior to the release of *Going My Way*, in fact, they were developing an entirely different screenplay – but the phenomenal popularity of their first collaboration subsequently led them in this direction.[76] McCarey later explained that his decision to produce a sequel had been a result of the many letters he received from the public asking for another picture 'of the same kind'.[77] Regardless of his motivation, it is clear that the director was able to use the commercial value of his working relationship with Crosby, in com-

bination with the tantalising commercial prospect of a sequel to *Going My Way*, to further assert his independence. Thus, rather than simply returning to RKO to fulfil his existing commitment, he instead established his own company, Rainbow Productions, the creation of which was no doubt partially inspired by the fact that *Going My Way* had boosted McCarey's 1944 earnings to such an extent that he had crossed into a 90 per cent income tax bracket, something that could be avoided using the capital gains tax loophole. In agreements finalised in January 1945, McCarey committed to directing two pictures for Rainbow, while RKO committed to: distributing these two pictures for a fee; reassigning its one picture deal with Crosby

Bing Crosby and Ingrid Bergman in the hugely successful *The Bells of St. Mary's* (1945)

to Rainbow; and reducing McCarey's contractual obligation to the studio from three pictures to two.[78]

Although the success of Going My Way certainly smoothed the path for his subsequent dealings with RKO, that McCarey was able to swiftly proceed with a sequel was also the result of the agreements he and Crosby had signed back in 1943. While Paramount owned Going My Way outright, their agreement with McCarey included no mention of either sequel rights or underlying rights to the characters or story, thus enabling the director to produce a sequel without Paramount's involvement. The studio was probably also motivated by the fact that the sooner Crosby fulfilled his obligation to RKO, the sooner he would be back on their lot. Perhaps the only real obstacle was David O. Selznick, who drove a very hard bargain when McCarey approached him to procure the services of Ingrid Bergman for the role of Sister Mary Benedict. The reported $175,000 paid to Selznick goes some way to explaining the inflated budget for The Bells of St. Mary's, which ultimately cost around $600,000 more to produce than Going My Way.[79]

Released in time for Christmas 1945, and again winning critical plaudits, The Bells of St. Mary's was not only that year's biggest hit but also, when adjusted for inflation, remains one of the highest-grossing films in US box-office history. Even prior to Going My Way, McCarey and Crosby were working on somewhat better terms than many of their contemporaries, with contracts based on a number of pictures rather than the standard seven-year term. Still, while they were able to leverage both their pre-existing reputations and their combined association to dictate their own working conditions, the fact that this freedom was partially facilitated by RKO and Paramount suggests the uneasy balance of power between creative talent and the studios that would increasingly hold sway as one set of industrial practices began to give way to another. And, as we shall see in Chapter 4, that a sequel was involved in this particular negotiation foreshadows a trend that would only intensify in subsequent decades.

Elegant repetition: industry-wide trends

The above case studies give some indication of the diverse range of circumstances in which sequels were produced during the studio era and the extent to which the form's deployment was both studio- and time-specific. There are, nonetheless, several broader trends to observe, many the direct result of historically specific circumstances and industrial organisation.

Talent and overheads

As already demonstrated, one of the key factors which distinguishes sequel production practice in this period is the luxury afforded the studios by the long-term contracts under which most talent worked. On the one hand, this meant that a sequel was always a viable option and could in theory be rushed through with little of the potentially complex negotiation that would be required after the move to the package-unit system. While a star might resist a sequel, there was very little they could do if the studio demanded it. Conversely, the repeated combinations of stars and/or genres that followed movies such as The Thin Man, Frankenstein, Dracula and Three Smart Girls indicate how a winning formula might be exploited without immediate recourse to a sequel proper. Other examples from the period include: Judy Garland and Mickey Rooney, who, after the breakout success of Love Finds Andy Hardy, were teamed together not in another Hardy picture but instead as new characters in *Babes in Arms* (1939); and Greer Garson and Walter Pidgeon, whose hugely successful pairing in *Mrs. Miniver* (1942) saw them reunited as on-screen husband and wife in *Madame Curie* (1943), *Mrs Parkington* (1944) and *Julia Misbehaves* (1948) before *The Miniver Story* appeared in 1950. There are, of course, several star combinations which never generated a sequel and, as Steve Neale has argued, 'the types of stories in which stars appeared were by no means always identical, hence that star-genre formulations were by no means always fixed'.[80] William Powell and Myrna Loy, for example, were not always cast together as carbon copies of Nick and Nora, but it is clear that their combination formed a kind of guarantee to audiences, reducing perceived risk to MGM and improving a film's commercial chances. The case of Universal underlines this: the relative narrowness of the films in which Deanna Durbin, Boris Karloff and Bela Lugosi appeared is a function of the studio in which they were produced, which had both more limited economic means and a more limited talent pool, leaving it more likely to closely mimic a prior success than diverge from it. All of which is to say that, because stars and directors were under long-term contract, the sequel was one of a menu of options from which a studio could select if it wished to capitalise on the success of a particular film.

Why, then, choose to make a sequel over an equivalent star–genre combination, or some other variation on the same formula? One answer to this question relates back to the studio system and its large overheads. As with the B-movie, a sequel might fill a useful gap in a production schedule, ensuring that contract staff were kept busy and that resources were in constant use. Such logic is evidently at work in a memo from Jack Warner to Warner production chief Hal Wallis in which the former urges the latter to get *Brother Rat and the Baby* – a sequel to the previous year's *Brother Rat* (1938) – prepared because, as he puts it, 'the whole cast will be idle'.[81]

Even as the old system was coming to an end, economies of scale could still be employed to make a sequel an attractive prospect. Work on *Demetrius and the Gladiators* (1954), a sequel to *The Robe* (1953) was already underway before the former film started shooting, with screenwriter Philip Dunne officially contracted by Daryl F. Zanuck at Twentieth Century-Fox to write a sequel on 4 December 1952.[82] With Dunne under contract, only a few thousand dollars were required to produce a screenplay, a modest investment relative to the money due to be expended on *The Robe*. Having finished principal production in July 1953, the *Demetrius* crew returned for two days of additional shooting on the 16 and 17 September on the Fox lot, just as *The Robe* was premiering to an audience of 6,500 at New York's Roxy Theater, beginning a phenomenal run which would see it gross $16,500,000 in the United States alone by the end of the year.[83] Recycling sets, costumes and even some footage from the original production, in combination with a shorter running time and shooting schedule, *Demetrius and the Gladiators* cost $1.99 million, just under half that of its predecessor. That was hardly a small investment, making *Demetrius* the ninth most expensive film released by Fox in 1954, but, released when *The Robe* was still fresh in audience memory, and marketed with the tagline 'IT BEGINS WHERE "THE ROBE" LEFT OFF', the film still notched up domestic rentals of $4.25 million, making it the third most successful Fox release of the year.[84]

While stressing the importance of the studios' free-ranging control of their talent and resources, we must also acknowledge that there were other limitations, albeit again the result of the factory conditions under which they operated. The annual release schedules set and overseen by the New York office meant that certain quotas had to be met, and the variability of production timelines and unforeseeable human-resource issues meant constant juggling on the part of production heads. This was particularly the case when the talent involved was in high demand, as with Mickey Rooney in the late 1930s. The production files for the Hardy films are littered with instances of shooting dates being adjusted according to Rooney's increasingly tight schedule, such as a memo from J. J. Cohn to Lou Ostrow on 30 December 1938, in which the former explains:

> If at all possible we want to cut Rooney's hair at the very last moment so as to allow Joe Mankiewicz [producer on The Adventures of Huckleberry Finn, in which Rooney was due to star] all possible time for retakes, etc. Please check with Mankiewicz the day before you cut Rooney's hair.[85]

The source material

Another potential hindrance came from the only key talent not under studio contract: the writer who generated the source material for the original film. The potential problems inherent in working with a free agent were crystallised by the acrimonious dealings between Fannie Hurst and Warner Bros. in relation to Four Daughters and its sequel Four Wives, dealings which marked a significant shift in the industry's understanding of how intellectual property rights might affect sequel production.

Hurst's dispute with Warner came when she discovered that they were attempting to make a sequel to Four Daughters, which had been based on her short story 'Sister Act', without paying her an additional fee. Arguably Warner's response to the success of A Family Affair and Three Smart Girls, Four Daughters charted the trials and tribulations of a group of musically talented sisters, and had become one of the studio's biggest hits of the 1938–9 season.[86] Unlike their multi-property contracts for the Nancy Drew and Perry Mason stories, Warner had not anticipated the need to include a sequel clause in Hurst's contract. Nonetheless, shortly after Four Daughters' release, Jack Warner was advised by his legal team that he could proceed with a sequel without further consulting Hurst, on the proviso that they 'put as much Sister Act material in new story as possible'.[87] The proposed solution was similar to that adopted by William Parsons for The Romance of Tarzan: use material for which you have already paid so as to avoid any issues with story credit.

Evidently they felt sufficiently secure in this regard to push ahead with production, with the Four Wives shoot beginning in August 1939 despite legal objections from Hurst. As a point of contrast, it is worth noting that John Garfield, who had made his screen debut in Four Daughters, was equally resistant to the concept of Four Wives. Under studio contract, however, Garfield was forced by Warner's production team to return to work.[88] Hurst's concerns, conversely, were not so easily dismissed. Her fiction had become a staple source for Hollywood over the preceding decade, including adaptations of Imitation of Life (1934) and Back Street (1932), and she was a savvy and staunch defender of her rights. President of the Authors Guild until 1938, she had in fact submitted a report to the Guild two years earlier, recommending that all movie deals for literary works go through a 'negotiator'.[89] According to Variety, this recommendation was finally due to become a reality, ironically due to the problems Miss Hurst was herself now encountering with Warner.

While not quite on a par with its predecessor, *Four Wives* was another critical and com-mercial success for the studio following its release in December 1939.[90] The dispute with Hurst, however, was not settled until late February 1940, when the studio agreed, first, to pay retrospectively for sequel rights, and, second, to pay additional amounts for any further sequels which followed.[91] As a further gesture towards their ongoing partnership, Warner went on to purchase a further Hurst story, 'Mannequin', just two weeks later.[92]

Although the matter was settled out of court, the dispute between Fannie Hurst and Warner Brothers still had industry-wide ramifications, raising questions about how multiple films might be produced from any single literary work, and potentially altering the entire negotiation process for all story acquisitions. In November 1939 *Variety* reported that the Screen Writers Guild had 'instructed members not to sign studio contracts carrying a clause by which perpet-ual use of characters goes with the story sale, such as is now in effect at Metro'. MGM, appar-ently inspired by Warner's issues with *Four Wives*, had added a new clause to its contracts with writers, meaning that they were in effect buying 'the characters as well as the yarns, with the right to use them in sequels'.[93] In this regard MGM and Warner Brothers were in the same boat, with a shared set of assumptions about what story rights should entail, but only Warner had acted on these assumptions, whereas MGM had heretofore been paying separately for each new Thin Man and Hardy family instalment. In fact, Hurst's was not the only dispute of this sort in which Warner was then involved, with a similar claim being made by Booth Tarkington over the studio's production of *Penrod and His Twin Brother* (1938), a sequel to *Penrod and Sam* (1937). Tarkington's claim actually predates that of Hurst, having been raised as a query in November 1937 before culminating in a court summons in April 1938, but it had been pro-ceeding very slowly until Hurst's claim surfaced, suggesting the wider influence of the latter.[94] In response to such attempts on the part of the studios, *Variety* later noted that 'an increasing number of writers have been inserting protective clauses into their contracts to cover such con-tingencies'.[95] Warner's attempts to further exploit Hurst's characters made writers of literary works aware that they would have to either account for or guard against unauthorised sequels in contracts with studios – and marked the beginning of a shift in industry practice regarding story acquisitions and character rights, whereby Hollywood studios legally formalised their hope that any single story might be just the beginning of something larger and more profitable.[96]

While the Hurst case marked a clear turning point, many authors were willing accomplices in the process of sequelisation. In their contract with Fox for their family autobiography, *Cheaper by the Dozen* (1950), Frank Gilbreth, Jr and Ernestine Gilbreth granted the studio a first-look option on the sequel they were then planning to write. That literary follow-up, entitled *Belles on Their Toes*, was published in June 1950, a matter of months after the release of the original film, with a film version appearing the following year.[97]

A sequel also became a practical option if there was no direct copyright over the source of the original. This might involve a work of fiction in the public domain, as in the case of *Frankenstein* or *The Adventures of Tom Sawyer*, or the mythologised life stories of Old West leg-ends such as the James brothers, as featured in *The Return of Frank James* (1940). Sequelising a life story was a more complicated business when your subject was alive and well, however. Even if the subject was a willing participant, one might have to work on their terms in order to get a sequel made. In the wake of the hugely successful *The Jolson Story* (1946), a biopic of Al

Jolson starring Larry Parks in the title role, Columbia was keen to produce a sequel. Parks, how-ever, was in dispute with the studio over his contract and had also testified that he had once been a member of the Communist Party in front of the House Committee of Un-American Activities. Thus in April 1948 it was reported that Al Jolson himself had made a deal for a sequel with MGM in which Gene Kelly would take on the lead role.[98] Why that deal fell through is unclear, but it seems that Columbia may have won Jolson back with more favourable terms, with *Variety* reporting that Jolson and Columbia would share equally in profits from *Jolson Sings Again* (1950), with each party handing over 5 per cent of their share to producer Sidney Buchman.[99] These even-handed terms seem an apt reflection of the mutually beneficial arrangement between Jolson and his cinematic biographers: the first film bolstered his fame, which lay the grounds for a second film, which was in turn enabled by his involvement.

If the original author were unwilling or unable to assist in such endeavours, the studio would be forced to look elsewhere, as evidenced by another recurrent trend of this period (and one which has persisted in subsequent decades), whereby an original source or screen-play was repurposed as a sequel to an entirely different property. When MGM was looking for a sequel to *Whistling in the Dark* (1941), the first starring vehicle for Richard 'Red' Skelton, it had no pre-prepared source material to draw on (the original having been based on a one-off stage play by Laurence Gross and Edward Childs Carpenter). It did, however, have an unused screenplay entitled 'Thin Man Story' in which Nick and Nora visit a small Southern town for a friend's wedding and inevitably find themselves embroiled in a murder case, revolving around the town's key inhabitants – Ellamae (Diana Lewis), Hattie (Celia Travers), Bailie (Peter Whitney) and Judge Lee (Guy Kibbee) – all of whom appear in the finished version of *Whistling in Dixie* (1942). 'Thin Man Story' was submitted as a treatment by Jonathan Latimer in December 1940, before ultimately being reconfigured as a mystery to be solved by Wally Benton, Skelton's char-acter from *Whistling in the Dark*.[100]

Sometimes even less work was required to transform an original screenplay into the sequel to another film, as exemplified by *Hot Pepper* (1933), Fox's third and final sequel to its silent comedy hit *What Price Glory* (1926). Directed by Raoul Walsh, *Glory* introduced Victor McLaglen and Edmund Lowe as Captain Flagg and Sergeant Quirt, a successful comic part-nership that would see the actors appear together again multiple times. By the autumn of 1932 they had not only appeared in two sequels to *Glory*, *The Cock-Eyed World* (1929) and *Women of All Nations* (1931), but also in *Guilty as Hell*, a comic murder-mystery as entirely different char-acters; the latter suggesting that they were sufficiently established as a comedy pairing for that joint persona to extend beyond the fictional world from which it had originated. Duly, *Hot Pepper* began its life in September 1932 as an uncredited story idea titled 'Hell to Pay' in which the two main characters, a down-on-his-luck gambler and a racketeer, are referred to not as Quirt and Flagg but as 'Eddie' and 'Vic', in reference to the actors for whom the script is intended. No mention is made of the army connection which defines the Quirt and Flagg films, suggesting this was intended as an original vehicle, albeit one which draws on an established star–genre combination. Gradually, however, connections are forged with the earlier films. First, in a screenplay also entitled 'Hell to Pay', submitted by Dudley Nichols and Henry Johnson on 12 September 1932, 'Eddie' and 'Vic' have become characters described as 'Duke Flagg – a big shot' and 'Harry Quint', in obvious reference to their earlier roles. The connection to *What Price*

Glory alluded to in that draft becomes explicit in a revised version dated 8 October 1932, in which the character dynamic is retained, but only develops after a new opening scene in a marine corps barrack, where Quirt and Flagg are being discharged from their military duties.[101] Here, then, we see how the narrative tropes of an existing series might be grafted, little by little, onto an original work.[102] Again, the scheduling demands of the studio system encouraged such a practice: if no source material for a sequel were readily available, and if the schedule was tight, it was quicker and cheaper to reconfigure an existing story or screenplay than create one from scratch.

Life goes on, film after film

These latter examples feed into a broader characteristic of the studio-era sequel, whereby narrative development and life development go hand in hand. In some respects this is the crux of any sequel from any era, the distinction being that so many sequels from this period focus on what are posited as ordinary lives in everyday situations. The Hardy family represent the apex of this particular trend, and one might hypothesise that it was partly under the influence of this hugely successful series that so many family-centred series were established. It was, after all, in the wake of *A Family Affair* that studios saw the commercial potential in occasionally returning to, or delivering regular reports from, the lives of the *Three Smart Girls*, the *Four Daughters*, Henry Aldrich, Blondie, Torchy Blane, Dr Kildare, Maisie, Ma and Pa Kettle and *Henry, the Rainmaker* (1949) among others. Even when the lives documented are more extraordinary, the events linking one film to another tend to be relatively mundane – the advent of parenthood, biological or surrogate, in the respective cases of Nick and Nora and Tarzan and Jane, for example. This trope for intertwining genealogical advancement with narrative continuation finds an almost parodic echo in the era's horror films: just as the *Four Daughters* became *Wives* and then *Mothers*, so *Frankenstein* finds a *Bride* before delivering a *Son*.

It would be inaccurate to suggest that Hollywood has entirely neglected 'average' family life in subsequent decades, but it has only rarely found occasion to sequelise it. One might speculate that this has something to do with the industry's waning interest in the adult female moviegoers who were central to its success in the 1930s and 40s, and its subsequent preference for courting the attention of teenage boys. A more concrete rationale would be that the virtual disappearance of such fare in the late 1950s can be explained, as with the disappearances of the big-screen serial and series film more generally, by its migration to television. There are clear formal differences between the sequel or series film and the episodes of a soap opera or sitcom, but these television formats, for which series such as the Hardy family and Ma and Pa Kettle were obvious prototypes, were quickly colonised by the new, domestically situated technology.

Two contemporary exceptions to Hollywood's aversion to sequelise everyday family life come, perhaps not coincidentally, in the form of remakes from the studio era: *Father of the Bride* (1991) and *Cheaper by the Dozen* (2003), both of which starred Steve Martin and spawned sequels. *Cheaper by the Dozen 2* (2005) bears little relation to *Belles on Their Toes*, but *Father of the Bride Part II* (1995) follows the path of *Father's Little Dividend* (1951) by introducing a grandchild into the life of protagonist George Banks. Whereas its remake in some respects stands apart from other contemporary sequels, *Father's Little Dividend* exemplifies much of what was distinct about sequelisation in the studio era, not only in terms of its subject matter, but also the swift, efficient manner in which it was produced. Based on a novel by Edward Streeter, directed by Vincente Minnelli and starring Spencer Tracy, Elizabeth Taylor and Joan Bennett, *Father of the Bride* was released in June 1950 to critical acclaim and very healthy box-office returns.[103] Within two weeks of shooting on the first film having finished, screenwriters Albert Hackett and Frances Goodrich (now freelance, but still regularly employed by MGM) had delivered seven pages of notes headed 'Sequel to Father of the Bride'.[104] By April those notes had become a treatment and by July a finished screenplay.[105] In early October, seven months after shooting completed on the first film, the original cast and director were back on the MGM lot, shooting the sequel. *Father's Little Dividend* was released in April 1951, less than a year after its predecessor, to warm critical notices and decent box office.[106] The ease and efficiency with which *Dividend* was produced was in part due to Goodrich and Hackett's ready-to-go screenplay, which we must assume was the result of foresight on the part of someone at the studio. We might also surmise that the original contract with Streeter included some contingency for a sequel. Nonetheless, the established studio machinery at MGM clearly played a major part. Minnelli, Tracy and Taylor were all under long-term contract and available for work, the very fact of which was increasingly anomalous in an industry busy responding to the end of vertical integration. For while Warner Bros. and Paramount were laying off department heads and releasing major stars from long-term contracts, MGM was still maintaining a large overhead, replete with production supervisors, musical specialists and a full complement of stars.[107] One cannot ignore the film's relatively modest logistical requirements (particularly when compared with the studio's hugely complex musical productions) as a factor in its speedy turnaround, but without the studio's traditional infrastructure, it seems highly unlikely that the film would have emerged as quickly as it did. *Father's Little Dividend* may be a minor work, worthy of little more than a footnote in histories of Hollywood's Golden Age, but, in the broader context of what I hope to have conveyed about the studio-era sequel in this chapter, its production context feels oddly elegiac: a studio clinging to an outmoded organisational model, producing a film whose brand of homely narrative continuation would soon be more commonly found on television.

3 | The uncertainty principles, 1955–77

The history of the sequel in the twenty years which followed the full implementation of the *Paramount* decree is, in volume terms at least, relatively short. As Figures A.1 and A.2 indicate, cinematic seriality as a whole went through a fallow period, with sequels, series and serials becoming far less prevalent on the big screen than they were in either the forty years before or the thirty-five years following. Whereas Hollywood released more than 500 sequels and series films between 1935 and 1954, there were fewer than 130 such releases between 1955 and 1974. Breaking these numbers down into five-year intervals, we can see that the low-point for big-screen seriality was the decade between 1955 and 1964, during which time only forty-three sequels and series films appeared; a stark contrast to the 285 equivalent releases in the ten years prior. The following ten years indicate a gradual increase, with seventy sequels and series films appearing between 1965 and 1974, but this is still markedly short of the rate of output prior to the major studios' divorcement from their cinema chains.

One might assume a different picture would emerge when these figures are examined proportionally, not only because the major studios dramatically cut back on production as a whole in the aftermath of the divorcement but also because the total number of releases began to decline, from an average of 670.8 films per annum in the 1940s to an average of 424.3 per year during the 1960s and down to 227.2 for the 1970s.[1] This process had effectively begun in the early 1940s, when the outlawing of blind-bidding and large-scale block-booking had the immediate effect of discouraging the majors from B-movie production. Following a brief upturn in the early 1950s, the majors cut back again in the middle of the decade, and their output continued to follow a downward trend thereafter. Although these cutbacks were offset to some degree by independent and/or foreign productions, there were generally fewer films on release in US cinemas after the demands of the *Paramount* decree had been met. The fall in sequel production, therefore, would seem to be reflective of a broader industrial pattern. In fact, even on a proportional basis the 1950s and 60s represent a marked low-point for the form, as indicated in Table 3.1. One of the central thrusts of this chapter, therefore, is an exploration into why this might be so.

For anyone even casually familiar with Hollywood history, and with the dramatic changes the industry underwent in this period, the major causes of this shift will be readily apparent. Nonetheless, considering the effects of these industrial undulations on the sequel form seems valuable; in part because observations about the increased prevalence of cinematic seriality over the past thirty years are often based in under-interrogated assumptions about the role it had played in previous decades. The oft-quoted statistics provided by Joseph Dominick, for example, indicate that there was an upswing in sequel production between 1964 and 1983,

Table 3.1 Sequels and series films as a percentage of total US releases[2]

Decade	Total no. of feature films released	Total no. of sequels and series films released	Sequels and series films as % of total releases
1940s	6,708	397	5.89
1950s	4,984	107	2.03
1960s	4,243	62	1.37
1970s	2,272	92	4.09

but these fail to take into account the extent to which the early 1960s marked an uncharacteristic slump for the form, undermining in turn the notion that this upswing represented an unprecedented shift in industrial practice.[3] Rather, from the mid-1950s through to the early 1970s, Hollywood temporarily moved away from the mass production of the series films, serials and sequels that had been one of its staples since the birth of the feature film, with the period thus representing what we might now understand as a brief interlude in the prevalence of cinematic seriality. It would be unnecessarily teleological to describe this era as 'transitional', but it is nonetheless evident that the role of the Hollywood sequel was in flux during this period; neither what it had been in the years of vertical integration, nor what it would go on to become in the late 1970s, as horizontal integration became a fact of Hollywood life. What follows, then, considers the causal relationship between those factors affecting Hollywood as a whole, and the manner in which the systemic changes they wrought also came to bear on the place of the sequel form within the industry. Film historians have tended to describe this period as a series of endings (the disintegration of the 'classical', vertically integrated studio system), beginnings (the rise of independent production, the 'blockbuster syndrome' and of the industry's conglomeration), and one complete narrative arc; that of the years between the releases of *Bonnie and Clyde* (1967) and *Jaws* (1975) sometimes dubbed the 'New Hollywood',[4] in which, so the story goes, the industry briefly embraced a more challenging, auteur-led cinema. I have chosen to begin in 1955, the year in which the major studios moved into television production and end in 1977, the year in which *Superman* (1978) began shooting; the former because it marked the point at which multi-part storytelling became vastly more prevalent on the small screen than in cinemas; the latter because it represents the point at which the blockbuster philosophy and increased conglomeration of the previous twenty years officially converged with the production-line approach of the B-movie. There were, of course, several noteworthy sequels released in the interceding twenty-three years, and the latter part of this chapter will consider some key examples, whose production histories either reflect the realities of sequel production during this period or hint at the direction the form would take in the decades to come.

To be continued ... elsewhere

Although there was no direct connection between the rise of television and the outcome of the Justice Department's antitrust suit against the Big Five, their combined impact on the industry was immense, not least because of their concurrence. On 3 March 1949, when

Paramount signed the consent decree which committed it to creating a separate exhibition company by the end of that year, just over 1 million television sets had been sold. But as the year progressed, with the Federal Court ruling that Warner Bros., MGM and Twentieth Century-Fox would have to join Paramount and RKO in signing a consent decree, sales were increasing rapidly. By the time MGM (the last of the majors to sign a decree) had at last begun divesting itself from Loew's Theatres in 1954, the small screen had reached a water-shed, with 55.7 per cent of US households containing at least one set.[5] In tandem with divestiture, the television boom contributed to the erosion of the nation's moviegoing habit, on which both the studios and theatres had previously been able to rely. While admissions had already begun to decline prior to 1949, and while other factors clearly played their part – in particular the increased migration to the suburbs, away from the cities which tradition-ally housed the largest first-run cinemas – television's central role in this process is strikingly demonstrated by Frederic Stuart's direct comparison of regional correlations between per capita box-office receipts and television penetration, which clearly indicates that moviegoing declined most quickly in those regions of the US where television ownership was more widespread.[6]

The ramifications for cinematic seriality were both immediate and multifarious. Television was quickly becoming the dominant form of entertainment, stealing away the regular audience who made box-office receipts on B-grade series films so predictable. Crucially, by the late 1950s it had also colonised the series format, becoming the dominant provider of multi-part, audio-visual storytelling. The latter shift, ironically, is at least in part due to the involvement of the stu-dios themselves in television production; which is in turn, in a further irony, an indirect result of the *Paramount* decree.

Because the Big Five were implicated in an antitrust suit, the Federal Communications Commission (FCC) (which, as a result of the 1934 Communications Act, had the power to refuse applications for television broadcasting licences from any party involved in monopolis-tic practices) was able to legitimately block their entry into television ownership. Meanwhile, their attempts to develop equivalent alternatives to the network model, in the form of 'Theatre TV' (the broadcast of exclusive television programming in cinemas) and 'pay' or 'subscription' TV (effectively a pay-per-view model for film and sports programming with which we are now very familiar), both failed to take off.[7] Thwarted both in their attempts to take ownership of television networks and in their struggle to provide commercially viable alternatives, the stu-dios were effectively forced to adopt a policy of both beating *and* joining their new competi-tors. This bifurcated approach required, on the one hand, that the studios further differentiate both the experience of moviegoing and the movies themselves from that which television offered and, on the other hand, that they exploit the established networks' need for program-ming in order to more effectively monetise both their existing studio facilities and their film libraries. I will return to the first part of this business equation, what might be called the 'big pic-ture' approach, in the following section, but first we must consider what the studios' engage-ment with the television industry meant for the sequel.

Writing on the studios' response to the television boom, Janet Wasko has suggested that, by the end of the 1950s, 'the Hollywood film companies were becoming media companies'.[8] This somewhat underplays the extent to which, as Douglas Gomery has argued, Hollywood had already diversified when it bought into the popular-music industry in the late 1920s and subsequently forged a mutually beneficial relationship (albeit usually of a promotional nature) with radio networks.[9] It is clear that the increased intertwining of the television and film industries in the second half of the 1950s represents an intensification of this strategy, but it is also evident that the studios were less interested in pioneering new formats than they were in putting pre-existing materials and business practices to new uses.

Hollywood's new role as the hub for television production was in fact initiated by Columbia, which, although not involved in the antitrust ruling, was seriously affected by the decline of the B-movie and so needed to swiftly establish an alternative source of revenue. Its Screen Gems subsidiary began producing television commercials in 1950, securing a contract to produce a half-hour anthology series for the Ford Motor Company in 1951.[10] This early start gave Screen Gems a considerable lead in the field, but it was not alone for long, joined late in 1954 by Disney, whose *Disneyland* (1954–92) premiered in September of that year, and shortly thereafter by Warner Bros., Twentieth Century-Fox and MGM, all of whom produced studio-branded anthology series for the 1955–6 season.[11] Although *Disneyland* had significant promotional value for its studio, intended to drive attendance for both its cinema releases and its newly opened theme park, for the other studios the principal benefit was that, in Christopher Anderson's words, 'supplying television programs to the networks offered a new rationale for standardized, studio-based production'.[12] By the mid-1950s, the majors had, to a greater (Warner) or lesser (MGM) extent, moved their feature-film business away from in-house production and towards the financing of projects put together by independent (or semi-independent) producers, leaving their backlots underutilised. The newly established Warner Bros. Television justified the maintenance of Warner's existing production facilities, and enabled it to replicate many of the organisational methods of the old studio system, with actors placed under long-term contract, and a *de facto* revival of the producer-unit mode. Contracted to provide a thirty-nine-episode series to ABC beginning in September 1955, Warner Bros. was justified in adopting such methods, given that it would be churning out programming at an even greater pace than it had done during the days of Bryan Foy's B-movie unit.[13]

As it was for the mode of production, so it was too for the programme content, with the low budgets dictating in part the nature of the material. Warner Bros.' contract with ABC stipulated that it could extend a plot across two episodes but no more, thus distinguishing the series from the open-ended serial structure of daytime soap operas. The network's rationale, according to Anderson, was that it

> seemed to believe that audiences could be engaged by the daily episodes of a prime-time serial, but that too much time passed between the weekly episodes of a prime-time series for audiences to remain engaged by stories left perpetually unresolved.[14]

Established later than CBS and NBC, and thus financially the weakest of the three national networks, ABC turned to Hollywood largely in order to save money on producing its own programming.[15] In doing so, it made a major contribution to establishing the episodic series as a prime-time staple. As Anderson explains:

Episodic series were not necessarily what many of the studios had imagined producing when they began, but their participation in the industry ultimately reorientated their efforts in that direction and in many ways solidified the networks' commitment to the episodic series as prime time's dominant programming form.[16]

It is arguably no surprise, then, that when tasked with producing a huge amount of episodic content, the studios would turn to the kind of material previously employed for series-film production. During its first two years of broadcast on ABC, Warner Bros. Television had helped successfully establish the Western (with *Cheyenne* [1955–63]) and the detective series (with *'77 Sunset Strip* [1958–64]), genres both traditionally associated with B-level productions, as central features of the television schedule, with these two series much imitated by other networks.

Having long been in the business of securing television rights when purchasing literary properties for film adaptation (as evidenced by Warner's 1934 contract for the Perry Mason stories, for example), it is equally unsurprising that several of the earliest television series produced by the studios were directly based on properties which had been the basis for either series films or sequels. Warner's initial thinking, when tasked with producing four different generic strands for *Warner Bros. Presents* [1955–6], was that it would base its 'teenage comedy' strand on either *Janie* (1944) or *Brother Rat*, both of which had inspired sequels.[17] Ultimately it abandoned these as templates, but other equivalent material made it to air from other studios. Following its unsuccessful emulation of the *Disneyland* format with *The 20th Century-Fox Hour* [1955–7], Fox first ventured into the episodic series format with *My Friend Flicka* (1955–8), which launched in February 1956 and was based on a studio-owned property which had already generated an original film and two sequels. Having similarly failed with the heavily self-promotional *MGM Parade* (1955–6) on ABC, MGM Television launched itself into episodic series fiction with *The Thin Man*, which ran for two seasons from 1957 to 1959, and subsequently continued to raid its back catalogue of multi-part narratives. Some of these translated better than others: *Dr. Kildare* ran for five seasons from September 1961 to 1966, and generated 190 episodes; starting that same September, *Father of the Bride* was less popular, lasting only one season; while, at the other end of the spectrum, *Maisie*, with Janis Paige taking on Ann Sothern's signature role, failed to make it past the pilot stage after premiering in September 1960. Examples such as these point to the manner in which television adopted not only the mode of production from which cinematic seriality had so frequently emerged in the past quarter-century, but also the genres with which it had hitherto been most frequently associated during that same period.

Furthermore, in part because the studios retained all rights, both to pre-existing properties and to newly created ones, such transferrals could work both ways. MGM exploited the success of television's *I Love Lucy* (1951–7) by combining Lucille Ball and Desi Arnaz in a big-screen release, *The Long, Long Trailer* (1954), while Warner Bros. moved to directly adapt *Dragnet* (1951–9), one of the small screen's most popular series, into a feature film of the same name (1955), following it up with *The Lone Ranger* (1956) and *Our Miss Brooks* (1956).[18] The rights for these films were purchased from independent producers, but by the early 1960s, with the Hollywood studios established as the networks' primary providers of fictional content,[19] there was an increasingly symbiotic relationship between the two. Witness the seamless transition made by Flipper the dolphin, whose friendship with a boy named Sandy Ricks (Luke Halpin) formed the basis for two MGM feature films, *Flipper* (1963) and its sequel, *Flipper's New Adventure* (1964). Released theatrically in June 1964, the sequel was followed in September of that year by the NBC broadcast of a TV series (1964–7) based on the same characters, in which Luke Halpin and Brian Kelly (playing Sandy's father) reprised their roles from the film. In tandem with the first season, a plethora of merchandise (including boardgames, colouring books and lunch boxes) was created; the co-ordination of these three, mutually promotional elements thus making *Flipper* a fully fledged multimedia franchise.

Although the early advent of big-screen TV adaptations makes it clear that there was a degree of circularity at work, most such transitions during this period went in one direction: a film might become the basis for a TV series, but thereafter it was unlikely to make it back onto the big screen. While this tendency seems to suggest the extent to which television, by the early 1960s, had come to be perceived by the motion-picture studios as the natural home for their sequential narrative properties, it is just as probable that this was more a matter of logistical and economic convenience than it was of design. With studios such as Warner Bros. and MGM needing a steady supply of story material which could be easily reiterated or extended, it stands to reason that they would turn to those properties which they both already owned and whose potential to generate multiple episodes had already been proven in the feature-film market. Roger Hagedorn has argued that serial fiction tends to take precedence when there is a need to establish a habitual audience for a new medium, but the example of Hollywood's early ventures in television production suggests an additional, if not alternate, explanation.[20] Following on from the rise of the double bill and subsequent series-film boom in the 1930s, here we have another instance in the Hollywood sequel's history in which seriality prevails in circumstances where the sheer level (and urgency) of demand for content makes it an effective solution to the problem of creating sufficient supply. Seriality, in other words, becomes a means of quickly bridging the gap between supply and demand, a pattern we will see repeated in the following chapter with the rise of video in the 1980s.

In gravitating away from both anthology series and the live broadcasts which had distinguished the new technology in its first few years,[21] moving instead towards prerecorded episodic fiction, television had, with considerable assistance from Hollywood, effectively become more like the movies. Meanwhile, as they helped bring the episodic series to the forefront of the networks' prime-time schedules, the studios were simultaneously seeking to make their movies less like television; one of the side-effects of which was to minimise the role of seriality in their production schedules over the coming decade.

The 'one-of-a-kind' epic

Looking back from the vantage point of 2013, in which many of the highest-budget, highest-earning films are either sequels or attempts to initiate a multi-film series, it is hard to conceive of the extent to which the equivalent releases from the early 1950s through to the late 1960s were, with a handful of noteworthy exceptions, standalone events. This does not mean they were not imitative of earlier successes, nor that they were not imitated by competitors, but it was rare that they spawned direct follow-ups, and it was rarer still, as in the case of *Dr. No* (1962), that the first film was evidently intended to represent the beginning of a series. This situation seems even more unlikely given that the budgets for the hits of this era were increasing dramatically, thus upping the level of risk on each individual production. Why, in these circumstances, didn't Hollywood rely more regularly on sequels, whose longstanding economic rationale is that they reduce risk by ensuring a 'built-in' audience? The answer, it seems, lies with the historically spe-cific characteristics of the blockbuster during this period.

As Tino Balio has suggested, when Hollywood sought to differentiate its output from tele-vision, 'the formula became "Make Them Big; Show Them Big; and Sell Them Big"'.[22] Although there had always been standout films (both in terms of cost and box-office returns) within their release schedules, following the success of films such as *Quo Vadis* (1951) and *The Robe*, the stu-dios concentrated their financial resources on fewer, costlier productions, seeking to reinforce the prominence of these films via a boutique mode of distribution and exhibition.[23] The 1950s and 60s were what Sheldon Hall has termed the 'roadshow era', a period when Hollywood's premium products were 'distributed and exhibited in a manner similar to that of a live stage performance at a legitimate theatre'.[24] There were several economic downsides to the road-show model, including a slower return on investment because of the limited number of show-ings (usually only one or two per day),[25] but these were at least partially offset by higher ticket prices and the perceived need to bestow event status upon the industry's most expensive pro-ductions and so entice audiences away from their television sets. Hall's work, along with that of Steve Neale and Peter Krämer, acts as an important corrective to earlier Hollywood histo-ries by pointing to the continuities between the blockbusters of this era (which in fact marked the first point at which the term 'blockbuster' was regularly employed within the industry) and those of more recent decades.[26] As a result, they pay less attention to the discontinuity involved in the near-absence of large-scale sequels during this period. (Krämer does point to the success of the sequels *Jolson Sings Again* and *Cinerama Holiday* [1955],[27] but the former was not roadshown and neither was hugely expensive, somewhat differentiating them from many of the key hits of the roadshow era.)

One reason for this disparity lies in the nature of the source material which the industry deemed appropriate for this theatrical mode of presentation. Given the strengthening associa-tion between television and the series format, we might posit that the studios deemed the sequel, with its longstanding reputation for being a cheap copy subject to diminishing artistic returns, unworthy of the unique event status of a true blockbuster. One of the purposes of the roadshow strategy was to attract an older, more affluent audience for whom cinemagoing was no longer a weekly ritual; appealing to that audience also meant deploying notions of quality to which the concept of seriality, at least as embodied by the B-movie and television, was inimical.

A more quantifiable hypothesis would suggest that the industry was merely doing what it had always done: following the hits. Many of the preferred genres for roadshow presentation, in particular the Biblical or historical epic and the musical, had long been regular components of Hollywood production, but became particularly favoured because they had proven them-selves at an early stage to attract large audiences. Films such as *The Robe*, *Oklahoma!* (1955), *The Ten Commandments* (1956), *Around the World in Eighty Days* (1956), *The King and I* (1956) and *The Bridge on the River Kwai* (1957), all among the top-five grossing films of their respec-tive release years, effectively set the template for Hollywood's most expensive productions over the following ten years.[28] These genres were not easy targets for sequelisation, for both formal and logistical reasons. Most of the musicals of the era, for example, were based on hit Broadway shows, many by Richard Rodgers and Oscar Hammerstein. In order to capitalise on the success of *Oklahoma!*, therefore, it was evidently easier to produce a film based on another successful Rodgers and Hammerstein production (*The King and I* or *South Pacific* [1958]) than to originate a sequel to *Oklahoma!*; a process which would require creating not only a new story and screenplay but also a new set of musical numbers. Similarly, many of the most popular roadshow attractions represented challenges to sequelisation at a narrative level, either because they were based on public-domain properties (i.e. the Bible) and/or portrayed historical, often exceptional events (in which case, the audience might already know what happened next, and the reality could not necessarily be shaped to fit the needs of a sequel), or because the conclusion of the original largely precluded future continuation, as with the tragedies *West Side Story* (1961) and *Doctor Zhivago* (1965).

At work here is a self-reinforcing relationship between a particular mode of exhibition and distribution and a certain type of content: the epic scope of these films justified this prestige mode of presentation and its inflated ticket prices, which was in turn the only way in which such expensive productions could hope to turn a profit – a strategy which was untenable in the longer term. Because these films proved the most successful of their era, so the number of releases seeking to emulate their success by imitating their content proliferated, ultimately culminating in an overcrowded roadshow sector towards the end of the 1960s which contributed – alongside a dropoff in film sales to television networks – to Hollywood's precipitous state in 1969–72.[29]

One other recurrent characteristic of the roadshow-era hits warrants some comment in relation to sequelisation: their frequent use of a large 'all-star' cast. Films such as *Around the World in Eighty Days*, *The Longest Day* (1962) and *It's a Mad, Mad, Mad, Mad World* (1963) featured ensembles top-heavy with either outright stars and/or well-known leads. Given that the majority of these stars were no longer under long-term contract, reassembling all or even some of them presented a major logistical headache. The possibility for Stanley Kramer and United Artists to capitalise on the success of *Mad World* with a direct sequel, therefore, was unlikely from the outset; leaving the door open for competitors to produce generic imitations, as Warner Bros. did with *The Great Race* (1965). The end of long-term studio contracts and the rise of the agent-packager impeded any attempt to carry over the cast from one film to another, no matter how few stars were involved, thus presenting a significant and hitherto unaccustomed barrier to sequel production.

Principal uncertainties

As documented in earlier chapters, the studios' contractual arrangements with key talent made it relatively easy, if not downright propitious, to produce a sequel to a newly minted box-office success – or an equivalent star–genre combination. Not all stars worked under these restrictions, and, equally, a star might resist, as John Garfield attempted to do with *Four Wives* – but the studios' standard punitive measures strongly discouraged such behaviour. The only real obstacle in this process, as Warner Bros. found out in its dealings with Booth Tarkington and Fannie Hurst, were those key talent not under studio contract. The available evidence suggests that, by the early 1950s, the studios were taking such contingencies into account when negotiating for story properties. The contracts for *Peyton Place* (1956), *The Fly* (1958) and *Mister Roberts* (1955), for example, all explicitly lay out the terms for any potential sequels.[30] While these terms are far from uniform, with some authors securing more favourable arrangements for subsequent continuations of their works, the consistent inclusion of a sequel clause suggests both a standardisation of legal practice in this regard and also a new transparency between writers and studios.

This development is key to the history of the Hollywood sequel, but its initial impact was arguably muted because, around the same time, the certainties which had governed the studios' working relationships with actors and directors quickly disappeared in the wake of the *Paramount* decree. Of course, the fact that they were not initially contracted for sequels did not mean key talent were averse to being involved, but the changes in standard industry practice, and the power these gave to stars, directors and those who represented them, frequently led to a far more protracted development process. As David Pirie notes, 'Each film became the product of long and frequently tortuous negotiations to establish whether, and on what terms, and with whom, it would be made.'[31] To understand the manner in which stars' increased influence and involvement directly impacted on sequel production in the post-studio era, let us consider the production histories of *True Grit* (1969) and its follow-up, *Rooster Cogburn* (1975), which mark a collaboration between a producer (Hal Wallis) and a star (John Wayne) who were attempting to operate within an industry quite different from that of the old studio system of which they were both products.

Although *True Grit* has a distinctly Old Hollywood pedigree, its production was driven by film-makers who had long since adopted New Hollywood ways. John Wayne was among the first stars to successfully untether himself from the disadvantageous strictures of the long-term contract, striking a deal with Republic in 1945 which gave him producer credit and 10 per cent of the gross box office.[32] In 1951 he went one step further by establishing Batjac, his own independent production company. With these foundations already in place, Wayne transitioned into the post-*Paramount* era with remarkable ease, remaining hugely popular throughout the following two decades, despite both the arrival of a raft of newcomers and the wave of revisionism which swept through his signature genre, the Western, in the latter half of the 1960s.[33] One of the key players in the factory-style system at Warner, Hal B. Wallis had, like Wayne, gradually moved towards independence: first, stepping down as Warner's head of production to become an in-house unit producer with profit participation;[34] then, in 1944, leaving the lot to set up Hal B. Wallis Productions. The two men had successfully collaborated on *The Sons of Katie Elder* (1965), so it is understandable that they would wish to reunite for another project. It was not until 1967, however, that the right project arrived, in the form of Charles Portis's *True Grit*, a picaresque tale of the Old West due to be published in 1968 as both a novel and in serial form in the *Saturday Evening Post*. By this time, Wallis and business partner Joseph Hazen (previously a lawyer at Warner Bros., who had left with Wallis in 1944), were ensconced at Paramount. Indicating the extent to which their financial clout remained essential to 'independent' production, it was Paramount who funded the purchase of Portis's novel in early February 1968, when it was still in galley form, as part of a joint venture between the studio, Wallis and Hazen. Although Wayne was technically a star for hire in this instance, loaned out from Batjac to Paramount, he was integral to the deal. Simultaneous to the purchase of story rights, Wayne signed on to star as Rooster Cogburn – *True Grit*'s hard-bitten but ultimately sympathetic protagonist – taking a one-third share of all rights in the film upon completion of production, with Paramount and Wallis–Hazen dividing the remaining share equally between them.[35] As befitted his role as co-owner, Wayne remained heavily involved in the production, offering Wallis notes on the script, and on a rough cut of the finished film screened in January 1969.

Sequel rights were accounted for in the original agreement with Portis, with the author receiving 50 per cent of the original purchase price for any sequel produced.[36] Thus, when *True Grit* became one of the ten highest-grossing films of 1969, with John Wayne going on to win his first and only Academy Award for Best Actor in a Leading Role, a sequel seemed a very real possibility. And so it was, shortly after Wayne's Oscar win, that Paul Nathan, associate producer and Wallis's righthand man, reported to Wallis in 1970 that Wayne's agent had confirmed that the star was 'eager to play Rooster' again and would commit on the basis of a treatment alone – the catch was that he would not be available for shooting until early 1972 due to other commitments.[37] In his old role as head of production, Wallis would have been free to reshuffle the star's schedule in order to capitalise more swiftly on *True Grit*'s currency; now, this was impossible. Despite the wait, Wayne clearly remained keen on the idea, because in June 1971 Nathan again reported to Wallis that 'Duke' was 'available in the spring and would love to play ROOSTER COGBURN'. There was clearly no lack of enthusiasm on Wallis's part, but he, too, was busy with other projects, and progress continued to be slow due to a number of false starts on the screenplay.[38]

With the various scheduling conflicts, it was not until January 1974, when Wallis himself penned a brief treatment based on an idea generated by Nathan, that the project finally moved ahead. Nathan's memo proposed that Rooster come to the aid of a woman 'like Katharine Hepburn' in the sequel, a comment which became reality in the spring of 1974 when Wallis contracted Hepburn herself to star alongside Wayne as Eula Goodnight. Hepburn had been one of the first stars to realise some form of independence, when she engineered a comeback by purchasing the film rights to *The Philadelphia Story* and then auctioning them off (with herself attached to star) in 1940. Like Wayne, she was therefore able to achieve a modicum of creative control early on, before the collapse of the studio system. Accordingly, even after the screenplay had been tailored on the basis of her involvement, Hepburn

John Wayne and Katharine Hepburn exerted their influence in a post-studio-system world in the production of *Rooster Cogburn* (1975)

had many suggestions as to how both her character in particular and the screenplay in general should develop, rewriting portions of dialogue and even whole scenes.[39] Coupled with a change of distributor-financier, the sheer number of interested parties (including Wallis, Wayne, Hepburn, Nathan and Portis among others), all of whom had some vested interest (usually in the form of profit participation) in the success of the project made for an extremely protracted production process that would have been almost unthinkable three decades earlier, when these veteran film-makers were part of a standardised and vertically integrated system in which creative input and contractual obligations were rarely allowed to slow the pace of the production line.[40]

Crosscurrents: From 'A' to 'B' and all points in between

Although I have stressed the extent to which television siphoned off much in the way of cine-matic seriality, it would be remiss to suggest that it was entirely absent from the big screen. After the low point between 1955 and 1964, in fact, there were new signs of life in the Hollywood sequel, with a clear upturn towards the end of the 1960s. More to the point, closer inspection indicates that it was during this fallow period in which two often overlapping but subtly distinct strands of attenuated storytelling – both of which derived from earlier practices and both of which would ultimately become more prevalent in the early 1970s – re-emerged as commercially viable responses to the new industrial realities of the television age.

B-sploitation

The first of these strands was the product of what came to be commonly known as the 'exploitation' field; a low-budget, high-volume strategy born of the aforementioned gap between supply and demand. While often discussed as a distinct category, the exploitation film was in effect the B-movie recalibrated for the post-divorcement era. Although many would eventually be forced to close, in the mid-1950s there were still a large number of cinemas in business whose demand for features was no longer being met by the major studios and their low-volume, high-budget mindset. This created a window of opportunity for independent pro-ducers, the most enduringly successful of which was American International Pictures (AIP), established in 1954 as American Releasing Corporation by James H. Nicholson and Samuel Z. Arkoff and initially part-funded by theatre-owning interests and Pathé Labs.[41] The new breed of low-budget films were different less in terms of production, for they were made as quickly and cheaply as the Bs of the studio era, than in terms of marketing and distribution. As Thomas Doherty has observed, 'Without the luxury of a guaranteed audience or an A attrac-tion host on which to attach itself, the secondary fare of the 1950s required a special "hook" to entice audiences, a gimmick or "exploitation angle".'[42] Crucially, too, 'exploitation' here does not denote a particular type of content, but rather the tailoring of that content to appeal to a particular *audience*. This is an important distinction, because it helps clarify the point of con-tinuity between the teen-targeted output of the late 1950s and early 60s, and the harder-edged films which were to follow. While he overemphasises the extent to which studio-era B-movies had a 'guaranteed' audience (if that had been the case, there would have been fewer failed or stalled series during the 1930s and 40s), or indeed the extent to which the Big Five had always relied on exploitation hooks, Doherty usefully identifies the degree to which both

independent producers and (to a lesser extent) the established studios deployed an exploitation approach not to attract the older patrons who were staying at home to watch television
and raise families, but instead to catch the attention of teenagers, the one audience segment
who were still regular moviegoers and who were also fuelling the only growth area in the
exhibition sector, the drive-in.

There were of course many facets to the emergent teen-movie genre, from its synergistic
cross-pollination with the concurrent explosion of rock 'n' roll music to its sometimes sincere,
sometimes salacious examinations of the much reported problem of juvenile delinquency,[43]
but relevant here is that it was one of the few sources of cinematic seriality on the big screen
between 1955 and 1964. Aside from final episodes in previously established series such as Ma
and Pa Kettle and Francis, the few recurrent characters emerging in the late 1950s were under
twenty-one. Columbia's *Gidget* (1959) and Universal's *Tammy and the Bachelor* (1961) both
spawned two sequels apiece, albeit with casting changes, while *Rock, Pretty Baby* (1956) continued the story of Jimmy Daley (John Saxon) in *Summer Love* (1958). For their part, AIP inau-
gurated and maintained one of the most successful teen cycles with *Beach Party* (1963),
teaming Annette Funicello and Frankie Avalon in a beach-set, music-driven romantic comedy.
Four further Beach movies from AIP followed: *Muscle Beach Party* (1964), *Bikini Beach* (1964),
Beach Blanket Bingo (1965) and *How to Stuff a Wild Bikini* (1965), all directed by William Asher
and starring Funicello, three pairing her with Avalon. With both returning cast members and a
distinct narrative formula, but without either continuing storylines or returning characters, the
Beach cycle in effect represents a conceptual series, much like the Gold Diggers and Road films.
While it falls outside the sequel bracket on formal terms, the Beach series is noteworthy for
the extent to which AIP so successfully deployed exploitation techniques (in particular opening on multiple screens and spending disproportionately on marketing) to target a youth audience, and the extent to which that audience was apparently willing to come back for more of
the same, albeit for a limited period. In November 1965, less than three years after the release
of *Beach Party*, Arkoff was telling the *New York Times* that '"The bikini beach cycle has had it."'[44]
Nonetheless, with each of the series reportedly grossing more than $2.5 million on produc-
tion budgets of less than $500,000, the industry was provided with yet more proof of what
most had already acknowledged. As the *Times* put it,

> The success of these pictures has given support to a theory circulated by some low budget
> moviemakers … that perhaps two-thirds of all movie tickets are purchased by people in the 15 to
> 25 age group. This theory relegates the adult audience to a minority group.[45]

Although it was a long time coming, the MPAA's replacement of the outmoded Production
Code with a ratings system in October 1968 meant that the notion of exploitation, while
clearly still geared towards younger audiences, took on a more distinctly adult edge.[46] David
A. Cook has noted that

> the early 1970s witnessed the rapid deployment of three exploitation genres that trafficked in both
> [sex and violence]. They were, in ascending order of market strength, the black action film, the martial
> arts films, and … the feature-length hardcore porno film.[47]

As with the teen movie, the boom in the 'black action film' – more commonly (and pejo-ratively) known as 'Blaxploitation' – in the early 1970s was the result of a coincidence between the needs of the struggling exhibition sector and the interests of a demographic who had not previously been directly catered for. Here, a historically underserved African-American audi-ence proved a financial boon to inner-city exhibitors who were struggling to survive following the migration of middle-class white audiences to the suburbs. And, as with their address of the teen audience, film-makers turned to the series and the sequel in order to most effectively and swiftly meet the apparent demand for a particular type of film. The Blaxploitation cycle was sequel-heavy, with *Cotton Comes to Harlem* (1970), *Shaft* (1971), *Superfly* (1972), *Slaughter* (1972), *Blacula* (1972) and *Cleopatra Jones* (1973) all inspiring follow-ups. In this instance, how-ever, the cycle was driven as much by major studios as by independents, first by United Artists' release of *Cotton Comes to Harlem*, and then by MGM with the release of *Shaft*. Although MGM was clearly following UA's lead in pushing ahead with *Shaft*,[48] it was not caught off-guard by the film's success. No doubt encouraged by the enthusiastic response from a preview screen-ing in Inglewood, MGM lost no time in commissioning a follow-up.[49] The studio announced plans for a sequel in May 1971, and an initial treatment by Stirling Silliphant and Roger Lewis was delivered on 11 June, all prior to *Shaft*'s 25 June premiere in Los Angeles.[50] In January 1972, *Shaft's Big Score* was going into production and in June of that year, before most of his numerous competitors had made it into cinemas, Richard Roundtree's hardbitten P.I. was back on the big screen. A further sequel, *Shaft in Africa*, went into production almost as swiftly, with a treatment by Silliphant ready in September 1972 and the shoot beginning in December. It is worth underlining the speed with which MGM turned these productions around, on the one hand because it indicates that a studio was still capable of B-level production practices, and on the other because it reflects the state of that particular studio at that particular moment in time. Having purchased MGM in 1969, primarily with an eye on its real-estate holdings, Las Vegas financier Kirk Kerkorian downsized the studio's production operations significantly. These new strictures, in combination with a recession which contributed to losses that totalled $72 million in 1969, meant the studio was momentarily in a position where it was better placed to support multiple low-risk projects than standalone blockbusters.[51] *Shaft* and its sequels, with their minimal budgetary requirements and seemingly assured audience, were exactly what MGM needed as its old business model faltered.

Although it warrants further study, there is no space here to address the role of the sequel in pornography in any detail. It is worth noting, nonetheless, that both *Deep Throat* (1972) and *Emmanuelle* (1974), two of the largest crossover successes from the 'adult' sector of the period, both begat sequels with returning female leads (Linda Lovelace and Sylvia Kristel, respectively) as recurring protagonists. There is, however, another offshoot from the exploitation field which had a more direct influence on the mainstream: the vigilante revenge film, as represented by *Billy Jack* (1971) and its two sequels and *Walking Tall* (1973) and its two sequels. One might query the extent to which these films led the way in terms of content, especially given Warner Bros.' and Twentieth Century-Fox's almost simultaneous releases of *Dirty Harry* (1971) and *The French Connection* (1971), which ploughed similar thematic ground in their representations of Harry Callahan (Clint Eastwood) and, to a lesser extent, Popeye Doyle (Gene Hackman) as police officers with vigilante urges. Rather, *Billy Jack* and its first

You liked it before,
so he's back with more,

SHAFT's BACK IN ACTION!

SHAFT's! BIG SCORE!

a brand new caper.

METRO-GOLDWYN-MAYER Presents "SHAFT'S BIG SCORE!" · Starring RICHARD ROUNDTREE · Co-Starring MOSES GUNN
Written by ERNEST TIDYMAN · Based Upon Characters Created by ERNEST TIDYMAN · Produced by ROGER LEWIS and
ERNEST TIDYMAN · Directed by GORDON PARKS · METROCOLOR · PANAVISION®   [R]   MGM

sequel *The Trial of Billy Jack* (1974) were influential primarily in relation to future marketing and distribution strategies.

Although *Billy Jack* was an independent production by writer-director-star Tom Laughlin, it was originally picked up and given limited distribution by Warner Bros. in the summer of 1971. Unhappy with what he deemed its inadequate release of his film, Laughlin filed suit against the studio, which, in an out-of-court settlement, agreed to relaunch the film under new terms more favourable to the film-maker.[52] Laughlin chose to resissue *Billy Jack* via a strategy known as 'four-walling', whereby the distributor rents a theatre from an exhibitor for a predetermined flat fee, and subsequently collects 100 per cent of the box-office takings, and supported it with a saturation television advertising campaign targeted at specific demographic groups – the use of TV advertising being particularly noteworthy, given that the studios in the early 1970s tended to devote most of their marketing budget to press.[53] Laughlin's release of *The Trial of Billy Jack* largely abandoned the four-walling approach in favour of a saturation release, opening the film simultaneously in 1,100 theatres, again backed with television advertising. According to Justin Wyatt, 'Laughlin was able to extract strict terms from exhibitors for the sequel: a 90/10 split toward Laughlin and a minimum cash guarantee adjusted for a low house nut for each the-ater.'[54] This saturation approach, coupled with a TV advertising spend of $3.5 million, $1 mil-lion more than the spend for the original, delivered a then-huge gross of $10.5 million in the first week of release, a figure which eventually led to rentals in excess of $30 million, making the film the fifth highest earner of the year.[55]

While the recordbreaking grosses of Universal's *Jaws* in 1975, released six months later, are often taken as the inaugural moment of the modern Hollywood blockbuster,[56] its release strat-egy now looks rather cautious when compared to that of *The Trial of Billy Jack*: Spielberg's mon-ster was accompanied by the requisite advertising onslaught, but it opened on less than 500 screens, indicating the extent to which the major studios were still some way from fully embracing the distribution logic of exploitation. As Dade Hayes and Jonathan Bing have argued, Laughlin has been unfairly overlooked in most accounts of the birth of the blockbuster and it is clear that he was in this respect rather ahead of his time – even if the films themselves are very much products of that era.[57] Still, the comparison between *Trial* and *Jaws* is slightly unbal-anced, for Laughlin had at his disposal something that Universal did not, something that pro-vided a surer guarantee of audience attendance than a mechanical shark: the sequel to a prior success.

A-sploitation

Although Hollywood's developmental arc in the 1970s is commonly described, as in David A. Cook's account, in relation to the major studios' adoption of production and release strategies pioneered in the independent sector for the exploitation film, it is clear that this was not strictly a one-way street. The place of the sequel in late 1970s Hollywood, for example, was as much down to pre-existing studio practices as it was the result of innovations by maverick outsiders such as Tom Laughlin. And, as with the low-budget exploitation model, we can trace its origins in part to the early 1960s.

Poster for *Shaft's Big Score!* (1972)

In the summer of 1963, just as AIP was heading to the beach, United Artists was launching *Dr. No* in the United States, the first in a proposed series of films to feature author Ian Fleming's fictional secret agent, James Bond.[58] Operating much as it had always done, but in a manner that was relatively new to other studios, United Artists signed a production finance and distribution agreement with producers Harry Saltzman and Albert 'Cubby' Broccoli, which gave the latter a large degree of creative freedom and a share in the profits. In this case, creative freedom had little to do with lofty artistic ambitions, but it enabled Broccoli, Saltzman and their team (including director Terence Young and screenwriter Richard Maibaum) to devise what they deemed to be a successful formula, which could be reiterated and augmented from film to film. So concerted was their effort to create a consistent formula, Maibaum claimed, that their efforts extended to the number of 'bumps' (a term used by Hitchcock to describe shocks or thrills) per film: 'Mr. Broccoli and Mr. Saltzman … and myself have not been content with 13 bumps [Hitchcock's preferred number]. We aim for 39.'[59]

Furthermore, like the Hardy family and Thin Man series before them, but quite unlike most sequels of the post-studio era, the Bond films had gone from strength to strength at the box office. *Dr. No* had grossed a respectable $16 million at the US box office, but the grosses thereafter were far more noteworthy: *From Russia with Love* (1964) grossed $24 million; *Goldfinger* (1964) $51 million; and *Thunderball* (1966) took $63 million, making it one of the biggest hits of that year.[60] Accordingly, in another reverse of the standard series trajectory, the ever-improving box-office returns allowed UA chairman Arthur Krim to increase the scale of the approved production budget from film to film.[61]

United Artists was also behind two other series in this period, producing multiple follow-ups to *The Pink Panther* (1964) and *The Magnificent Seven* (1960), but the development of these series was far more haphazard and erratic than that of 007.[62] The Bond series would in many ways become the template for the production and distribution practices which would later govern Hollywood's approach to blockbuster-scale seriality in the coming decades: new instalments released at regular intervals, but with a sufficient gap (usually around a year) between each to warrant its marketing as an event. Nonetheless, while Broccoli and Saltzman's successful innovations clearly contributed to the changing sense of how seriality might function at the high-budget level, their eschewal of narrative continuity between instalments indicates a debt to the studio-era series film which would increasingly seem, if not outmoded, then certainly no longer the norm.

Rather more prescient, in this respect among others, were *Planet of the Apes* in 1968 and its four sequels. It would require a considerable budget to bring Pierre Boulle's original source novel to the screen, so it was not easy for producer Arthur P. Jacobs to find a studio willing to take the risk. Jacobs developed the project initially with investment from Warner Bros., but in spring of 1965, when the studio baulked at a proposed budget of around $11 million, the project entered limbo. It was not until September of the following year, when Jacobs's production company, Apjac, entered into an agreement with Twentieth Century-Fox that *Apes* once again began to develop again in earnest,[63] with the finished film eventually premiering in New York in February 1968, prior to a nationwide release in April.

It is not clear who originated the idea to produce an *Apes* sequel, but there is no doubt that Fox and Apjac were quick to react to the film's extraordinary success. *Variety* columnist

Army Archerd claimed on 27 March 1968, the date of the film's Los Angeles premiere, that Fox had approached Jacobs about a sequel and that the producer would be speaking to Boulle about the possibility that same day.[64] Twelve days later Rod Serling, creator of The Twilight Zone (1959–64) and one of the many writers to have worked on the original screenplay, sent two pages of suggestions for a sequel to Jacobs. Dissatisfied with Serling's suggestions, which he felt lacked any equivalent to the final 'shock' revelation of the Statue of Liberty, Jacobs contracted Boulle to write a treatment. The author was clearly enthused by the prospect of a sequel, and had turned out some initial thoughts by mid-April 1968, while the original film was still rolling out across the country. Although the original contract with Boulle is not accessible for research, it is clear that his financial motivation regarding the sequel revolved not around an already agreed fee from the original contract, but rather because he might be paid to write it.[65] Not all of the original participants were quite so eager, however. Charlton Heston's oft-reported disinclination to return as Taylor, the original's principal protagonist was compounded by his subsequent insistence that he would only take part if his role were kept to a minimum and if he were killed off in such a way as to preclude further sequels, a problem solved by a climax in which the planet and its inhabitants are wiped out in a nuclear apocalypse.[66] While Heston's resistance made the process more tortuous than it might otherwise have been, Jacobs was clearly (and rightly) convinced that Beneath the Planet of the Apes (1970) would be a success, because in December 1969, a full five months before its release, he began discussions with screenwriter Paul Dehn about picking up the pieces for another sequel. 'If it does as well as we hope they [Fox] would like a sequel', he explained to Dehn, before acknowledging the challenge facing the writer: 'I don't know how to solve this. We did kill absolutely everyone.'[67]

Beneath was not quite as successful as its predecessor, but it had been produced on a smaller budget (with savings made, much as they would have been in the studio era, via the recycling of sets, ape masks and costumes) so a sequel was indeed commissioned. Although the industry was superficially very different in 1970, the efficient regularity with which the subsequent three films (Escape from the Planet of the Apes [1971], Conquest of the Planet of the Apes [1972] and Battle for the Planet of the Apes [1973]) were produced by a team of regular collaborators (Jacobs, Dehn, actors Roddy McDowall and Kim Hunter, make-up designer John Chambers and art director William Creber among others), financially supported by a single studio, recalls the factory-like approach of the Seitz Unit at MGM. As with Kay Van Riper and the Hardy family, Dehn became increasingly proactive in his generation of further story material, to the extent that he had sent suggestions for a fourth Apes film to Jacobs before the third had even finished shooting.[68]

In these echoes of the studio system, the Apes series feels quite unlike the shape of sequels to come, but there were also noteworthy divergences from the series film production mode of yore. First, although production expenditure was significantly reduced as the series progressed (reflecting, in turn, Fox's reduced box-office expectations), these could not (with the exception of Battle, the last and cheapest instalment) be classified as low-budget productions. Second, as had been the case with Bond (whose car had become a Corgi toy in 1965), merchandise and spin-offs were very much a part of the process. Although sales of Apes-related products did not peak until the launch of a spin-off television series in 1974, Fox had begun to move ahead with a concerted programme of tie-ins in early 1969, in the hope of launching products to coincide with the release of *Beneath*.[69] Last, unlike both Bond and many of the studio-era series films, there was a concerted attempt to create a continuity (however tenuous) between the films. While Fox production chiefs Richard D. Zanuck and David Brown, along with associate producer Mort Abrahams, had expressed concern that the early drafts of the screenplay for *Beneath* relied too heavily on knowledge of the original, as the series developed, there was an increasing need to clarify the grey areas in this fictional universe, prompting Dehn to pull together a chronological list of events, beginning in 1973 and ending in 2000, so that he and Jacobs could maintain some consistency between cause and effect.[70]

In its commingling of production practices reminiscent of the old producer-unit system with more contemporary commercial and aesthetic concerns, *Apes* gives the lie to any notion of the sequel's linear trajectory from B to A. Like the apes themselves, on the surface these films seem to signal a new phase in the evolution of the Hollywood sequel, but beyond that surface lie some very familiar patterns of behaviour.

Waiting for *Superman*

If there is commonality between the sequels discussed in this chapter, it is that they indicate the extent to which the status and purpose of the sequel diversified in the twenty-five years following the *Paramount* decree, just as the industry itself had destabilised and diversified as a result of the decree and in response to television. Despite a considerably reduced output from the studios, the sequel continued to be the product of a high-volume, low-budget response to exhibitor demand, a low-risk filler for whatever gaps appeared in the shifting marketplace. But, from the late 1960s onwards it also, in the case of Bond, the *Apes* films, *The Godfather Part II* and *The Trial of Billy Jack*, took on the status of an event, whether in terms of production values, release strategy or both. As earlier chapters have demonstrated, this duality had always been a facet of the Hollywood sequel, with each era throwing up both low-budget cash-ins and more considered (or at least more expensive) continuations. It might seem that the sequel's path had bifurcated, but in effect this was little different from the distinction between A and B films in the studio era. And, like those earlier categories, there was always a degree of crossover, often as not driven by a like-minded opportunism among producers at all levels of the industry.

Equally, the types of story most frequently sequelised in the studio era (crime and mystery thrillers, horror and fantasy), and the characters leading those stories, continued to be those most prone to continuation after its passing; the only noteworthy absence being the gentle, family-centred comedy-dramas which had become the almost exclusive preserve of television. The most significant distinction was that these stories were no longer being brought to the screen as B-level products. Budgets that would once have been reserved for the production of 'specials', prestige epics and musicals were now being spent on science fiction and horror stories. Detectives who might once have been personified by character actors such as Warner Oland or Basil Rathbone were now played by A-list stars such as Clint Eastwood, Sidney Poitier and Gene Hackman. Bond and *Apes* clearly played a significant role in this realignment of generic priorities, but it was not until 1977, the year in which *Star Wars* broke box-office records and in which producer Ilya Salkind embarked on the production of both *Superman* and *Superman II* (1980), that these exceptions would come to resemble the rule.

4 | The end is just the beginning, 1978–2010

We've grown the business of event movies – multi-quadrant product for the global market .... .
At first blush, it seems more risky, but it's actually less risky if you do it right.[1]

Alan Horn, President and COO, Warner Brothers Entertainment

The past three decades have been boom time for the Hollywood sequel. While one aim of this historical account has been to underscore the importance of the sequel to Hollywood *throughout* the past century, it is equally undeniable that, from a purely commercial perspective, the form has flourished since 1977. This was more a resurgence than a new phenomenon, however, the difference being one of visibility. The industry had always been prone to sequelitis, but its symptoms were now more pronounced, as cinematic seriality began to more regularly lead the way at the box office: on all but three occasions since 1980, at least one sequel has been among the ten highest-grossing films of the year in the United States; in six of the past ten years, a sequel has been the highest-grossing film; and in 2007, sequels accounted for no less than six of the top ten. Even once adjusted for inflation, twenty of the 100 highest-grossing films of all time are sequels, of which only one (the formidable *The Bells of St. Mary's*) was made prior to 1977. So while it may remain an object of derision for film critics, the sequel has established itself as a vital, positive influence on the studios' year-end reports; a situation which seems unlikely to change in the near future.

How did this come to pass? Alan Horn's comments, made while announcing the end of his tenure at Warner Brothers in autumn 2010, hint at some of the intermeshing industrial developments which have contributed to the sequel's newly fortified position: the growing importance of generating revenue from outside North America; an ever-increasing focus on expensive event movies designed to appeal to all audiences, everywhere; and a need to minimise the high-level risk involved in such a strategy. Minimising risk, of course, has always been one of the film industry's organising principles, particularly because producers are involved in an inherently risky business in which success is never guaranteed; an ugly truth which, as Arthur DeVany has observed, is the economic corollary of William Goldman's 'nobody knows anything'.[2] The business of minimising risk has changed, however. Whereas the studio era saw the majors prosper because their exhibition holdings enabled them to profit from their competitors' triumphs as well as their own, effectively spread-betting across a wide range of *films*, the media conglomerate era (which began in earnest in 1985 with News Corporation's purchase of Twentieth Century-Fox) has seen the studios spread-betting across a wide range of *outlets*, from cinemas worldwide, free and pay television, the various video formats and now digital delivery systems. Because each of these outlets tend to be driven by theatrical success, the perceived (as opposed to actual) predictability of sequel revenues at the box office brings with it the perceived predictability of success in these ancillary markets, thus further reinforcing the perception of the form's earning potential.[3]

It would be somewhat too neat, however, to cast the function of the sequel in this period as simply one of the cornerstones of a pre-planned franchise; the glue binding together the multimedia interests dominating the film and television industries. Understanding the sequel's growth from the mid-1970s in relation to 'an upswing in defensive market tactics' is not enough.[4] That is certainly *one* of its functions, but to focus exclusively on this facet would be to ignore the plural influences on sequel production over the past thirty years, including: generic trends (particularly those relating to horror and comedy); the power of stars and star directors; and, most importantly, the burgeoning home-video market.

This chapter will consider the manner in which cinematic seriality has become one of the industry's preferred strategies for offsetting risk on its most expensive productions, while also acknowledging that other strand of cinematic seriality, low budget and high volume, which had been so central to studio-era Hollywood and which was given new life by the home-entertainment boom. The emergence of video as a new, hugely profitable market for filmed entertainment was truly transformative, inspiring both the revival of the independent sector and a new wave of mergers and acquisitions which, encouraged by the Reagan administration's penchant for deregulation, saw the establishment of what Edward Jay Epstein has dubbed 'the sexopoly',[5] a cartel of six vertically and horizontally integrated media conglomerates – Sony (owner of Columbia), News Corporation (Fox), Time Warner Inc., the Walt Disney Company, Viacom (Paramount) and NBC-Universal – with the kind of ubiquity and global reach that the erstwhile Big Five could only dream of. These two strands of sequel production are not discrete, of course. Understanding the role of the sequel from 1978 onwards means acknowledging that the development of cinematic seriality over the past three decades has taken paths which, like the form itself, are both novel and familiar.

Straight to video
Part 1 – tape

> Because the world is withdrawing to the safety and protection of the home, you're going to find a lot of advancement in television broadcasting, high resolution and sound … . The world is going inside. But they'll go out if you make it worth their time. All the pressure is on us.[6]
>
> Steven Spielberg

If television was the defining influence on the Hollywood sequel from the early 1950s through to the late 70s, there is no question that video has taken up the mantle over the past three decades. Unlike television, however, home video stimulated feature-length seriality to an extent that had not been seen since the 1930s. Made in 1982, Steven Spielberg's observations on the future of filmed entertainment are at once prescient and short-sighted: prescient because he foretells the dominance of the home-entertainment market; and short-sighted because his invocation of an 'us' assumes much the same opposition between the home and the cinema which inspired Hollywood's 'big picture' approach of the 1950s and 60s – an opposition between staying in and going out which somewhat obscures the extent to which the industry would, from the early 1980s onwards, become ever more invested in and financially reliant upon how audiences spent their time at home. This transition was well underway in 1982, but the full extent of its influence on the future structure of the film industry, which would in turn shape the development of the Hollywood sequel, was yet to become clear.

In 1974, the only way to watch movies at home, at a time of your choosing, and free of stringent network censorship, was to hire a 16mm film print. Although contemporary reports suggested there was a relatively healthy market for 16mm rentals, it was still a niche pursuit, largely the preserve of cinephiles.[7] Before the decade was over, however, a technologically and industrially streamlined version of that niche was on its way to becoming a mass-market activity. The year 1975 saw the debuts of both Home Box Office (HBO), a subscription-based cable television channel offering Hollywood movies free of network censorship, and Betamax, a videotape format launched by Japan's Sony Corporation, whose principal advantage, according to Sony CEO Akio Morita, was its capacity for time-shifting; allowing users to record television programmes and replay them at their leisure and convenience.[8]

Consensus among historians of the video revolution is that the Hollywood majors were hugely resistant to the rise of the new technology and that their realisation of its potential as a new market for their feature-film product was very much led by consumer demand.[9] The studios' resistance had nothing to do with an inherent conservatism but was instead because, as with television, they failed to see how they could possibly profit from a technology which enabled audiences to watch and rewatch their movies effectively free of charge. As Frederick Wasser notes, the majors 'were more interested in the expansion of cable channels leasing their film products' than they were in the new format, because they could exert some measure of control on how and when their movies were consumed.[10] Tape might replace 16mm rentals, but that was a small market, for connoisseurs only. Seeing little in it of benefit, the industry (or at least elements of it) went on the offensive. Jack Valenti described video as 'parasitical' and, in 1976, MCA (later joined by Disney) launched a lawsuit against Sony which was to drag on for eight years, before the US Supreme Court eventually ruled in Sony's favour.[11] Sony's victory was bittersweet, however: by the time the Supreme Court vindicated its right to exploit Betamax technology in 1984, it was well on its way to losing a battle for the consumer market with Matsushita, whose lower-quality VHS format had the dual advantages of both better distribution and greater flexibility, allowing users to record two hours on a single tape.[12] Crucially, all of the major studios (including Sony's two chief combatants, MCA and Disney) had by this time embraced video as a vital new source of revenue, with each having established an in-house home-video department by 1981.[13] As Morita reflected several years later, the lawsuit had 'been good for the lawyers', but ultimately for no-one else.[14]

The video revolution, on the other hand, proved to be good for everyone: by 1988, 60 per cent of all US households with a television also contained a VCR; sales of prerecorded videocassettes increased more than tenfold between 1981 and 1985, reaching 207.5 million in 1989;[15] and, by 1987, revenue from video had overtaken that from the domestic theatrical box office – all of this occurring without any apparent negative impact upon the mainstream theatrical market. Admissions remained steady and rentals, largely because of ticket-price hikes, continued to grow. In part this was due to pre-emptive action by the four key exhibition chains,

United Artists Theaters, Cineplex Odeon, American Multi-Cinema and General Cinema, who each embarked on expansion and refurbishment plans to increase and improve cinemagoing facilities across the country.[16] Of greater importance was the manner in which producers might utilise the new ancillary revenues: as J. Atwood Ives, company treasurer of General Cinema, correctly predicted in 1980, the potential for additional revenue would lead to an increase in the number of pictures produced. 'We need more product!' he declared – and he got it, with the annual number of releases in the United States climbing from 209 in 1980 to 515 in 1986.[17]

How did this shift in both viewing habits and the movie industry's business model affect the development of the sequel? First and foremost, it created a new market for film in which, initially at least, consumer demand was not being met by the majors. Bruce A. Austin has described home video as the contemporary equivalent of the 'second-run' cinema, but this doesn't quite capture the manner in which video not only provided additional revenue for pre-existing titles (as second-run cinemas had done) but also created a gap in the market which producers leapt to fill. Some of this product came from new genres such as the fitness video, but much of it was feature film. As had occurred with the emergence of the double bill as a standard exhibition format in the 1930s, the sudden increase in demand for feature films provoked a concurrent increase in (mostly) low-budget seriality. Video was not only the second-run house, therefore, but also the new home of the B-movie and those genres traditionally associated with exploitation, not least the pornographic sector, whose theatrical outlets swiftly shut down as private viewing on video inevitably came to dominate that market.[18]

Most of the additional output came not from the majors, but from independents both large (Orion Pictures, Cannon Films and De Laurentiis Entertainment Group) and small (Vestron, Hemdale, New World Pictures and New Line Cinema). Some of these companies (such as New World, originally founded by Roger Corman, New Line and Hemdale) had existed long before video was a viable source of revenue, some (Orion, established in 1978 by ex-UA executives Arthur Krim, Robert S. Benjamin and Eric Pleskow; Vestron, founded in 1981) were relatively new, but all were energised or revived in the early 1980s as the market took off, driving a boom in production from 1985 through to the early 90s.[19] As the figures in Table 4.1 indicate, sequel production increased between 1985 and 1991, almost entirely accounted for by independents. At first, indie sequels such as *Exterminator 2* (1984), *Hardbodies 2* (1986) and *Slumber Party Massacre II* (1987) enjoyed a modest theatrical run (usually on fewer than 500 screens) before moving swiftly to what was seen as their natural home on video. From the late 1980s onwards, however, an increasing number of independent distributors bypassed the theatrical market altogether. In some cases, a direct-to-video (DTV) release was an economically viable route to the market for a series which could no longer command attention in a theatrical arena where even earlier instalments had been also-rans at best, as was the case with *Ghoulies 2* (1987), *Howling IV: The Original Nightmare* (1988), *Maniac Cop 2* (1990), *Bloodfist IV: Die Trying* (1992) and *House IV* (1992). By the end of the 1980s, however, an entire series could originate from a video release alone, as was the case with *Puppet Master* (1989) and *Witchcraft* (1989), with the former spawning four follow-ups through to 1994, before being revived a few years later with *Curse of the Puppet Master* (1998) and then again as the DVD format hit its stride with *Puppet Master: The Legacy* (2003). The *Puppet Master* series, alongside *Trancers* (1985) and its five

Table 4.1 Independently produced and distributed sequels, 1984–93

Decade	Total no. of US sequels released	Total no. of sequels from indies	Indie-produced sequels as % of total
1984	16	5	31
1985	22	12	55
1986	17	9	53
1987	29	19	65
1988	37	22	59
1989	37	24	64
1990	46	29	63
1991	39	28	71
1992	35	25	71
1993	32	21	66

Note: Figures tabulated using the sequel database (URL).

sequels (1991–2002) and *Subspecies* (1991) and its three sequels (1993–8), were the products of Empire Entertainment and subsequently Full Moon Entertainment, both established by Charles Band. After filing for bankruptcy and dissolving Empire, Band set up Full Moon in 1988 with the sole intention of creating DTV product,[20] a move which suggests the extent to which video, in less than a decade, had come to dominate the market for low-budget genre fare.

Given the generally low level of financial investment, and perceived low-quality threshold for video fare, it is understandable that the definition of what constituted a sequel in this field was somewhat loose. This was in part a function of the genres most frequently represented in the straight-to-video sphere. It is hard to gauge the extent to which viewers of *Chained Heat 2* (1993) were concerned that it neither followed the narrative nor reprised the characters of *Chained Heat* (1983), and was rather a reiteration of the 'woman in prison' scenario sold as a vehicle for Brigitte Nielsen, a conceptual sequel, as it were. Occupying generic territory somewhere between conventional narrative cinema and pornography, this and equivalent entries in the erotic thriller cycle of the late 1980s and early 90s – including *Night Eyes* and its three sequels (1990–5), and *Body Chemistry* and its four sequels (1990–6) – were therefore less committed to the storytelling conventions of the mainstream.[21] Continuity of narrative and character was certainly not universally ignored: the *Puppet Master* series was inevitably committed to centring on the character of Andre Toulon, the Puppet Master, in film after film, even though the actors portraying him changed on multiple occasions. Sometimes, however, these were sequels in name only, as exemplified by the now-infamous *Troll 2* (1990), which was made as another film entirely, in which the antagonists are referred to as goblins rather than trolls, before being hastily retitled for its release in the hope of generating business on video from unsuspecting fans of *Troll* (1986).

Not all independents were created equal, and so not every independently produced sequel was created with the kind of modest budget or ambition that marks out *Troll 2*. Just as there were clear distinctions between a Little Three studio such as Universal, a top-rung B-producer such as Monogram and shorter-lived Poverty Row entities such as Mascot or Chesterfield, so the independent sector of the 1980s and early 90s had its own fluctuating social strata, dependent upon which type of production strategy each company adopted. Cannon Films, for example, under the aegis of Israeli producers Yoram Globus and Menahem Golan, who had purchased the company in 1979, opted for quantity over quality. Observing the huge demand not being met by Hollywood, Golan proclaimed in 1986: 'There is space for the mediocre!'[22] As the video market blossomed, they dramatically increased their output, putting twelve films into production in 1982 (more than most of the majors) building steadily to a roster of forty-one films in 1986.[23] Although their interests extended beyond 'the mediocre', into projects as varied as John Cassavetes's *Love Streams* (1984) and Neil Jordan's *The Company of Wolves* (1984), it was unsurprising that, given the sheer volume of output, sequels were particularly well represented in Cannon's line-up. Nineteen out of the ninety films they produced between 1979 and 1993 were sequels, including multiple instalments of the *Missing in Action* (1984), *American Ninja* (1985) and *Delta Force* (1986) series and follow-ups to films which had originated elsewhere, including *Superman IV: The Quest for Peace* (1987), *Texas Chainsaw Massacre 2* (1986) and four sequels to *Death Wish* (1974).

At the other end of the spectrum was Carolco, established in 1979 by Andrew Vajna and Mario Kassar, which gravitated towards a low-volume, high-budget approach following its breakout success with *First Blood* in 1982. Vajna and Kassar were able to trade on the respect earned by turning what was seen as a risky project into one of the highest-grossing films of the year, garnering financial support for a sequel from a coterie of outside backers, including Crédit Lyonnais, which had established a reputation for investing in independent productions. With *First Blood* as the anchor, Vajna and Kassar intended to build a slate of ambitiously budgeted projects in the $18–20 million range, most of which would be in the 'action-orientated field that we know how to make best'.[24] The *First Blood* series aside, sequels accounted for only a small proportion of the films Carolco produced between 1984 and its bankruptcy declaration in 1995, but they were disproportionately vital to the financial health of the company as a whole: *Rambo – First Blood Part 2* (1985) and *Terminator 2: Judgment Day* were, by some margin, the company's most commercially successful films in that period, although the huge budget for the latter, of which a reported $14 million went to Arnold Schwarzenegger,[25] certainly limited its short-term profitability.

Having first established New Line Cinema as an independent distributor of arthouse and 'midnight' movies in 1967, Bob Shaye had taken a rather different approach to either Carolco or Cannon, but, as the 1980s progressed, his company became similarly reliant upon sequels. Venturing into production in 1977, Shaye, alongside old college friend Michael Lynne, gradually augmented that aspect of the business while keeping budgets at $2 million or less per film.[26] It was not until 1984 that New Line's production investments really began to pay off. In November of that year *A Nightmare on Elm Street*, directed by Wes Craven and produced for just $1.8 million,[27] grossed more than $25 million in the United States alone, becoming one of two, independently produced 'sleeper' genre hits that autumn (the other being *The Terminator*), which would become the bases for multiple sequels. 'I had no idea of making it into a series,' Craven recalls, 'it was actually Bob Shaye who asked for a hook, as he called it, for a possible sequel – and I thought he was being overly optimistic.'[28] Rather than end with the monstrous Freddy Krueger (Robert Englund) disappearing into a black abyss, as in Craven's original version of the screenplay, the shooting script would instead, at Shaye's behest, leave open the possibility for his return – a decision which, in Craven's words, proved how 'very pre-scient' Shaye was about the film's potential to spawn sequels, not least when the director's con-cept had been rejected by numerous other studios. Intent on getting a sequel underway with or without Craven's involvement, Shaye reassembled several of the external financiers involved in the first film, including Media Home Entertainment, an independent video distributor who would again take North American video rights in exchange for its investment.[29] Released just fifty-one weeks after the theatrical debut of the original, A Nightmare on Elm Street 2: Freddy's Revenge (1985) bucked the trend among horror sequels by improving upon the box-office per-formance of its predecessor, with a gross of $29 million and rentals of $12 million against a budget of $2.2 million.[30] As Justin Wyatt has noted, Shaye and Lynne, unlike Vajna and Kassar, chose to funnel the Nightmare profits 'back into the company rather than into hasty and size-able production and distribution expansion'. Still, the boost Nightmare provided was significant: as Shaye remarked, 'One Elm Street annually' could cover their overhead costs.[31] From 1985 onwards, New Line effectively grew in tandem with the Nightmare series: A Nightmare on Elm Street 3: Dream Warriors (1987) became the company's first wide (1,000 screens or more) release, outgrossing the second film; and in 1988 Shaye produced both a TV series for Lorimar called Freddy's Nightmares and A Nightmare on Elm Street 4: The Dream Master, which outgrossed all previous instalments. Its success with these sequels paved the way for New Line to acquire the rights to what would become its biggest commercial hit film to date, Teenage Mutant Ninja Turtles (1990), which in turn allowed it to establish an in-house home-video arm, rather than sublicense those rights to Media Home Entertainment or another third party which would cut into its profits.

As these varied histories suggest, regardless of the intended market or scale of budget, independents throughout the 1980s and into the early 90s were reliant on sequels for their financial survival. Their drive to establish franchises, whether for video or otherwise, is reminis-cent of the kind of commercial vulnerability that inspired Universal's dedication to its horror formula in the 1930s. It is also, however, indicative of a new trend in film finance largely driven by the video boom: the presale. Preselling was an innovation of producer Dino DeLaurentiis in the early 1970s, who raised finance for films such as Death Wish by selling rights to distributors in various territories prior to the film actually entering production.[32] As the appetite for video grew, so did the value of the distribution rights a company such as Cannon could presell, thus increasing the budgetary scope for the production slate. At newly established film markets such as MiFed in Milan (first running in 1980) and AFMA in Los Angeles (formed in 1981), the pre-sale of international home-video rights contributed an increasingly large proportion of all rev-enues. Frederick Wasser has suggested that, because preselling created opportunities for new producers to enter the industry, 'Pre-buying was the primary activity that reinforced diversity in video distribution and film production.'[33] While the emergence of Cannon, Carolco, New Line and Vestron among others as substantial forces within the US film industry during the 1980s bears this out, it is also clear that a diversity of competitive distributors did not automatically lead to a diverse output of films. By its very nature, preselling favoured those properties which offered distributors some reassurance about the reliability of a return on their investment. Whatever its budget level, a sequel provided (or at least seemed to provide) precisely that measure of predictability, enabling an independent such as New Line or Carolco to more easily presell rights and raise production finance. Of course, given the predictable unpredictability of the market, there was no such thing as a completely safe investment, but it enabled independents such as Carolco to invest ever-increasing sums of money in their valued relationships with talent such as Sylvester Stallone and Arnold Schwarzenegger and the films in which they starred. Hence the budget for *Rambo III* (1988), which, at around $63 million, was more than double the budget for the second film, was offset by a reported $80 million in presales for foreign theatrical and video rights to a variety of distributors, investments no doubt made primarily on the basis of the superlative financial results delivered by its predecessor.[34]

By focusing exclusively on the independent sector here, I do not want to suggest that sequelisation during this period was entirely or even largely driven by these companies. Although they produced fewer sequels in total, the major studios were, of course, just as keen to capitalise on their prior successes. Yet it is hard to ignore the striking fact that the combination of financial insecurity and a newly voracious video market meant that, for an independent in the 1980s, repeating oneself was a commercial necessity, a matter of survival. Needless to say, preselling was not a flawless strategy, placing huge pressure on films to succeed, it ultimately provoked the downfall of companies such as Vestron and Carolco after a series of commercial failures. By the early 1990s, the window of opportunity opened up by video, an opportunity the independents exploited in part through the production of sequels and series, was beginning to close. The next video revolution would belong to the studios.

Part 2 – disc drive

The rise of the Digital Versatile Disc provides a bellwether of just how the industry had changed since the late 1970s, and how those changes had impacted upon trends in sequel production. First, contrary to their stance on the arrival of Betamax, the major studios did not merely welcome the launch of DVD in 1996, but were in fact a driving force in bringing it to market. Warner Bros. Home Video, as represented by its president Warren Lieberfarb, was part of the DVD Forum, a collective of European and Japanese electronics manufacturers (including the principal combatants in the original video-format war, Matsushita and Sony) whose aim was to create a universal standard for the launch of the new disc-based video technology. With Lieberfarb leading the charge, Warner convinced the other major studios to get on board with the new format, establishing the 'Ad Hoc Studio Committee' to request that Sony and Toshiba (who were independently developing rival versions of the technology in the early 1990s) came to an agreement about a single format, thus ensuring a relatively smooth launch,[35] which no doubt contributed to the speedy take-up by North American consumers when it debuted in 1997.[36] Second, not only were independent distributors a far less potent force within the marketplace for DVD than they had been during the early days of the videotape, but the very notion of what constituted an independent had become muddied by a series of mergers and acquisitions. These developments were already in progress when DVD arrived, having begun in earnest in 1993 when Disney bought Miramax and Turner Broadcasting Corporation acquired New Line and Castle Rock Productions, with the last three entities being subsumed by Time Warner in 1996. Although these acquisitions are indicative of the growing scale and ambition of multimedia conglomerates during this period, they also bespeak a broader, somewhat contradictory trend: the major studios' return, albeit indirectly, to low-budget feature-film production and distribution. In a master narrative which accentuates the upward spiral of production budgets and the industry's increasing focus on blockbuster event movies, accounts of contemporary Hollywood tend to assume that low-budget studio production begins and ends with recently absorbed independents or 'speciality' divisions, thus ignoring another trend: the striking growth of the studio-produced direct-to-video movie from the 1990s through to the 2000s.[37]

Just as the independents had done in the mid-to-late 1980s, from 1994 onwards the major studios began to embrace the direct-to-video market. And, just as the independents had done, the studios relied on the sequel to fill out their release slates. It is a sign of just how swiftly times had changed that it was the Walt Disney Company, originally so opposed to the new format, that proved just how lucrative the direct-to-video market could be. Disney had begun to roll out its back catalogue for home viewing in 1980,[38] while still mired in legal action against Sony, but had only released two of its classic animated features, *Dumbo* (1941) and *Alice in Wonderland* (1951), by the time the lawsuit was finally settled in 1984. It was not until Disney began to embrace the 'sell-through' model pioneered by Paramount (which had reduced the retail price of *Star Trek II: Wrath of Khan* (1982) from the standard $80 to $39.95 in a successful attempt to encourage direct sales to consumers over those to rental dealers) that the company came to fully realise the commercial potential of the new format.[39] It had some success with the video edition of *Pinocchio* (1940) in 1985, but it was the release of *Sleeping Beauty* (1959) in 1986, priced at $29.95, which indicated that Disney's longstanding strategy of reissuing classic animated features in cinemas could be replicated in the video format with considerably higher financial returns.[40] *Beauty* went on to sell 1.2 million copies, a feat subsequently dwarfed by the release of *Bambi* (1942) in 1989, which generated 10.5 million sales and $168 million in revenue, making it the second highest-selling video of all time after *E.T.: The Extra Terrestrial* (1982). Over the course of a decade, the studio became the leader in the sell-through video market and, by 1997, eight of the ten bestselling video releases of all time were Disney titles.[41]

By 1994, most of the Disney back catalogue had received some form of video release, and the long lead times involved in animated feature production meant that new, theatrically released 'classics' such as *Aladdin* (1992) and *The Lion King* (1994) were only appearing at the rate of one per year. It is unsurprising, therefore, that the studio should choose to create additional, bespoke material to feed its video distribution arm. This they did with *The Return of Jafar* (1994), a sequel to *Aladdin*, which bypassed cinemas and launched on VHS on 20 May 1994, less than a month after copies of its predecessor had been withdrawn from retail and rental shelves as part of the company's 'moratorium' strategy.[42] Produced for around a fifth of the cost of *Aladdin* ($6 million versus $33 million), *Jafar* sold more than 7 million copies in its first month, and, in the process, instantly legitimised the commercial viability of the direct-to-video market for the major studios.[43] Although Disney had made the first move, it was not the only studio to have sensed that there was serious money to be made in DTV productions. The previous summer, Universal had announced that production had begun on a DTV sequel to *The Land before Time* (1988), an animated feature which had been a reasonable (if not exactly spectacular) theatrical success for the studio five years earlier, but had proved a strong performer on video. *The Land before Time: The Great Valley Adventure* (1994) had in fact been on the cards since 1992, so Universal was not reacting directly to *The Return of Jafar*, but was clearly inspired by Disney, or rather Disney's dominance of the children's market, which at the time accounted for more than 50 per cent of all video sales and looked set to grow in the coming years.[44] Although its focus was on family fare, Universal simultaneously announced production of *Darkman 2: The Return of Durant* (1994), a sequel to *Darkman* (1990), another modest theatrical release which had proven itself more durable as a piece of home entertainment. Neither of these scaled the heights of *Jafar* in terms of sales, but both were sufficiently profitable to prompt further sequels. Like Cannon and their ilk in the 1980s, and not dissimilar to the studios' approach to B-film production in the 1930s, Universal and Disney had minimised the risk of entering into the DTV market by keeping production costs low and exploiting prior successes which had some form of built-in awareness among consumers. Furthermore – and here again this is not dissimilar to the studios' attempt to attract younger viewers to B-movie series such as the Hardy family and Nancy Drew – Universal and Disney were targeting an audience (children) whose considerable capacity for repeat viewing made the parental purchase of a video more cost-effective than recurrent rentals.[45] For Disney's production of *Jafar*, the budget limitations meant avoiding the computer-generated set-pieces which had become a staple of their animated features from *Beauty and the Beast* (1991) onwards, farming out the labour-intensive animation to their television animation production units in Japan and Australia, and replacing expensive talent with cheaper alternatives;[46] hence Dan Castellaneta in place of Robin Williams providing the voice of the genie, and an assortment of lesser-known composers in place of Alan Menken furnishing the musical numbers – including the aptly titled 'You're Only Second Rate'. This was not, however, simply a belated attempt to replicate the production model pioneered by the independents. Rather, the studios had watched and waited until the sell-through market had grown sufficiently to ensure that its returns would more than justify its investment. By 1993, the balance between rental and sell-through had begun to tip: in that year, 41 per cent of the $12.8 billion spent on video in the US came from sales, as opposed to just 24 per cent in 1988; and, whereas rental growth was slowing, retail sales were gathering momentum.[47]

Disney and Universal expanded their DTV production slates immediately following their initial forays into that sphere in 1994,[48] with the former producing a second sequel to *Aladdin* alongside follow-ups to *Honey I Shrunk the Kids* (1990), *Beauty and the Beast*, *The Lion King*, and *Pocahontas* (1995), and the latter delivering four more instalments of *The Land before Time*. Although their competitors were less quick to react, by the end of the decade all of the majors had released, or had in production, some form of DTV feature film, most of which hewed close to the Disney template by sequelising a family-orientated property which had first been given a theatrical release. In 1998 alone, as Disney established a new sales benchmark for the DTV market with the release of *The Lion King II: Simba's Pride* (1998) (14 million copies sold and revenues of $300 million), Warner Bros. launched *Dennis 2: Dennis Strikes Again* (1998) and *Richie Rich's Christmas Wish* (1998); Twentieth Century-Fox released *Addams Family Reunion* (1998) and *Ferngully 2: The Magical Rescue* (1998); and MGM released *The Secret of Nimh 2: Timmy to the Rescue* (1998).

This gradual move into DTV production was visibly accelerated as DVD began to establish itself as a new force in home entertainment. Not only did the format take hold more quickly than VHS, but by 2003 it was generating considerably more revenue than VHS ever had and, by 2004, was contributing more than $20 billion to studio coffers, almost as much as the combined total revenue from free television, pay television and theatrical exhibition.[49] As Paul McDonald has observed, this was in no small part because the studios had priced their DVD releases for sell-through competitively from the outset, in order to steer consumers away from rental and towards the more profitable retail sector.[50] In evident recognition of just how profitable DTV sequels had proved to be, Disney ramped up its production in 2001 and then, in 2003, split out the unit overseeing their production from its WDTV division to create a standalone entity, 'DisneyToon Studios'.[51] Universal, meanwhile, had already promoted Louis Feola (who had spearheaded its DTV efforts back in 1994) to head up a newly created division titled 'Universal Family and Home Entertainment Production' (subsequently renamed Universal Home Entertainment Productions), with plans to increase the number of DTV releases to between five and eight per annum.[52] By the middle of the decade, most of the major studios had followed Disney and Universal's lead by establishing divisions dedicated specifically to DTV production, and all were to some degree invested in the format.[53] By 2007, the market had grown to such an extent that DTV titles were estimated to contribute around $1 billion (or 6 per cent) of all DVD sales revenue.[54]

Although family-orientated titles continued to be the largest winners (alongside animation, these included live action such as Fox's three sequels to *Dr. Doolittle* [1998] and *Dr. Doolittle 2* [2001] and *Beethoven's 3rd, 4th, 5th* and *Beethoven's Big Break* [2000, 2001, 2003, 2008]), as an increasing number of studios entered the fray (most of them without the kind of family-friendly cachet of Disney), so the remit broadened to include teen movies (Columbia's *Cruel Intentions 2* [2000] and *Cruel Intentions 3* [2004] Universal's four *American Pie*[55] and four *Bring It On* [2000] sequels), science fiction (MGM's *Species III* [2004] and *Species IV: The Awakening* [2007]; Sony's *Starship Troopers 2: Hero of the Federation* [2004] and *Starship Troopers 3: Marauder* [2008]), action (Columbia's *Sniper 3* [2004]; Universal's *Smokin' Aces 2: Assassins' Ball* [2010]), and horror (Warner's *Lost Boys: The Tribe* [2008] and *Lost Boys: The Thirst* [2010]; Fox's *Wrong Turn 2: Dead End* [2007] and *Wrong Turn 3: Left for Dead* [2009]; Lionsgate's *American Psycho II: All-American Girl* [2002]). Independents such as Full Moon Entertainment and Concorde-New Horizons were still producing and releasing DVDs throughout this period, contributing further to the variety of films present on video shelves. Now, however, their efforts were increasingly dwarfed by those of the studios. The only fully independent distributor to come close to rivalling the studios during the past decade has been Lionsgate (formerly Lions Gate), which, like its major competitors, has been heavily invested in the DTV market, with a strong emphasis on sequels.[56]

The explanation for the prevalence of the sequel form in the studios' direct-to-video production rosters is similar to that of the independents in the 1980s: the logic of the presale. In this case, however, this logic prevailed less because of the need to raise production finances than because it ensured consumers knew what it was they were purchasing: 'They're not going to buy something they don't know anything about', observed Universal's Ken Graffeo; 'To be successful in the home video original programming market, you have to have a recognizable franchise', concurred Fox's David Bixler.[57] Without a presold element, there was little chance that the largest retailers (of which Wal-Mart was by far the most powerful) would buy sufficient units to deliver the required level of revenue. This was of particular concern because marketing budgets for DTV releases were generally far lower than for those titles which had been given a successful theatrical launch, meaning that the capacity to raise audience awareness via advertising was limited. Further insurance was provided by minimising production budgets, which were generally set at between $2 million and $10 million (Universal and Disney, which had been in the business longer and therefore had proven track records, were generally more willing to budget at the higher end of that spectrum than Fox or MGM), equivalent to 5–10 per cent of what the studios spent on producing their theatrical releases.[58]

With their low budgets, reliance on long-running series, often based on known properties, and particular genres, the studios' production of DTV films over the past fifteen years is hugely reminiscent of their approach to B-movie-making in the 1930s and early 40s. This was not quite the return of the producer-unit system, but with dedicated in-house departments strictly determining the annual number, type and scale of DTV productions, it bore some striking similarities. The talent were not under long-term contract as in the 1930s, but they nonetheless frequently returned to work on multiple instalments.[59] Sometimes A-list talent was involved (as when Robin Williams returned to voice the genie for Aladdin and the King of Thieves [1995]) but more often these were the products of film-makers well practised in the low-budget sphere, from director P. J. Pesce (director of From Dusk till Dawn 3: The Hangman's Daughter [1999], Sniper 3 [2004], Lost Boys: The Tribe and Smokin' Aces 2: Assassins' Ball), to proven DVD stars such as Wesley Snipes and Steven Seagal. As with the studios' earlier B-movie units, DTV films married a loose approach to the material with extremely tight schedules and budgets. 'You don't get to go over schedule, not even by an hour', Pesce explained in interview. And, much as Bryan Foy might have done back in the 1930s, studios adapted liberally from material they already owned. Thus Hans Rodinoff's original screenplay for Lost Boys: The Tribe bore no relationship to the original film, instead centring on a group of surfers who were also werewolves.[60] While many of the films for this market were sequels proper, some, like their independent predecessors in the 1980s, were closer to spin-offs, in which a supporting character from the original took centre stage (as in the three DTV sequels following Dr. Doolittle 2, where Kyla Pratt reprises her role as Doolittle's daughter) or to conceptual series films (Bring It On Again [2003] and The Butterfly Effect 2 [2006], for example), which recycle the basic narrative situations and trajectories of their predecessors with an entirely new and unconnected set of characters. Last, as per the B-movie model of the studio era, DTV production and the steady, relatively reliable profits it generated helped to justify the overhead incurred by maintaining an in-house department – albeit in this case a home-entertainment division dedicated to marketing and distribution, rather than a studio-based production facility.

The DVD boom's influence on sequels was not limited to the DTV arena, however. It was not only the key profit driver for feature film, but also a motor able to improve studio fortunes in other sectors. This was most evident with films which had generated only moderate box-office returns, but were then able to reach a larger audience on DVD, because they remained on shelves longer than they played in cinemas and could therefore benefit from word-of-mouth recommendation. This newly bolstered, built-in audience might then in turn be relied upon to come out and boost the box-office returns for a sequel. This dynamic was already evident towards the end of the VHS era, when Austin Powers: The Spy Who Shagged Me (1999) grossed more in its opening weekend than *Austin Powers: International Man of Mystery* (1997) had achieved in its entire run; a phenomenal result credited largely to the success of the original on video. As Russell Schwartz, marketing chief at New Line, noted of *Rush Hour 2* (2001): 'Our audience was expanded through video.'[61] DVD made such occurrences far more common, with sequels such as *Transporter 2* (2005), *Harold and Kumar Escape from Guantanamo Bay* (2008) and *Saw II* (2005) all benefiting from the popularity of their predecessors on disc, sometimes as much as doubling the box-office gross of the original.[62]

Such benefits worked in both directions, with the release of a sequel in cinemas (and subsequently on DVD) often creating a substantial increase in DVD sales for previous instalments. To give just one noteworthy example, *American Pie* saw sales leap from 37,800 total in July 2001, to 219,593 August 2001, the month in which *American Pie 2* (2001) premiered in cinemas. This pattern was repeated with the theatrical release of the third instalment, *American Pie: The Wedding* (2003), with sales of *American Pie* and *American Pie 2* leaping from 10,631 and 9,404 in July to 92,371 and 80,840 respectively. These figures are merely one indicator of the commercial power of cross-promotion, given that they do not include the various iterations of the *Pie* series in boxset form which were similarly boosted by the releases of new DTV instalments such as *American Pie: Band Camp* (2005), *American Pie: The Naked Mile* (2006) and *American Pie Presents Beta House* (2007).[63] Such cross-promotional activity across a series of films was not new – each new *Planet of the Apes* sequel prompted theatrical reissues of previous instalments – but its commercial potential had grown dramatically.

Last, because of its status as a physical product with a presence in retail stores across the US, a DVD release could be used to drive sales of other, related consumer items stocked in those outlets. Since the late 1970s, when *Star Wars* and *Superman* ushered in a new era in related licensed products, such activity has become a huge, multibillion dollar business for the Hollywood studios.[64] The concurrent rise in sell-through video meant that retailers became increasingly invested in the products of the film industry, leading to a situation in which the DVD launch could be as vital a platform for sales of merchandise as the theatrical release. Here again, the sequel is seen to be a particularly valued commodity. As Disney's head of consumer products observed,

> *Wal-Mart* is pushing bigger programs on DVD release than film – because DVD is an event in the store … . The first time out for a brand-new property … retailers will mitigate risk and invest modestly. They'll only ante up for a so-called second-run intellectual property, a known entity, like 'Toy Story 2,' 'The Chronicles of Narnia' or 'The Lord of the Rings'.[65]

As the numerous commercial interconnections forged by the rise of DVD indicate, there is one further parallel between the B-movie cycle of the 1930s and 40s and the DTV movie cycle of the past fifteen years, which suggests the considerable differences between the two versions of Hollywood which produced them. The B-movie was advantageous to the studios not only because it kept their production facilities busy, but also because their monopolistic stake in the exhibition sector meant that they had a vested interest in keeping their cinema chains supplied with a steady stream of films, regardless of type. For DTV titles, however, the economic boost they gave to the outlets stocking them was of secondary importance to the studios. Paramount aside (which, as part of Viacom, was indirectly affiliated with the Blockbuster video chain between 1994 and 2004), none of the majors had a direct stake in either the rental or retail businesses; they benefited from these outlets only insofar as their own individual video products were successful. The real benefit of the studios' DTV sequel output was the manner in which it generated revenue while also increasing the value of an existing film (or films) with which it was associated. As Universal's Craig Cornblau observed, 'We discovered we could keep franchises alive with made-for-DVD movies if we made them feature quality.'[66] The comparison between the B-cycle and the DTV cycle thus brings into focus an important transition within the industry: whereas the studios' overall profitability in the 1930s was a result of their ability to maximise the potential of their *physical* property (in terms of studio space, cinema chains and, arguably too, talent under long-term contract), their profitability from the late 1980s onwards was increasingly dependent on their ability to fully exploit their *intellectual* property (including originary material such as novels, plays, comic books, videogames, television shows, old movies and theme-park rides, and the characters or situations featured therein).[67] The rise of DVD further increased the value of the studios' intellectual property by fortifying the commercial interconnections, originally forged in the first video boom, both between films and sequels, and between films and their ancillary incarnations, whether as home video, novelisation, CD soundtrack, videogame or merchandise. By greatly enhancing the potential profits to be made in exploiting these interconnections, DVD further enhanced Hollywood's pursuit of what had become, since the early 1980s, its primary objective: the cultivation of the franchise.

The rise of the franchise

It's become downright gauche to acquire a plain old property anymore – it always has to be a series of properties.[68]

Peter Bart

In its coverage of the departure of Frank Price from Columbia Pictures in late 1983, the *New York Times* consulted with financial analyst Emanuel Goldman. According to Goldman, Price's departure was precipitated by the fact that Columbia's new corporate owner, the Coca-Cola Company, failed to understand the nature of the film industry: 'Coca-Cola made a large commitment to get into a business far afield from syrup', he explained. 'There is no brand name franchise in the movie business. A moviegoer doesn't care if a picture is labelled Columbia or Paramount.'[69] Though accurate in some respects, Goldman's observations failed to anticipate the extent to which, while their value as brands in their own right would remain mostly elusive (with Disney, of course, the notable exception), each of the studios would increasingly become committed to positioning their films as parts of a larger commercial whole that might best be described as a franchise. This was not a new concept *per se* – and it is arguable, as Peter Bart has suggested, that this is little more than a 'convenient buzzword',[70] often used more in the spirit of opportunism than semantic accuracy. Nonetheless, it is clear that, from the late 1970s onwards, studios began pursuing this strategy with a greater dedication than they had in the past, largely because of their gradual absorption into larger conglomerate structures. As we have seen, DVD would become an important cornerstone for this business model, but the studios' ambitions for franchise construction, and their understanding of how this might be achieved, preceded the arrival of the new format by many years.

Although *Star Wars* is consistently portrayed as the watershed, marking, in David A. Cook's words, 'the creation and nurturing of the first true film franchise',[71] the George Lucas space opera's primary influence on both the industry as a whole and the development of the franchise in particular arguably took the form of a cautionary tale for the studios, rather than a positive example in how to proceed. True, *Star Wars* launched an unprecedented merchandise bonanza, which had generated more than $2.5 billion in revenue by 1997, but Lucas's deal with Twentieth Century-Fox, in which he took a low salary in exchange for merchandising and sequel rights, meant that he, rather than the studio, was the main beneficiary of this extraordinary and sustained success.[72] One can only speculate as to what extent Lucas conceived of *Star Wars* as a trilogy from the outset; he has in fact claimed that it developed as such only because he had too much material for a single film.[73] Regardless, as the primary creator, Lucas's control over this newly minted fictional universe meant that he, as the film-maker, was able to dictate the pace and extent of its subsequent development as a franchise – a model which the studios were understandably keen to avoid becoming the norm. The fact that the industry failed to recognise the potential of *Star Wars* stems from the ways in which it was both alike and dissimilar to the franchise template as it would develop: alike in its eschewal of expensive stars in favour of expensive special effects; dissimilar in its avoidance of any other presold elements, such as a basis in well-known source material. The absence of both stars and a presold property explains the lack of confidence the studio displayed right up until the film's release, which in turn explains why Lucas was not able to embark on producing a sequel until after the original had proved itself at the box office. It is for this reason, too, that *Star Wars*, with hindsight, seems less central to the history of the Hollywood sequel than three other blockbuster productions, all distributed by Warner Bros.

Appearing more than a decade apart from each other, *Superman*, *Batman* (1989) and *Harry Potter and the Philosopher's Stone* (2001) were representative of where the industry was situated at their respective points of production, and also indicators of what it would strive to become. *Superman*, produced by father-and-son team Alexander and Ilya Salkind, had been in the works long before *Star Wars* arrived in cinemas. The Salkinds' multiple attempts to acquire film rights to Jerry Siegel and Joe Schuster's comic-book hero finally came to fruition when Warner Bros. merged with DC Comics' owner National Comics in 1969. Warner seemingly had little interest in pursuing the project, and so granted the producers a broad spread of rights, essentially allowing them free rein to produce films and television programmes featuring the character. Although the studio would have approval on budget and casting, this would be what was known as a negative pick-up, in which the Salkinds independently financed the film, delivering a finished product for Warner Bros. to distribute.[74] The studio's attitude might seem improbable in retrospect, given that the character is now perceived as one of its most valuable intellectual properties, but is less so when one considers that no comic book had hitherto received the full big-budget treatment. Warner's initial reticence aside, the Salkinds' approach to the production of *Superman*, and the studio's rather more enthusiastic approach to launching the finished product, more clearly reveals the beginnings of the franchise mentality in three key respects.

First, they were drawing on an enduring, presold property which was both serial in nature and which had hitherto been brought to screen only via low-budget productions, the presold element helping the Salkinds raise production finance more quickly.[75] Second, the expansive nature of their contract with Warner Bros. enabled the enterprising Salkinds to think beyond a standalone film. Earlier in the 1970s, they had shot *The Three Musketeers* (1973) and *The Four Musketeers* (1974) back to back, enabling them to enjoy some economies of scale across the two. Given the huge potential expense of bringing Superman to life, the Salkinds decided to adopt the same approach, with a sequel to be shot simultaneous to the first film. Making this happen meant that the talent involved were contracted accordingly and it s this contractual foresight which has subsequently become an integral part of franchise production. A 400-page treatment from *The Godfather* author Mario Puzo detailed the story for both the first and second films, making it easier to secure commitments from director Richard Donner and principal cast members Marlon Brando, Christopher Reeve, Margot Kidder and Gene Hackman for the sequel before production on the first film had commenced. Although the Salkinds' multi-film approach was attractive in theory, its realisation encountered numerous barriers which made it seem less than ideal in practice. There were much publicised conflicts with Marlon Brando, footage of whom was excised from *Superman II* in order to avoid his participation in 11 per cent of the sequel's profits, and Richard Donner, who was replaced by Richard Lester, allegedly without being informed. These battles meant that shooting on the sequel drew to a halt before the release of the first film, only to resume towards the end of 1979.

Last, although initially unenthusiastic, having subsequently witnessed not only the success of the *Star Wars* merchandise but also Fox's error in failing to anticipate that windfall, Warner orchestrated a huge campaign, involving not only the usual promotional blitz but also the anticipatory manufacture of various forms of merchandise – an initiative that would eventually grow to generate around 1,200 licensed products – which benefited each of the divisions of what was now Warner Communications Inc. The studio was particularly well placed to push ahead with a merchandise effort because WCI's chairman Steve Ross had incorporated the Licensing Corporation of America, a company specifically dedicated to that activity, when creating the new conglomerate in 1969.[76] It was, claimed Warner's head of distribution, Terry Semel, 'the biggest interdivisional effort we have ever done as a company'.[77]

Semel's words find their echo, some years later, in his description of *Batman* (1989) as 'the first time we utilized the whole machine of the company. The marketing, the tie-ins, the merchandising, the international'.[78] This was not simply an empty repetition of his mantra from the *Superman* era: by the summer of 1989 Semel was CEO and the 'whole machine' had been reconfigured in the wake of another phase in Warner's corporate history. Whereas the studio behind *Superman* was part of a conglomerate with an extremely diverse set of holdings, financial difficulties in 1984 had prompted Steve Ross to sell off those entities (including the Gadgets restaurant chain and the Pittsburgh Pirates baseball team) not directly related to the entertainment or communications industries. On 23 June 1989, as *Batman* was breaking opening weekend box-office records, WCI was not only a more streamlined, focused entity, one whose every division could profitably be put to work on a synergistic blockbuster such as this, but it was also (despite a major challenge from Paramount) well on its way to merging with Time,

Inc., a publishing giant which, crucially, had a considerable investment in the cable television arena via its ownership of HBO and the American Television and Communications Corporation.[79] *Batman* was a new archetype for what could be achieved when a multimedia conglomerate put the whole machine to work.[80] Merchandise, for example, was now incorporated into the production and development process, with potential licensees paying visits to the Pinewood set.[81] In terms of commercial results, furthermore, it played a major role in establishing what Dade Hayes and Jonathan Bing call the 'opening weekend paradigm',[82] in which the full power of a multimedia entertainment conglomerate is utilised to generate as much box-office revenue as possible in as short a timeframe as possible, pushing the industry visibly closer to a model in which a film's theatrical lifespan grows shorter and shorter.[83]

While the above suggests the extent to which *Batman* represented an intensification of the Salkinds' approach to *Superman*, it was notable, too, for establishing a template in which a studio combined a presold property with relatively untested film-makers (in this case director Tim Burton and actor Michael Keaton in the title role) who might offer a distinctive take on familiar material. As Will Brooker has indicated, Warner's choice of Burton may have been partially inspired by the edgier depictions of the character in graphic novels by Frank Miller and Alan Moore – but the notion that this was Burton's *Batman*, regardless of where the true 'vision' for the film derives from, was an influential addition to the franchise model.[84] As the casting of Jack Nicholson in the role of the Joker makes clear, however, Warner was clearly not willing to rely on the popularity of the character alone, resorting to a more traditional deployment of a star's marquee value in an attempt to offset risk.

While *Batman*'s success suggested that Warner's gamble had paid off, the sequel, *Batman Returns* (1992), again revealed the strategy's limitations. Speculation about a sequel began almost as soon the original had premiered, and the studio clearly intended to move ahead as soon as possible, having spent hundreds of thousands of dollars keeping the Gotham set in storage at Pinewood. It seems, however, that it had not factored plans for a sequel into its initial contractual negotiations with either Burton or Keaton. The latter held out purportedly because he did not want to commit without seeing a script,[85] but also secured a salary increase from $5 million to $10 million. The issue with Burton was officially less one of salary (although it seems likely that he, too, secured a higher fee for the sequel) but his reluctance to revisit Gotham City.[86] This reticence, coupled with the studio's desire to involve him , led to a longer-than-expected interval between productions and also, more crucially, to the director being given more free rein creatively.

By the early 2000s, Warner's approach to *Batman* clearly continued to influence franchise film-making. Directors whose commercial track records were as yet unproven, but who had established something resembling 'auteur' credentials, were increasingly twinned with the studios' biggest releases, as was the case with Jean-Pierre Jeunet and *Alien: Resurrection* (1997), Peter Jackson and *The Lord of the Rings* trilogy, Sam Raimi with *Spider-Man* and its two sequels, Bryan Singer with *X-Men* (2000) and *X2* (2002), and Paul Greengrass with *The Bourne Supremacy* (2004) and *The Bourne Ultimatum* (2007). Warner itself briefly diverged from this path in replacing Burton with Joel Schumacher, widely perceived as a journeyman, as director for *Batman Forever* (1995) and *Batman and Robin* (1997). Following widespread derision from critics and fans (and considerably reduced box-office returns) for the latter, however, the studio reverted to its original approach in hiring Christopher Nolan to revive the franchise with *Batman Begins* (2005).

Furthermore, although the phrase had yet to be officially coined in 1989, *Batman* was also arguably influential in terms of the 'reboot' strategy, the starting anew of a franchise which usually involves a move away from the look, feel and tone of previous incarnations of a character. Burton's *Batman* was (alongside the Miller and Moore graphic novels) a quite explicit attempt to start afresh, in the process erasing the memory of the lighthearted approach of the *Batman* television series (1966–9) in the 1960s. There is a parallel here with an earlier industrial practice which again suggests the distinctions between old and new Hollywood. Equivalent to the 'off-casting' of stars in the studio era, Warner's approach to *Batman* effectively involved the off-casting of source material; with the intellectual property, the character of Batman in this case, as the star. Chapter 6 will further explore the notion of character as star and its effects on sequel production, but in the meantime it need only be remarked that this approach foregrounded the practice of interpretation – in this instance, Tim Burton's personal interpretation of the Batman character and mythos – as a means of stressing that the film would deliver the new alongside the familiar.

A more recent turning point, once again provided by Warner, came in 2001 with the launch of *Harry Potter and the Philosopher's Stone*. As with *Batman*, this high-budget adaptation of the first in J. K. Rowling's series of novels for children came hot on the heels of another phase in Warner's corporate development, in this case the merger in February 2000 between Time Warner and internet powerhouse America Online (AOL).[87] And, as with *Superman*, *Philosopher's Stone* was based on a well-established fictional property, whose lead character was played by an unknown who was contracted from the outset for multiple films. The newly forged relationship with AOL added another layer of in-house synergy and cross-promotion, but this was effectively an extension of the multi-divisional efforts which had characterised the launches of both *Superman* and *Batman*.

What, then, did Harry Potter add to the franchise formula? Crucially, it cultivated the notion of the 'saga', a version of seriality whose formal, aesthetic properties had important ramifications for the manner in which it was approached by the studio. For these purposes, the saga consists of an explicitly predetermined and finite number of multiple, separately released instalments. What Harry Potter's status as a preordained seven-part saga more fundamentally altered, rather, was the perception of the level of investment required for both the studio and the audience. If Potter was to succeed from a corporate perspective, Warner Bros. would have to deliver a product which viewers would be willing to follow and invest in over several years. It was not unusual for a studio to simultaneously acquire multiple, connected literary properties, but it was rare that these properties were part of a single, larger narrative whole. The implications of Rowling's endeavour (which by 2000 was one of the biggest literary success stories in memory) meant that Warner Bros., who had acquired the rights to the first four novels via a first-look deal with British producer David Heyman, would have to approach this as a long-haul business venture rather than an opportunity for short-term financial gain.[88] That meant, in the words of Warner Bros. marketing executive Diane Nelson, setting 'guidelines to ensure that we're protecting the brand's integrity for the long term'.[89] This was not simply a case of building in sequel potential, or preplanning a follow-up from the outset, but rather the

Daniel Radcliffe, Rupert Grint and Emma Watson, young stars of the Harry Potter franchise,
in *Harry Potter and the Prisoner of Azkaban* (2004)

creation of a brand which might, if handled correctly, continue to deliver revenue to the studio
for a decade or more.[90] The notion of 'brand management', of developing a long-term strategy to ensure the cultivation of a loyal audience, was not simply a marketing strategy.
Presumably taking note of the damage done to the Batman franchise in the 1990s by both
casting changes and a shift in directorial vision, the studio and Heyman kept *Harry Potter* casting consistent and allowed different directors to subtly modify the look and feel of each instalment without radically altering the appearance of the fictional universe.

In tandem with *The Lord of the Rings* trilogy from Warner subsidiary New Line, the sustained
financial bonanza provided by *Harry Potter*, whose eight instalments have amassed more than
$2.3 billion at the US box office alone,[91] clearly influenced a wave of somewhat less successful
attempts to replicate it: *The Golden Compass* (2007), *The Chronicles of Narnia* (2005–8) and *Percy
Jackson and the Lightning Thief* (2010). Despite these disappointments, encouragement has come
from the phenomenal success of *The Twilight Saga* and *The Hunger Games* (2012–) which,
although targeted from the outset at a slightly older audience than the initial Potter episodes,
are both also based on a finite series of novels with a fantastical slant and huge fanbase.

Superman, *Batman*, *Harry Potter and the Philosopher's Stone* and their respective sequels
were certainly not the only films to fuel the studios' desire for franchise cultivation over the
past thirty years, but they afford a useful indication of the manner in which multi-part storytelling, refined and modified according to the standard business practices of the time, has gradually moved to the centre stage of studio release schedules, becoming the art-form of choice
for the contemporary multimedia conglomerate. In the past decade in particular, the franchise
has come to be a holy grail in the studios' quest for huge, sustained and reliable profits. Barely
a week passes without *Variety* reporting the studios' latest attempts (or struggles) to create a
new multimedia phenomenon.[92] But, as the example of *The Golden Compass* suggests, there is
often some distance between the conglomerate dream and the commercial reality. While this

intensification in the pursuit of franchise-ready properties distinguishes contemporary Hollywood from its earlier incarnations, certain persistent trends have also driven sequel production for the best part of a century, and a review of these will conclude this chapter.

Back in the habit: the contemporary sequel and opportunism

While franchise film-making is indicative of conglomerate Hollywood's shift towards the ever more calculated deployment of its intellectual property, with the sequel forming part of a pre-conceived commercial strategy, it has not entirely replaced pre-existing patterns of sequel production. Even outside the home-entertainment sphere, a particular form of economic logic has persisted, driving much sequel production over the past 100 years, a logic which assumes that the sequel form is one of the most effective means of capitalising on a film's success. This logic might best be understood under the rubric of opportunism, a term whose use here implies no negative value judgment, but instead describes an attitude underpinning certain aspects of Hollywood's approach to the sequel. This opportunistic element manifests itself in sequel production in various ways, but here I want to discuss three broad areas in which it has played a part over the past thirty years: the sequel and the studios; the sequel and stars; and the sequel and generic trends. Each of these areas displays a clear continuity with Hollywood practice in earlier decades, albeit one refracted through the prism of a reconfigured industry.

The studios

While the studios have increasingly adopted the franchise model, they have also continued to produce sequels to films whose success (or at least the *scale* of whose success) was to some degree unanticipated. This was particularly evident during the 1980s and early 90s, when a steady stream of movies became surprise or 'sleeper' hits. Films such as *Airplane!* (1980), *The Cannonball Run* (1981), *Porky's* (1982), *48 Hrs.* (1982), *National Lampoon's Vacation* (1983), *The Karate Kid* (1984), *Police Academy* (1984), *Romancing the Stone* (1984), *Crocodile Dundee* (1986), *Lethal Weapon* (1987), *Three Men and a Baby* (1987), *Look Who's Talking* (1989), *Home Alone* (1990), *City Slickers* (1991), *Beethoven* (1992), *Ace Ventura: Pet Detective* (1994) and *Speed* (1994) were all major studio releases with relatively modest budgets which became unexpected hits, precipitating one or more follow-ups. For reasons discussed in Chapter 3, the studio executives and producers behind these films were rarely able to move ahead with a sequel as quickly as they might have done in the studio era, meaning an interval of around two years, and sometimes more, between the original and its sequel. Occasionally, however, circumstances coalesced to facilitate a swifter response. Disney's Touchstone division,[93] for example, was able to rush *Sister Act 2: Back in the Habit* into cinemas just over eighteen months after the release of *Sister Act* (1992). The availability of talent, in particular the star, Whoopi Goldberg, was of course a key issue, but the speed with which the sequel came together arguably had much to do with Disney's approach to its source material. Much as had been the case during the 1940s, the studio saved time on the development process by simply refashioning a finished screenplay already at its disposal, rather than starting from scratch. In 1990 Disney had signed Dawn Steel, one-time president of Columbia Pictures and subsequently an independent producer, to an exclusive deal in which she would develop properties for Disney to distribute. As part of that arrangement, Steel had been developing a screenplay by Judi Ann Nelson entitled *Knocking at Heaven's Door*, a dramatic gospel musical based on real-life events at a high school in Crenshaw. Shortly after *Sister Act*'s success, Steel was instructed to rework *Knocking* into a sequel to the Goldberg hit. (Although she 'understood their agenda of needing a sequel', this was one reason Steel cited for the premature termination of her agreement with Disney in September 1992).[94] With Mason's screenplay duly repurposed by James Orr and Jim Cruickshank, Bill Duke was assigned directing duties in February 1993, shooting began in May, and the film was released in December of that same year.[95] While not quite as swift as the turnaround on a studio-era sequel such as *Father's Little Dividend*, *Sister Act 2: Back in the Habit*'s prompt arrival confirms that the major studios were still capable of reacting dynamically to cap-italise on a hit if the opportunity presented itself.

As the franchise mentality became more ingrained, and, crucially, as front-loaded release strategies and shortening theatrical windows began to reduce the opportunity for positive word of mouth to build over a number of weeks, such surprise hits from the studios became less frequent. Nonetheless, films such as *Rush Hour* (1998), *American Pie*, *Big Momma's House* (2000), *Legally Blonde* (2001) and *Step Up* (2006), all of which have begat sequels, proved that there was still a willingness to exploit an unexpected box-office result. More recently, this prac-tice has been exemplified by *Paranormal Activity* (2009) and *The Hangover* (2009), although in both cases the studios' approach indicates how the industry has shifted. *Paranormal Activity* was an old-fashioned negative pick-up, with DreamWorks (by then a subsidiary of Viacom, distrib-uting through Paramount) acquiring all US distribution, along with remake and sequel rights at the Slamdance Festival in January 2008. The intention was to release the supernatural thriller, produced for less than $15,000, straight to DVD, before remaking the film on a considerably larger budget, a plan which won favour by a commitment to hiring the director, Oren Peli, to remake his own film.[96] Plans changed following a series of test screenings, which the produc-ers had insisted upon as part of the acquisition agreement, and the resounding success of which convinced Paramount to release the original film theatrically. When the film grossed in excess of $100 million, Paramount established a micro-budget production fund, and of course pressed ahead with a sequel.[97] It maintained the original's independent production ethic for the sequel: although an industry veteran, Akiva Goldsman, was among its producer credits, *Paranormal Activity 2* (2010) was neither directed by nor starred any established Hollywood names; it was produced quickly, in time for release just eleven months after the original; and, although it represented a huge increase from the original, the budget was set at $3 million, less than 5 per cent of the 2010 average Hollywood production cost.[98]

The Hangover has a less unusual production history, with the original screenplay sold to Warner Bros. and Todd Phillips, who had a 'first-look' deal with the studio, attached to direct. Phillips wanted to 'mix things up' by casting three relatively unknown actors (Bradley Cooper, Ed Helms and Zach Galifianakis) as the male leads, but Warner was no longer willing to pro-vide the full budget without stars attached, capping production funds at $34 million – around half the current average for a studio release.[99] Insistent on his casting choices, Phillips worked for union scale and waived his contractual share of the gross in exchange for an equity stake in the production, alongside Warner and co-producers/financiers Legendary Pictures.[100] Phillips's new status as equity partner gave him 15 per cent of all revenues from *The*

Hangover, meaning that he ultimately earned a huge sum after it went on to gross more than $400 million worldwide.[101] While the fact that it had not initially foreseen the film's commercial potential might be taken as evidence of corporate conservatism at work, Warner Bros. was rather more proactive once it was completed. Following excellent test-screening results and a strong response to the trailer at exhibitor trade show ShoWest, the studio announced in April 2009, two months before *The Hangover* premiered, that it had commissioned Phillips to write a sequel and had made deals with Cooper, Helms and Galifianakis to reprise their roles.[102]

While often portrayed as lumbering conglomerate giants interested only in blockbuster production these examples indicate that the studios are still willing to support riskier productions at lower budgets on occasion, and are as capable of reacting as swiftly to a new, unexpected opportunity as were their studio-era counterparts. At the same time, of course, the speed of these reactions was predicated in part by arrangements which had pre-empted such eventualities, arrangements which in some respects recall the earlier studio system. Phillips's deal gives him considerably more freedom than a director under long-term contract in the 1940s, but it also puts Warner at a competitive advantage when bidding for his services, making it easier and quicker to secure his commitment to *The Hangover 2* (2011). Similarly, DreamWorks and Paramount may have had little faith in the original version of *Paranormal Activity*, but it was only because they had purchased remake and sequel rights upfront that they were able to deliver a sequel within a year of the original. The prevalence of such forward-thinking regarding sequelisation, which, as previous chapters have shown, had clearly begun to spread from the 1950s onwards, indicates that it is now at the contract stage that the studios (and indeed the independents) must establish their right to further capitalise upon a film's success, speculatively preparing the ground for opportunities their counterparts from the 1930s might have taken largely for granted.

The talent

The driving force behind the behavioural shift described above is largely a result of an equivalent shift in the relationship between creative talent (primarily stars, but also directors and writers) and the sequel form, which was in turn the result of the studio system's collapse. As Chapter 2 demonstrated, because the long-term-contract model meant that the stars were effectively their exclusive property, the studios were able to rely more heavily on star-orientated formulas as a means of maximising the return on their investment; swiftly exploiting the success of *The Gay Divorce* (1935), for example, not with a sequel but with multiple Fred Astaire and Ginger Rogers musicals. By the late 1960s, with that model a distant memory, there was less incentive for the studios to develop such combinations when they had no proprietary hold over the constituent parts. By the same token, for the talent locked into the studio system, there was little intrinsic benefit to being involved in a sequel to a prior success. Consistent popularity at the box office did tend to have a positive bearing on one's salary, but as there was no direct correlation between a star's earnings and the net revenue generated by any one film in which they appeared, they, too, had little reason to find reprising a role any more desirable than portraying a nominally different character who represented an equivalent variation on their persona. By the 1980s, however, it was becoming clear that the industry as a whole had developed a predilection for combinations of star and character/franchise which it was beginning to favour over those of star and genre.

It is no surprise that, as had been the case under the old system, the studios and their backers had a preference for a form of exploitation which was proprietary over one which was generic and therefore open to imitation. For the stars, however, this was essentially a new development, albeit one which had a precursor in the sequels starring Douglas Fairbanks and Rudolph Valentino in the 1920s. As discussed in Chapter 1, Fairbanks and Valentino were more obviously predisposed towards producing and/or starring in sequels to their earlier successes precisely because they more directly benefited (whether in terms of financial return, star status or both) from each film. For creative talent in the 1980s, while they may not have any legal hold over a given property, their public association with that property was often seen to be an essential component of its value. If a studio or independent producer wanted to reassemble the key creative personnel for a sequel, those personnel suddenly had something they may not have had previously, something their agents and managers prized above all: the leverage to demand more favourable contractual terms. Sequelisation, therefore, not only offered studios the opportunity to maximise the potential of their intellectual property, it also offered talent – and stars in particular – the opportunity to variously improve their 'quote' (the agent's term for a client's standard salary), the industry status accompanying that quote, and potentially also their creative control over projects.

This pattern had begun to develop during the 1970s, notably when, in order to secure his commitment to *The Godfather Part II* in 1974, Paramount had agreed to pay Francis Ford Coppola a then-phenomenal $1 million fee and 13 per cent of the gross receipts, also granting him time to first shoot *The Conversation* (1972) and the creative freedom to continue the Corleone saga as he saw fit.[103] It took on new life in the 1980s, however, as independents such as the Salkinds and Carolco became more involved in high-budget production. Because Carolco began to depend upon the *Rambo* series to fuel its other production activities, it needed Sylvester Stallone more than any other studio. As a result, it was willing to make ever greater displays of financial and contractual generosity in order to keep him on board. Thus, whereas for *First Blood* Stallone was paid $3.5 million, by the time of *Rambo III*, Stallone was commanding a salary of $16 million, and was also an official contributor to the screenplay.[104] Although there have been various instances in which high salaries have been paid out for standalone films (the $5 million Dustin Hoffman received for *Tootsie* [1982], for example), the increasing commercial importance of cinematic seriality across all sectors of the industry has clearly contributed to a situation in which sequels are one of the primary driving forces for such economic largesse. And, because spiralling star salaries create a domino effect on salaries for other creative personnel, they have therefore been one of the key inflationary pressures on production budgets which, even taking inflation into account, were sixteen times larger on average in 2003 than they were in 1947.[105]

Excessive as they may seem, the huge payouts for Stallone, Bruce Willis (a reported $20 million for *Die Hard: With a Vengence* [1995]), Tom Cruise (earning around $70 million in both salary and gross participation from *Mission: Impossible 2* [2000]) and Arnold Schwarzenegger ($29.5 million plus 20 per cent of the gross receipts for all forms of distribution for *Terminator 3: Rise of the Machines* [2003]), were testimony to the studios' belief that the appeal of these

stars in combination with a signature character provided a guarantee (or as close to a guarantee as was possible) of a large return on that investment. Although it was questionable whether
they could have commanded these fees for non-sequels (Schwarzenegger had proven particularly fallible in the years immediately prior to *Terminator 3*), each of these stars was nonetheless well established in their own right.[106] The power of the sequel is such, however, that even
less influential figures, or those with no proven track record outside the original film, are also
likely to benefit. Thus Tommy Lee Jones (a star, certainly, but not in the same league as Cruise
or Willis) was able, after lengthy negotiations which delayed production, to command $20 mil-
lion for *Men in Black 2* (2002), well above his usual quote; Whoopi Goldberg's salary leapt from
$2.5 million for *Sister Act* to a rumoured $6.5 million for *Sister Act 2: Back in the Habit*; and
Sigourney Weaver, who earned $33,000 for *Alien* (1979), was paid $11 million for *Alien:
Resurrection*.[107] Perhaps most striking of all was the leverage achieved by Macaulay Culkin following the phenomenal success of *Home Alone*. Aged just nine when that film was released,
Culkin had no sequel clause in his original contract, enabling his father and manager, Kit Culkin,
to demand that Twentieth Century-Fox supply not only a huge salary increase but also a cov-
eted role in *The Good Son* (1993), another Fox production, in exchange for Macaulay's services
in *Home Alone 2: Lost in New York*.[108]

As this latter example suggests, salary demands are often more important in terms of their
symbolic value, with other, less economically tangible rewards being equally desirable. Both
Leonard Nimoy and William Shatner were able to parlay the necessity of their continued presence in the *Star Trek* series into opportunities for greater creative input, with Nimoy directing
Star Trek III: The Search for Spock (1984) and *Star Trek IV: The Voyage Home* (1986) and Shatner
(who had also delayed production on *IV* by holding out for a higher salary) directing *Star Trek
V: The Final Frontier* (1989).[109] Wes Craven, who had signed over all his rights to the *Nightmare
on Elm Street* intellectual property in his original contract with Bob Shaye back in 1984, was
tempted back to the series when Shaye not only offered him a retrospective share in revenue
from the sequels, but also gave him the freedom to reinvent the franchise as he saw fit. Similarly,
Warner Bros. was so keen for Joe Dante to direct *Gremlins 2: The New Batch* (1990), and he
was so uninterested in the assignment, that the studio was willing to grant him complete creative control and final cut, an opportunity so rare he felt unable to turn it down, resulting in a
film which was less a straightforward follow-up than an anarchic satire on the very notion of
the Hollywood sequel.[110]

As indicated earlier, the growth of pre-emptive contractual arrangements for sequel participation has been one of the central developments of the franchise era. Although multiple-
picture deals between studios, producers and stars became increasingly common in the 1980s,
it was rare that they centred around a particular series or franchise.[111] Since the early 1990s,
however, the studios have become more proactive, at least in relation to any film which they
intend to build into a franchise. Ben Affleck, Christian Bale, Eric Bana, Robert Downey Jr, Shia
Leboeuf and Brandon Routh each had sequel clauses in their contracts for *Daredevil* (2003),
Batman Begins, *Hulk* (2003), *Iron Man* (2008), *Transformers* (2007) and *Superman Returns* (2006)
respectively – although only Bale, LeBoeuf and Downey Jr have actually been required to
honour those commitments.[112] As this list suggests, the Salkinds' multi-film approach to
Superman (and the contractual necessities that went with it) helped establish a template for

Joe Dante, granted creative free rein for *Gremlins 2: The New Batch* (1990)

blockbuster production generally, and for comic-book adaptations in particular, albeit one which took many years to become standard practice. Although most of these actors are better known than Christopher Reeve was back in 1977, only Affleck had really proven himself to be a box-office draw at the point of casting, suggesting the extent to which, as with *Superman*, multiple-film commitments tend to be more common with talent who are yet to achieve A-list status.[113]

Although such agreements appear to tip the balance of power back towards the studios in a manner recalling the age of the long-term contract, they can also benefit the creative talent involved. Marvel Studios has worked on precisely this basis since becoming more directly involved in production in the years following *Spider-Man*. Its deals with actors such as Samuel L. Jackson, Chris Evans and Robert Downey Jr involve low initial salaries, but include pay increases for subsequent films and bonuses should those films hit certain financial targets. Furthermore, commitments are built in for as many as nine appearances in their respective roles as Nick Fury, Captain America and Iron Man respectively, including a debut film, direct sequels and guest appearances in other related productions. As *Variety* observed, Marvel has been able to 'lowball' its salary payments in part by offering actors the chance 'to star in their own franchise', and in part by the more fundamental appeal of regular work over a number of years at a time of industrial uncertainty.[114] Aside from giving some degree of reassurance around production budgets, these arrangements also allow Marvel to build a long-range release schedule with more confidence, the first phase of which culminated with the release of

Avengers Assemble (2012). Underlining these logistics are the examples of other ensemble cast pieces from the past decade: *American Pie, X-Men* and *Scooby-Doo* (2003) all had sequel options in place for all or most key cast members, and sequels have duly followed; *The Italian Job* (2003) and *Hairspray* (2007) did not, and their sequels have either yet to appear or have stalled entirely, despite the stated intentions of their respective studios.[115]

Such agreements, however, are not necessarily the last word in any given negotiation. Tobey Maguire had options for two sequels in his original contract for *Spider-Man*, with his $4 million salary for the first film rising incrementally so that he would earn a further $23 million across two subsequent instalments. Following *Spider-Man's* phenomenal success his agents attempted to renegotiate the deal, a tactic which nearly misfired when Sony threatened to replace Maguire (whose salary demands were compounded when his back problems caused production delays) with Jake Gyllenhaal. Ultimately, the renegotiation strategy proved successful, with Maguire's salary for *Spider-Man 2* alone ballooning to $17 million.[116] Renegotiation is a familiar process in Hollywood deal-making, as exemplified by Eddie Murphy who, having signed an exclusive multi-picture deal with Paramount after the success of *48 Hrs.* in 1982, had his contract renegotiated twice: once following the success of *Beverly Hills Cop* in November 1984; and then again after the release of *Beverly Hills Cop II* in September 1987.[117] While they may not voluntarily initiate such renegotiations, the fact that the studios have historically acquiesced to such requests suggests that there is a benefit to them in future-proofing the viability of potential sequels. That said, the studios are not always willing to relent to such demands. When Kathleen Turner requested a larger salary for *The Jewel of the Nile* (1985), sequel to *Romancing the Stone*, Fox filed a suit against her, citing her prior contractual obligation to appear in a second film with no increase in pay.[118]

For the studios, then, the sequel represents an opportunity to maximise their intellectual property in a manner which seems relatively free of risk, while for the talent it represents the opportunity to improve their salary, status and potentially also their creative satisfaction. As encapsulated by contractual options and the negotiations which surround them, it is because the sequel offers advantages to both the studios *and* the talent, and because the realisation of such advantages creates a potential conflict of interest, that it has become – whether as an actuality or merely a future possibility – one of the recurrent flashpoints in the ongoing power struggles between those who finance films and those whose labour brings them to life.

The sequel and the genre cycle

As Rick Altman observes, studios have always preferred to emphasise their films' '*proprietary* characteristics (star, director and other related films from the same studio) over *sharable* determinants like genre'.[119] Whereas, thus far, I have pointed to the manner in which the sequel is often the product of the opportunistic logic of its makers, I would like to counterpose, last, that it is also a defensive act on their part, to guard against the opportunism of their competitors. While this was certainly a factor during the studio era, as with Universal's use of its repertory cast of monsters in the 1930s and 40s, the dissolution of the star system saw a narrowing in the range of convenient options for a studio seeking to capitalise on a hit by using material over which they had a proprietary hold. This new reality, coupled with the increase in demand for filmed entertainment brought about by video and an influx of independent producers, meant that the generic cycles which had always been central to Hollywood's output became more reliant upon cinematic seriality during the 1980s than they had been since the 1940s.

We can see this process at work most visibly in the horror boom years of the late 1970s and early 80s. While the genre had made a major return earlier in the decade with both big-budget studio productions such as *The Exorcist* (1973) and *The Omen* (1976) and independent breakthroughs such as *The Texas Chainsaw Massacre* and *Last House on the Left* (1972), it was with *Halloween* (1978) that horror took on a new market currency. As *Variety* noted, John Carpenter's film had 'changed the market potential for horror films by demonstrating that low-budgeters (as in the 50s) could compete with the big boys', precipitating a final, dramatic push in the decade-long growth of the genre which, combined with science fiction, accounted for between 35 and 37 per cent of US theatrical rentals in 1980, versus just 5 per cent in 1970.[120] The spike in horror production and the slasher cycle which followed has been well documented, as indeed has the increased tendency towards sequelisation, but the fact that, in Andrew Tudor's words, 'sequelling … has itself become a major convention of the genre', is due less to a sociocultural shift than to the hugely competitive market environment in the years following *Halloween*.[121] As was standard in the wake of any unexpected box-office triumph, a swath of generic imitators followed, many of them hewing closely to the stalk-and-slash template of Carpenter's film. It is no surprise, therefore, that the producers of *Halloween* should choose to make an actual sequel, rather than a generic variation likely to lack the sequel's edge over the numerous competing films. Nor indeed is it any surprise that when one of those imitators, *Friday the 13th* (1980), came close to replicating *Halloween*'s popularity, its producers (Paramount) should choose to rush ahead with a follow-up. Neither *Halloween II* nor *Friday the 13th Part 2* (1981) came close to their predecessors' box-office performance, but both were still hugely profitable due to low production costs, thus establishing a clear template for successful horror series. The popularity of *Friday the 13th* in particular, whose third instalment, *Friday the 13th Part III* (1982), outgrossed the second film and came close to equalling the original, was clearly the inspiration for Bob Shaye's approach to *Nightmare on Elm Street*. Following *Friday*'s lead, Shaye prioritised the prompt production of a sequel over other factors, a necessary strategy in a highly competitive market that would certainly attempt to capitalise on *Nightmare* if New Line did not move swiftly.[122]

A similar, if less pronounced, pattern is visible with teen-orientated comedy around the same period. Although *National Lampoon's Animal House* (1978) initiated the cycle, its immediate impact was not to generate sequels but instead to establish the big-screen viability of both its star John Belushi and his fellow *Saturday Night Live* alumni, including Dan Aykroyd, Chevy Chase and Bill Murray. The real turning point came in the spring of 1982, with the phenomenally popular *Porky's*, which became the fifth highest-grossing film of the year. Although distributed by Fox, *Porky's* was produced by independent Canadian company Astral Bellevue, which partially explains why *Porky's II: The Next Day* (1983) was ready for release little over a year later. Again, this proved a commercially judicious decision. While the sequel grossed only around a third of the amount of the original, it fared considerably better than its teen comedy competitors, *Spring Break* (1983) and *Valley Girl* (1983), that same year. Just as *Nightmare on Elm Street* followed the *Friday the 13th* template, which had itself followed *Halloween*, so *Police*

Academy mimicked the *Porky's* template. By far the most successful of the *Porky's* equivalents until that point, *Police Academy* was also the product of an independent, in this case Paul Maslansky, working with funding from the Ladd Company, as part of a joint venture with Warner Bros. As with the Seitz Unit and its Hardy family series, Maslansky quickly established a momentum, to the extent that he was ready to commission a screenplay for *Police Academy III: Back in Training* (1986) in January 1985, while still shooting *Police Academy II: Their First Assignment* (1985). Unlike Seitz, he was no doubt partially motivated by an agreement which gave him 30 per cent profit participation in each instalment, an attractive proposition when the films were budgeted at between $6 and $8 million and returned that investment many times over.[123]

Accounting for a significant proportion of all the sequels produced in the 1980s, horror and youth-orientated comedy have been particularly suitable for sequelisation because of voluminous, opportunistic competition for similar audience groups along with certain logistical advantages: they can be made quickly and cheaply, reliant neither on stars nor complex special effects. In this respect, much as with the yet-to-flourish DTV market, they echoed three aspects of series film production in the 1930s and 40s. First, while they operated in rather different generic territory, the detective movies, Westerns and sentimental family comedies dominating the series film in those years were similarly favoured because they required neither stars nor large budgets and could be turned out with factory-like efficiency. Second, these genres burgeoned as a result of opportunistic imitation, with one hit prompting a host of similar movies from other studios (Fox's Charlie Chan inspiring Warner's *Perry Mason* [1983], MGM's *A Family Affair* prompting Paramount's Henry Aldrich series [1939–44] and so on). Last, their narratives lent themselves to continuation and repetition, a transhistorical formal characteristic to be discussed further in Chapter 7. Although they have both ebbed and flowed in popularity, horror and youth-orientated comedy have continued to rely upon sequelisation with every new iteration. Thus the renewal of the slasher movie in the late 1990s with *Scream* (1996), the revival of the gross-out teen comedy with *American Pie* and the more recent, harder-edged 'torture-porn' cycle inspired primarily by *Saw* (2004) have each followed much the same pattern as their 1980s predecessors, with both the initiatory success and at least one subsequently profitable competitor (*I Know What You Did Last Summer* [1997] and *Urban Legend* [1998] in the former instance, *Road Trip* [2000] and *Dude, Where's My Car?* [2000] in relation to *American Pie*, and *Hostel* [2005] in relation to *Saw*) spawning one or more sequels.[124]

The franchise model, with its emphasis on proactively following a preconceived narrative and commercial scheme rather than reactively generating a series on a film-by-film basis, seems outwardly inimical to the mentality which drives these generic cycles. In fact, even here Hollywood is clearly still subject to a more reactive brand of opportunism. Witness the wave of comic-book movies following in the wake of *X-Men* and *Spider-Man*, the family-orientated fantasy films (*The Golden Compass, The Chronicles of Narnia, Percy Jackson* and *The Spiderwick Chronicles* [2008]) attempting to recreate the commercial magic of the *Harry Potter* series, and the slew of self-reflexive, star-voiced animated comedies (including *Ice Age* [2002], *Madagascar* [2005] and their respective sequels) which have taken their lead from DreamWorks' *Shrek*. Noting this generic tendency, Edward Jay Epstein has proposed that there is a clear, nine-point

'midas formula' for a successful franchise; ranging from the inclusion of child or adolescent protagonists, a fairytale-like narrative structure and happy ending, to the use of computer-
generated action sequences and inclusion of characters specifically intended for toy licensing.[125]
Encapsulating franchise production in this fashion does somewhat flatten the still considerable
aesthetic diversity among the blockbuster contingent: qualitative judgments aside, there are
clearly more distinguishable differences (in tone, structure and so on) between *Harry Potter*, *Ice
Age*, *Pirates of the Caribbean* and *The Dark Knight* than there are between movies which emerge
as the result of more recognisable generic cycles such as *Friday the 13th* and *Halloween*. While
his criteria are questionable, Epstein nonetheless effectively conveys the extent to which the
industry has adopted the notion of the franchise as a broad-based category, a mode of production which makes the most of available resources. Here again, of course, we bump up
against the series film, a model adopted by all of the studios in the 1930s for much the same
reason; and a historical precedent which suggests that however drastically altered the whole
equation of pictures may now be, those who appear to have solved it will continue to find their
competitors snapping at their heels.

Dangling cause: to be continued?

As I write this in summer 2013, the home-entertainment sector is beginning to stabilise after
a lengthy slump which began in 2008, simultaneous to the wider economic downturn. The
growth in sales and rentals via new digital-distribution channels is at last becoming a viable sup-
plement to the decline of revenue from physical DVD sales and rentals. Largely because of the
premium ticket prices charged for the increasing number of films screening in IMAX or 3D formats, the theatrical box office has held relatively steady – but, in the past twenty-five years, that
revenue has come to represent less and less of the major studios' total income. Despite the
continuing upheaval, it is clear that Hollywood is some way from the financial precipice at which
it stood in the late 1960s.[126] The manner in which audiences access movies and television is
changing, but their appetite for these forms of entertainment persists, despite a growing
number of multimedia distractions. As long as the studios are able to navigate this changing ter-
rain – and, because of the scale and influence of their parent conglomerates, they are advan-
tageously placed to do so – and as long as they remain directly invested in each of the rapidly
multiplying, synergistically linked distribution channels and sources of film-related revenue, it
seems likely that their passion for producing content which connects those channels, and which
generates revenue not only for itself but also for related, pre-existing content, will continue to
burn strong. The sequel, as one of the multimedia conglomerate organism's healthiest, most
durable forms of connective tissue, seems likely to do the same.

While tracing this history of the Hollywood sequel, I have consistently stressed the commingling of past practices and novel developments characterising each and every manifestation
of the form over the past century. This intertwining of progression and repetition is also, of
course, one of the persistent formal tropes of the Hollywood sequel, a more detailed examination of which forms the basis for the remaining three chapters. As I hope the developments
discussed in this final historical section make clear, it is something more than sophistry to suggest that the narrative work of the sequel as an aesthetic form – and the balance it strikes

between the novel and the familiar – is an apt metaphor for the actual historical developments of the sequel as a commercial product. At each and every turn, from its silent origins through to its privileged commercial status in the early twenty-first century, the sequel has played a crucial role in Hollywood's development, a feat it has achieved by drawing on successful aspects of the industry's past while simultaneously propelling it, inexorably, into its future.

PART 2 | *FORM*

5 | No end in sight: The classical narrative paradigm and the sequel

If, as I suggested in the introductory chapter, the sequel's place in writing on postclassical cinema is unfortunate, its relationship with accounts of classical Hollywood cinema is equally problematic. This uneasiness is perhaps best summarised by the following assertion from Kristin Thompson, made in relation to the spate of adaptations between film and television in the late 1990s and early 2000s:

> Such transfers of story material form part of a larger pattern that includes sequels, serials, spin-offs, and sagas – other trends that have burgeoned in recent decades. The circulation of plots among media reflects, I would argue, an important change in our conception of narrative itself – and specifically a loosening of the notion of closure and the self-contained work of fictional art.[1]

This comment encapsulates two broadly held assumptions, one historical, the other theoretical, which this book calls into question: first that the sequel is in any sense a characteristic phenomenon of contemporary Hollywood; second, that it is necessarily at odds with the notions of narrative unity informing the classical paradigm.

The historical case is straightforward enough: the account of the sequel's long history in the preceding chapters, alongside the statistics in the appendix, offer an empirical corrective to unchecked assumptions about the contemporaneity of the form. The sequel and the series have been standard practice in Hollywood for decades, and it is a historical fallacy to suggest otherwise. Given this evidence, Thompson is on shaky ground when proposing that our conception of narrative itself is only now shifting: audiences have long been familiar with protracted cinematic storytelling.

This brings us to the theoretical issues, which are a trickier matter – not least because of Thompson's central role in defining the critical understanding of narrative in Hollywood cinema – and to the questions I wish to consider further in this chapter:

- In what ways might the sequel challenge notions of classical narrative unity?
- To what extent does the in-built chronology of the sequel interact with the episodic qualities of the series film?
- And how might we measure closure versus open-endedness?

In asking these questions, I have a larger goal: to identify and describe those formal characteristics distinguishing the sequel from a standalone work. Combining discussion of these issues with analyses of a broad range of films, what I hope will emerge, both here and in the remaining chapters, is a poetics of the cinematic follow-up which is subtly different from, albeit complementary to, that of single artworks, a poetics which allows us to understand the negotiation between 'saying the same thing differently and saying another similarly' in which all sequels must engage.

Classical/postclassical and the primacy of narrative

In *Storytelling in the New Hollywood* (1999) and *The Way Hollywood Tells It* (2006) respectively, Thompson and David Bordwell have both argued for the persistence of the classical tradition in contemporary Hollywood, suggesting that their account of *The Classical Hollywood Cinema* remains largely robust and relevant, and taking to task those scholars who have posited the existence of a postclassical mode.[2] While both acknowledge that changes have occurred, they are consistent in asserting the continued structural and organisational primacy of narrative in Hollywood film-making. This becomes particularly apparent when we take into account Thompson's brief acknowledgment of the sequel in *Storytelling in the New Hollywood*, where she concedes that a film 'aimed at generating a sequel' might not achieve full closure in the classical manner, at least insofar as it might introduce a new 'dangling cause' late in the narrative, but is simultaneously keen to stress that this 'does not typically generate ambiguity but hints at the direction the sequel's action will take'.[3] In other words, such a strategy does not fundamentally challenge the tenets of classical storytelling; the new dangling cause being separate from and therefore not disruptive to the classical narrative arc.

Bordwell and Thompson suggest that the case for postclassical Hollywood cinema's existence rests on the assumption that coherent narrative and classical storytelling techniques have fragmented in the face of external forces, variously the influence of 'high-concept' marketing, advertising, the fragmentation of audiences post-1960 and subsequent emergence of a 'distracted' viewer, and of course the growing dominance of the blockbuster with its predilection for spectacle.[4] Although these shifts have indeed been characterised as influential by many critics, the extent to which it is assumed that said shifts have caused narrative traditions to collapse is highly questionable.[5] Insofar as he discusses a shift away from classicism, Thomas Schatz in no sense downplays the role of narrative in what came next. His description of *Star Wars* as 'so fast-paced ... and resolutely plot-driven that character depth and development are scarcely on the agenda',[6] is indicative of Schatz's argument that the emergent blockbuster mentality did not mean a disintegration of narrative, but rather a realignment of priorities whereby 'characters (even "the hero") are essentially plot functions'.[7] Even when discussing the 'intertextual' qualities of the blockbuster, qualities which mean it is 'purposefully incoherent', Schatz concedes that 'many (perhaps most) New Hollywood films still aspire to this kind of narrative integrity'.[8] Similarly, while Justin Wyatt stresses modularity and moments of excess within the high-concept film, at no point does he suggest that narrative has disintegrated or disappeared entirely. After all, in Wyatt's account it is the story that forms the starting point for any high-concept project, even if it can be 'easily communicated and summarized'[9] and, to paraphrase Spielberg, compact enough to hold in your hand.

This is not a defence *per se* of Schatz's or Wyatt's definitions. It is clear that the death of narrative has been overstated, and that moments of spectacle and excess are neither new nor necessarily disruptive of narrative flow.[10] The fact remains, however, that when Thompson claims that 'a number of critics and historians have come to believe that narrative has fallen apart', she is simplifying not only the postclassical argument of other scholars but also her own task of disproving it.[11]

As the above suggests, the classical/postclassical debate has effectively been reduced to an opposition between narrative coherence and narrative erosion in Hollywood cinema; and it is in this context which Thompson's more recent remarks on narrative redefinition and loosening closure initially appear to mark something of a shift. They do nothing, however, to alter the fact that this has always been a debate which assumes that change has occurred post-1975, rather than allowing for the possibility that the original model was itself too narrow. The very existence of the sequel and the series in the studio era indicates that Hollywood has always produced fictional artworks which are not 'self-contained' in the strict sense of Thompson's definition, but to what extent does the sequel form actually represent a challenge to closure? There is no easy way to answer this question, and this, it seems to me, is because the sequel amplifies the role of audience knowledge, destabilising certain assumptions at the heart of the classical model. To better illustrate this hypothesis, let us consider the closing scene of a recent Hollywood sequel: *Rambo* (2008).

The long road to closure

A companion piece of sorts to *Rocky Balboa* (2006) – in which Stallone revisited his other iconic role – *Rambo* comes twenty years after *Rambo III*. Like its two immediate predecessors (but notably not the original, *First Blood*), the latest film takes the form of a rescue mission behind enemy lines, with the Vietnam veteran once again coerced out of peaceful retirement (this time in a Thai fishing village) in order to ferry a group of missionaries upriver to wartorn Burma. When he later learns that the missionaries have been taken hostage by a vicious infantry unit, Rambo joins forces with a group of hardbitten mercenaries and sets out to bring them home. Despite his initial apathy, Rambo is particularly taken with the idealistic missionary Sarah (Julie Benz), and, although there is no time for a romantic interlude, the film makes it clear that her survival is his principal motivation for embarking on the rescue. After no less than 236 'kills', Rambo emerges triumphant. The enemy has been annihilated, the missionaries rescued.

The epilogue to this orgy of violence is in stark contrast with what has preceded it. We see (p. 108, overleaf) Rambo walking down a country road in the rural United States and, as he approaches the camera, we cut to a close-up of a rusty mailbox on the roadside marked 'R. Rambo'. The camera pans to reveal a dirt track leading away from the road, down to a farmhouse framed by trees and grazing horses. After a moment of contemplation, during which he looks back at the road down which he's just walked, Rambo's expression softens and we watch as he heads away from the camera and towards the farmhouse, at which point the credits begin to roll. The implication is clear: after more than twenty-five years of torment and bloody retribution, Rambo is returning home. In interview, Stallone described the scene as follows:

> He goes down and looks up the road and his journey was over. In other words it's like an odyssey, like, for lack of a better term, Ulysses who went through all these different trials and tribulations and in the end everybody sort of thinks, 'Can I ever go back and have one more chance at trying to relive my life even though there's not much of it left?' So to me it's a kind of happy ending.[12]

Rambo

First Blood

Even without this explanation, fans of *First Blood* may well perceive the resonance of the scene in relation to the opening moments of that original film (p. 109). In both sequences Rambo is dressed in jeans and army green jacket – civilian clothing with a nod to his military past – and in both he stops to take in a pastoral scene below him, before descending towards it and away from the camera in long shot. Music is key here, with the acoustic guitar signature from the opening moments of *First Blood* (also used in that film's closing song, 'The Long Road') coming in as Rambo decides to approach what we assume is his family home at the close of the new film. Viewed retrospectively, the initial moments from *First Blood* have the feel of a conclusion, but of course what Rambo learns when he reaches his destination – that his combat buddy Delmar has died as the result of Agent Orange contamination – sets him off on a different course, one which is clearly signalled as less welcoming in the subsequent shots: the weather is cold, the light grey, the road not made to accommodate him and the sign 'Welcome to Hope' under which he passes loaded with irony. *Rambo*, then, is Stallone's attempt to bring the character – in the words of Rambo's ex-commander, Colonel Trautman (Richard Crenna) – full circle, returning him to the country from which he has long been estranged.

Watching the epilogue initially, I was struck by two jarring thoughts. First, it seemed impossible to ignore how little the rest of the film prepares us for such a peaceful conclusion. There is no mention by Rambo or any other character of his desire to return home, nor any subsequent explanation of what motivates this return, or indeed how he achieves it. This is not the resolution to *Rambo* as an individual film, but rather to a larger narrative journey. If we can say that *Rambo* manages to convey the sense of an ending in these final moments, it is arguably because of our extratextual knowledge of the protagonist's twenty-five-year odyssey, acquired from viewing the earlier films.

My second, contrary, response was to wonder if Rambo was once again about to be pulled over by a local sheriff and told to leave town, thus recommencing the whole cycle of violence. Again, this owes a debt to extratextual knowledge, not only knowledge of the events from *First Blood* but also a broader understanding of the character to which each film in the series has contributed. The succession of sequels has, after all, underlined the repetitive nature of Rambo's behaviour, suggesting that, however much time passes, he is still and always will be scarred by his Vietnam War experiences. There is nothing in this latest instalment to suggest this has changed. As if confirming my suspicions, in his DVD commentary to *Rambo*, Stallone concludes by saying, 'Now he's come full circle. John Rambo goes home. The question is: will he stay there?'

These are conflicting responses: the former demonstrating how extratextual knowledge can enrich the sense of closure, the latter indicating how that same knowledge can undermine it. At the crux of this issue, I would suggest, are two relationships which the sequel, with its invocation of extratextual knowledge, has the ability to render disjunctive: the relationship between closure and resolution, and that between *syuzhet* and *fabula*.

Closure or resolution?

The Classical Hollywood Cinema does not explicitly distinguish between 'closure' and 'resolution', in fact deploying these terms in a manner which suggests a certain interchangeability. Thus we are told, variously, that characters 'constantly look forward to closure';[13] that in 'the classical

cinema, the narration's emphasis upon the future gears our expectations toward the resolution of suspense';[14] that 'classical narration's insistence upon closure rewards the search for
meaning';[15] that the 'classical ending, both as resolution and epilogue, tends to usher in the narration as self-conscious and omniscient presence';[16] and that The China Syndrome's (1979) 'eva-
sive double plot also yields classical closure'.[17] The same conflation occurs in Storytelling in the
New Hollywood, in which we are told that 'Virtually all Hollywood films achieve closure in all
plotlines and subplots',[18] and that, during the 'climax portion' of a film, 'the action shifts into a
straightforward progress toward the final resolution'.[19]

   If a distinction between closure and resolution is perceptible in The Classical Hollywood
Cinema it is in its description of the epilogue. Bordwell identifies the epilogue as a standard part
of the classical film, 'a part of the final scene, or even a complete final scene, that shows the
return of a stable narrative state'.[20] Insofar as it represents the return to stability, the epilogue
is 'the last effect' in the causal chain and contributes to the sense of 'classical unity' by creating
'an explicit balancing effect'.[21] In this sense, the purpose of the epilogue is to underline the
result of the preceding scene or moments and fulfils Bordwell's definition of the classical film's
ending, which 'need not be 'happy'; it need only be a definite conclusion to the chain of cause
and effect'.[22] The classical epilogue is not, therefore, necessarily the site of resolution per se:
although it may in some films serve to resolve one or more causal lines, it may alternatively reit-
erate the results of an earlier resolution. Bordwell elucidates his position in Narration in the
Fiction Film, stating that the epilogue is 'a brief celebration of the stable state achieved by the
main characters'. He proceeds to acknowledge that the classical ending may well leave some
minor issues unresolved and that on this basis it may be preferable to put aside the term 'closure' and instead 'speak of a "closure effect," or even, if the strain of unresolved issues seems
strong, of "pseudoclosure"'. Despite these equivocations, Bordwell maintains that, in terms of
classical norms, 'the most coherent possible epilogue remains the standard to be aimed at'.[23]
Here the relationship between resolution and closure in the classical paradigm comes more
fully into view: closure, or the closure effect, is the result of resolution. Thus we might usefully
untangle 'closure' from 'resolution', allowing us to better understand how these two closely
related elements of narrative interact. But there is more at issue here than semantics.
Inadvertently perhaps, Thompson's aforementioned comments highlight the potential useful-
ness of distinguishing clearly between narrative resolution at the micro level and a broader
sense of closure at the macro level.

   Rambo provides a clear illustration of how this distinction might aid our understanding of
the divergences between the sequel form and the classical model. In the classical film, closure
and resolution are tightly linked, the former specifically the result of the latter. In Rambo, on the
other hand, the epilogue serves not as the last effect in the causal chain of this individual film,
but rather aims to create balance and bring a sense of closure to the entire series. The conflicts
and issues introduced in Rambo itself – specifically the kidnapping of the missionaries – have
been resolved in the preceding scenes, as neatly as in any classical, 'standalone' film. The epilogue, conversely, furnishes answers to broader questions about Rambo's future and past which
were posed not in this film, but in earlier instalments. Rambo can be understood and enjoyed
without prior viewing of its predecessors – a characteristic of most Hollywood sequels, to
which I shall return – but it is also clear that the full resonance of its epilogue can only be taken

in with that prior narrative knowledge. That, as followers of the Rambo series, we may not be convinced by this display of closure, is merely an alternative result of that same knowledge base.

We might therefore conclude that Thompson is right to set the sequel in opposition to closure, but not necessarily because of qualities internal to the text itself. As *Rambo* suggests, while resolution can be interior to an individual film, closure in the sequel sometimes involves looking beyond the narrative at hand. The sequel form is thus particularly troubling to notions of classical unity, because the extratextual audience knowledge on which it draws can impact directly on the notions of narrative comprehension with which Bordwell and Thompson concern themselves. I introduce the problem of audience knowledge here as a dangling cause, the effect of which can be seen in the gaps between syuzhet and fabula which the sequel creates.

The burgeoning fabula

To borrow Bordwell's terminology (itself borrowed from the Russian Formalists), I wish to propose that one of the defining formal characteristics of a sequel is its complication of the assumed relationship between a film's syuzhet and its fabula. Bordwell's theory of classical narrative and narration rests heavily on these two terms, the definition of which he introduced in *The Classical Hollywood Cinema* and subsequently elaborated in *Narration in the Fiction Film*. The former publication defines fabula as 'story', 'the events of the narrative in their presumed spatial, temporal and causal relations', and syuzhet as 'plot', 'the totality of formal and stylistic materials in the film'.[24] Once again, Bordwell refines his definition in *Narration*, stating that 'The *syuzhet* … is the actual arrangement and presentation of the fabula in the film. It is not the text in toto' and thus extricates 'style' from the syuzhet.[25] While the latter is 'independent of the medium', with the same patterns potentially appearing in a novel or play, the former 'names the film's systematic use of cinematic devices', and is 'thus wholly ingredient to the medium'.[26] Style and syuzhet can interact in various ways, but both fall under the umbrella term 'narration', which Bordwell defines as 'the process whereby the film's syuzhet and style interact in the course of cueing and channelling the spectator's construction of the fabula'.[27] Thus while discussion of syuzhet and style inevitably leads us toward the activity and choices of the filmmakers, the fabula immediately brings us to the role of the audience. According to Bordwell, it is 'a pattern which perceivers of narratives create through assumptions and inferences. It is the developing result of picking up narrative cues, applying schemata, framing and testing hypotheses.'[28] Furthermore, the fabula 'is not a whimsical or arbitrary construct', and, like the process of applying schemata which produces it, is 'intersubjective', with viewers agreeing 'about either what the story is or what factors obscure or render ambiguous the adequate construction of the story'.[29] This core conceptualisation of the fabula in relation to the viewers and their cognitive activity has been the source of much consternation in film studies, with some scholars caricaturing Bordwell's model viewer as little more than an 'information processor'.[30] These critics incorrectly assume that in describing the act of fabula construction Bordwell is implying that this is the totality of viewer activity,[31] but the fabula's purported intersubjective status deserves further interrogation in relation to *Rambo* because it brings us to the issue of extratextual knowledge.

Bordwell and Thompson do acknowledge the role of extra- and intertextual information in *The Classical Hollywood Cinema*, but primarily in the form of what they label 'generic motivation', the most common type of 'intertextual motivation', which is itself one of four means by which a Hollywood narrative 'justifies its story material and the plot's presentation of that story material'.[32] Quoting generic motifs such as the musical's song-and-dance numbers, Bordwell suggests that 'such operations do not radically disunify the films, since each genre creates its own rules, and the spectator judges any given element in the light of its appropriateness to generic conventions'.[33] Generic motivation, then, is the catch-all for any event within a Hollywood film which appears to fall outside or be in excess of the carefully integrated chain of cause and effect which *The Classical Hollywood Cinema* posits as central to classical narrative. As with the issue of closure, Bordwell expands on these principles in *Narration in the Fiction Film*, replacing generic motivation with the more inclusive 'transtextual motivation'. This new term captures not only genre conventions, but also those conventions associated with star persona and authorial tendencies.[34] Vital as it may be to an account of narrative construction and comprehension, the concept of transtextual motivation raises many questions which Bordwell, Staiger and Thompson leave unanswered.[35] How well versed in every set of generic conventions was/is each and every spectator? And how many musicals, Westerns, Dietrich or Hitchcock films must one see before acquiring the necessary knowledge of their respective conventions? Geoff King has suggested, in defence of the endurance of classical narrative conventions in the sequel, that although a 'long-running series can develop a shorthand of its own, based on assumptions of familiarity', this 'does not constitute an "evacuation" of narrative, however, and is probably not qualitatively different from the intertextual operations of stardom, genre or auteurism'.[36] Although I join King in contesting any claim for narrative 'evacuation', the example of *Rambo* indicates that there is a clear distinction to be made between the intertextuality at play in a genre film and that at play in a sequel. In Bordwell's model, when the viewer 'motivates transtextually' they are referring to generic schemata about the *kinds* of activity in which Dietrich might engage and the *types* of event which might occur in a Hitchcock film. This is crucially different to the transtextual competence encouraged by a sequel, which may well utilise generic conventions, but which could also refer to specific narrative events in prior films. I shall return to debates around intertextuality, and to the interactions between genre and the sequel, in Chapters 6 and 7, but in the meantime it is clear that neither Bordwell's concept of transtextual motivation, nor King's comments on intertextuality, fully account for the more complex interaction between syuzhet and fabula I am attempting to describe here.

In the case of *Rambo*, the syuzhet must encourage the construction of a discrete microfabula that is nonetheless consonant with the macro-fabula established by its predecessors: it is this which I would posit as one of the recurrent formal characteristics of the sequel. The apparent disjunction between *Rambo*'s epilogue and the eighty minutes preceding it is arguably caused by the direct and explicit connection it establishes with the macro-fabula of the Rambo series, a connection which, aside from a brief, impressionistic flashback sequence, is absent from the rest of the film. Granted, the viewer can always make incorrect or outlandish inferences about the fabula from the syuzhet,[37] but I would argue that, aside from moments of intentional ambiguity, the basic act of fabula construction is more commonly intersubjective than it is either arbitrary or whimsical. The events presented in *Rambo*'s epilogue will still be comprehensible to those viewers who have never seen the earlier instalments, and remain intersubjective at a basic level, but the fabula those viewers construct as a result will be more limited and the moment may well resonate less than it does with those more familiar with the character and his prior history.

Not all sequels so overtly reveal the gap between the limited fabula of an individual film and the larger, ongoing fabula to which it contributes. Nonetheless, having identified this distinction, we might begin to understand the choices available to sequel producers and how these choices may have been governed by historically specific commercial and industrial concerns. Knowing the production history of *Rambo* and its predecessors, which began with the surprise success of *First Blood*, we might observe that the construction of its macro-fabula has resultantly been rather ad hoc, with no evidence of advance planning. No-one knew when the box-office success story would come to an end, which explains why *Rambo III* resolves only those causal lines it has itself established and does nothing to address its protagonist's ongoing issues. There is, after all, a direct commercial parallel to the issue of syuzhet and macro-fabula: the multi-platform structure of the entertainment industry is now such that the economic story is much larger than the success of any individual entry in a series. *Rambo* achieved moderate returns in cinemas (grossing £3.1 million in the UK and $45 million in the US), but these fell far from the heights scaled by earlier entries in the series. And yet the theatrical release gave a new lease of life to sales of its predecessors on DVD, thus underscoring the sequel form's ability to create an ongoing commercial narrative, with no apparent resolution in sight.[38]

There are, inevitably, gradations of these dynamics between syuzhet and fabula, and between closure and resolution, gradations explored in the following sections, as I attempt to delineate a broader typology of the sequel's narrative characteristics.

Endings as beginnings

In the preceding analysis of *Rambo*, and in proposing a distinction between micro- and macro-fabula, I have in effect assumed a division between those viewers who have seen the preceding films in the series and those who have not. But of course there are many intermediary distinctions: between those viewers who are conversant with other Sylvester Stallone movies and those who are not; and between those viewers who have recently rewatched *Rambo*'s predecessors and those who have not seen *Rambo III* since its initial release in 1988, for example. One of the problematic aspects of the fabula as a concept is that there are unquestionably limits to the intersubjectivity Bordwell suggests is one of its central characteristics, precisely because of the role memory plays both in its initial construction and subsequent maintenance. The fabula I construct in the course of watching any given film is likely to be relatively detailed and include nuances and specificities which will be gradually forgotten the more distant in time the viewing experience becomes. Six months or a year on, I will struggle to provide anything but the basic story information if asked to recall it. It is worth noting, too, that the Russian Formalists have been criticised for marginalising the fabula, and valuing it only insofar as it reveals the workings of the syuzhet,[39] indicating the extent to which these were terms devised

to better describe the strategies and working practices of prose writers, rather than to illuminate the deductive work of their readers. None of this, I would contend, undermines my
proposition that, whatever multifarious racial, sexual and socioeconomic differences there are
between sequel viewers, one can still assume a more basic distinction between those with
access to the macro-fabula and those whose knowledge is limited to the micro-fabula of this
individual film. Furthermore, I would propose that this same assumption informs the narrative
construction of most Hollywood sequels, and that, as a result, a recurrent characteristic of the
form is its attempt to address knowledgeable viewers without alienating the uninitiated. As the
example of *Rambo*'s epilogue suggests, while references to prior filmic events are common, they
are rarely employed such that they fundamentally derail the discrete narrative comprehensibility of the film at hand. The implications of this are numerous and, in order to investigate them
further, I will outline some common narrative tendencies of the Hollywood sequel, framed in
terms of the choices confronting the film-makers (by which I mean the screenwriter, director,
producers, actors, financial backers and so on) involved. If we conceive of narrative continuation in terms of problems and solutions, we can more easily navigate through the voluminous
and generically diverse range of sequels produced by Hollywood over the past century.

Beginning again

While issues of closure and resolution have dominated thus far, I will now turn from endings
to beginnings. Where to start, then? We can, broadly speaking, identify two recurrent solutions
to this problem: recommence immediately after the final moments depicted in the previous
film, as in *Bride of Frankenstein, After The Thin Man, Beneath the Planet of the Apes, Halloween II,
Quantum of Solace* (2008) and *Crank 2* (2008); or, as with *The Son of the Sheik, Father's Little
Dividend, Terminator 2: Judgment Day* and *Toy Story 2* (1999) insert a gap of weeks, months, years
or even decades. As the examples indicate, both strategies have coexisted throughout
Hollywood history. That the latter is seemingly more prevalent is probably in part a pragmatic
response to the passage of real time between films (how else to explain the ageing of certain
actors, the changing of fashions and so on?) but it also presents a challenge to narrative construction: how and to what extent to inform the audience of events that may have taken place
in the interval between the end of one film and the beginning of another? Most Hollywood
sequels avoid an elliptical approach, opting instead to fill in those gaps required to make explicable the events that follow, but the speed at which this information is meted out, and the time
and effort devoted to such exposition, differ considerably from film to film.

Thus within the first two minutes of *Die Hard 2*, via a conversation between John McClane
(Bruce Willis) and a traffic cop, we are given to understand that, following their reconciliation
at the end of *Die Hard*, John moved to Los Angeles to live with his wife Holly (Bonnie Bedelia);
that they still live together there; and that he is still in the police force. In other words, the equilibrium established by *Die Hard*'s resolution has been maintained until this point. *Ghostbusters II*
(1989) devotes more time to this process, opening with a title card reading '5 YEARS LATER'
and dedicating much of its first ten minutes to the reintroduction of both the Ghostbusters
and Dana Barrett (Sigourney Weaver), whose haunted apartment became the locus of the
action in the first film. A succession of brief scenes show that Ray and Winston (Dan Aykroyd

and Ernie Hudson) are now using their famous uniforms to entertain at children's parties; that Egon (Harold Ramis) has returned to other forms of scientific research; and that Venkman (Bill Murray) is host to all manner of ersatz paranormal devotees on a TV show entitled *World of the Psychic*. Unlike *Die Hard 2*, then, this sequel undermines the state of equilibrium established by the resolution of its predecessor. The Ghostbusters are no longer working as a team and whatever respect and fame they may have earned has now dissipated, the latter fact underlined by the attitude of the children Ray and Winston attempt to entertain in their opening scene: 'Who you gonna call?', they shout; 'He-Man!' the children retort.

In both cases, however, the exposition required to bridge the gap between the first and second films is integrated with the introduction of new information central to the progression of the sequel. *Ghostbusters II* follows its '5 YEARS LATER' title card with a shot of luminescent pink slime oozing through the crack in a paving stone, followed by the wheel of a cart rolling through it. The cart, the following shots reveal, is in fact a baby carriage being pushed by Dana. Seemingly possessed by the slime, it takes on a life of its own, rolling away at speed into traffic. Dana rescues her baby from the runaway carriage but this disturbing event prompts her to visit Egon, in the hope of a logical explanation, and, as they talk, it is established that she and Venkman (seemingly a romantic item at the end of *Ghostbusters*) have not spoken for some time, and that she is now married to someone else. This latter scene, which immediately follows the reintroduction of Ray and Winston and immediately precedes the scene reintroducing Venkman, serves both to further the trajectory of the new story and also to provide expository information about those five intervening years.

Not every sequel adopts such a linear or integrated approach to exposition. *Father's Little Dividend* begins with Spencer Tracy's Stanley Banks taking a carnation for his buttonhole from a vase, calling up to his wife and then, in an echo of *Father of the Bride*, sitting down in his armchair to address the camera. 'I'd like to say a few words about what's happened to me over the past year', he begins, and thereafter the film unfolds in flashback, beginning when Stanley learns that his recently married daughter Kay (Elizabeth Taylor) is now pregnant. The imminent birth is the new disruptive element, introduced to destabilise the equilibrium established at the end of the first film and reaffirmed in the opening voiceover, when Banks remarks: 'I was thinking what a lucky man I was, with a nice house all paid for, three children all paid for, and a beautiful wife.'

Motivating the action

Here, then, is another transhistorical tendency of the Hollywood sequel: its frequent use of a new agent or event to motivate its story. This disruptive force is often generically similar to that in the previous film (another group of terrorists, another killer shark, another crazed scientist), and tends to take one of six forms:

1 the arrival of a new character, such as a baby;
2 the departure (or death) of an existing character;
3 the relocation of existing characters to another setting and/or set of circumstances;
4 the emergence of a new case/mission/quest to be solved or undertaken;

5 the return of an old nemesis or problem; or
6 in a variation of the latter form, a repeat encounter between characters who were dramatically at odds in the previous film.

Clearly, some level of film-to-film causality might be at work in some of the above cases. The
antagonism between a protagonist and their nemesis may well stem directly from events in an
earlier film, as in the relationship between Kevin McCallister (Macaulay Culkin) and the burglars
Harry (Joe Pesci) and Marv (Daniel Stern) in *Home Alone 2: Lost in New York*, or that between
Demetrius (Victor Mature) and Caligula (Jay Robinson) in *Demetrius and the Gladiators*, sequel
to *The Robe*. By and large, however, these six, action-motivating disruptions only occasionally
have a causal connection with earlier events.

There is often, of course, more than one source of disruption at work in any given sequel.
The equilibrium established at the conclusion of *Boys Town* (1938), both by the successful assim-
ilation of troubled Whitey Marsh (Mickey Rooney) into the boys' reformatory school run by
Father Flanagan (Spencer Tracy), and the erasure of the school's financial debts, is duly unset-
tled on both fronts in the opening minutes of *Men of Boys Town* (1941). In the opening scene
it is established that Boys Town has once again run out of funds and that Flanagan must once
again use his wits to save it from closure. Shortly thereafter, a troubled youth named Ted
Martley (Larry Nunn) is sent to the school and begins to challenge its organisation just as
Whitey had done in the first film. Lastly, Whitey, who is now the 'mayor' of Boys Town, is
adopted by a rich couple, the Maitlands, and so is reluctantly forced to leave Flanagan and his
friends. The film therefore combines the return of an old problem (lack of funds) with the
arrival of a new character (Ted) and the departure of an existing character (Whitey), creating
a series of narrative dilemmas which are resolved by its conclusion.

Such an approach is evident even in those sequels which pick up immediately after their
predecessors. Although *Bride of Frankenstein* begins with the revelation (delivered in a prologue
by Mary Shelley, played by Elsa Lanchester) that the Monster has survived the fire which concluded the first film, and although some of the sequel's initial action is driven by his subsequent
rampage through the village, it is the arrival of Dr Frankenstein's deranged old tutor, Dr
Pretorius (Ernest Thesiger), that drives the narrative forward. It is Pretorius who initiates the
creation of the Bride, Pretorius who welcomes the Monster back into Frankenstein's life and
Pretorius's intervention that ultimately leads to the Monster's destruction.

Even in the horror genre, where one of the key (if not only) returning characters tends to
be the antagonist, the aforementioned sources of disruption are still utilised to motivate new
events. In *A Nightmare on Elm Street 2: Freddy's Revenge*, for example, a new set of characters
moves into the house previously inhabited by Nancy Thompson (Heather Langenkamp) in the
first film, initiating the return of Freddy Krueger. Then, in *A Nightmare on Elm Street 3: Dream
Warriors* we return to Nancy, now a psychiatrist specialising in sleep therapy, who is forced to
confront Freddy once again as he menaces her patients. The repeat encounter between a monstrous character or force and a survivor figure is a trope of not only *Elm Street* but also the
Alien and *Halloween* series and *Hannibal* (2001), sequel to *Silence of the Lambs* (1991), and will
almost invariably also involve relocating these characters to a new setting under different circumstances. Bereft of a central pair of antagonists, the sequels to *Friday the 13th* have – with

the exception of *Friday the 13th: A New Beginning* (1985), which focuses instead on the actions of a copycat killer – instead had to rely primarily on the arrival of new characters (read: victims) and/or the relocation of their one recurrent character, Jason Voorhees, to increasingly incongruous settings (a cruise ship in 1989's *Friday the 13th Part VIII: Jason Takes Manhattan* and a science-fiction future in 2002's *Jason X*). The absence of a new form of disruption in *Halloween II* provides noteworthy contrast here. It begins by replaying *Halloween*'s closing moments, in which it is revealed that the psychotic Michael Myers (Tony Moran in the first film) is still alive, and then seamlessly continues the action without an ellipsis. Laurie Strode (Jamie Lee Curtis), having fought off Myers (now played by Dick Warlock) in *Halloween*, is taken to hospital to recover while Dr Sam Loomis (Donald Pleasance) continues to search for the missing psychopath. Myers continues to stalk Laurie, who continues to evade him. Only when it is revealed that Myers is in fact Laurie's biological older brother does a new disruptive element come into play, but, coming as it does more than forty-five minutes into the film, this serves primarily to retrospectively explain prior events rather than to drive forward a narrative that is already in progress. Most of the action of *Halloween II*, therefore, results directly from the events of its predecessor: a quality that makes it the exception which proves the rule.

Thus we can begin to see how the micro-fabula of a sequel might be partially discrete from the pre-existing macro-fabula which it ultimately extends. I stress this primarily to indicate the limited extent to which a Hollywood sequel need rely on continuation proper, rather than to deny that it does so at all. Far from it: the extent and nature of that continuation is precisely what sets one sequel apart from another.

Film-to-film causality

As indicated by the manner in which they choose to initiate and motivate a new series of events, here is another central quandary facing the makers of a sequel: to what extent should story events be causally linked to those of the preceding film(s)? To what extent, in other words, should narrative past inform narrative present? Most sequels can be placed somewhere in the middle of a spectrum of causation ranging from those close-knit to their predecessors to those only loosely connected. The close-knit contingent is exemplified by films such as the *The Lord of the Rings* trilogy, *The Godfather: Part II* and *Return of the Jedi* (1983). Although there is an ellipsis between the latter film and the concluding scene of its predecessor, *The Empire Strikes Back* (1980), most of its key story developments are the direct effect of prior events. The film opens with the attempts of Luke Skywalker (Mark Hamill), Princess Leia (Carrie Fisher) and Chewbacca (Peter Mayhew) to rescue Han Solo (Harrison Ford) from the clutches of the monstrous Jabba the Hut, to whom he was sold at the end of *Empire* by the bounty hunter Bobba Fett (Jeremy Bulloch). Much of *Jedi*'s action thereafter is driven by the need to resolve those elements left open by its predecessor, specifically the revelation that the Empire's evil leader Darth Vader (David Prowse/James Earl Jones) is Luke's father and the culmination of the romantic subplot involving a love triangle between Luke, Leia and Han which has been gradually elaborated over the previous two films. New developments are either largely incidental (ergo the introduction of the Ewoks, a tribe of furry creatures who assist in defeating the Empire) or instead aid to resolve pre-existing conflicts: the revelation that Leia is Luke's sister emphatically removes him from the love triangle, while the Empire's construction of a new Death Star instigates the final confrontation between the forces of good and evil, including that between Luke and his father. By and large, then, *Return of the Jedi* is – in narrative as well as commercial terms – the effect of which *The Empire Strikes Back* is the cause.

Passing over the conceptual series films (such as the Gold Diggers and Road movies) discussed in Chapter 2, at the opposite end of this spectrum lie sequels which are connected to their predecessors by the barest thread, with little if any causal links. That thread tends to be a returning character who, while present, is of only nominal importance to narrative progression. *Grease 2* (1982) is, as with *Grease* (1978), set at Rydell High School and sees the return of ditzy student Frenchy (Didi Conn) and Principal McGee (Eve Arden) in supporting roles, but the film is centred instead on a new pair of star-crossed lovers, the clean-cut 'square' Michael (Maxwell Caulfield) and the hip, sassy Stephanie (Michelle Pfeiffer), whose relationship echoes (albeit with the gender roles reversed) that of cocky biker Danny (John Travolta) and sweet, virginal Sandy (Olivia Newton-John) from the first film. A similarly tokenistic use of returning supporting characters can be found in the *Airport* (1970–9) films, whose sole linking cast member is George Kennedy, and *Mannequin 2: On the Move* (1991), which reintroduces fashion window dresser Hollywood (Meshach Taylor) as comic support to a new romance between another man and another department store mannequin.

As per my discussion of Universal's horror films from the studio era in Chapter 2, the causal distance between a sequel and its predecessor often finds its symbolic reflection in the genealogical distance between its characters. Thus *The Son of the Sheik* follows directly in his father's footsteps, and is influenced by the patriarch's advice and actions, whereas, in *Teen Wolf Too* (1987), Jason Bateman plays Todd Howard, merely a cousin to *Teen Wolf*'s Scott Howard (Michael J. Fox), who has no role in the sequel and whose advice might have prevented Todd from repeating all of his lycanthropic mistakes in what is effectively a re-enactment of the first film.

With all of the survivors from the first film now dead, *Final Destination 3* stretches the inclusion of earlier characters to its limit point. Here a new, unconnected group of characters survive a new freak accident (a derailed rollercoaster at a fairground) because one of their number (Wendy, played by Mary Elizabeth Winstead) foresees the disaster and coaxes them away from the rollercoaster before it's too late, thus saving their lives. Having 'cheated death' in the opening scene, the survivors are once again targeted by death itself, which, according to the logic of the series, is determined to complete its 'plan' and dispatch them. Wendy becomes aware of this immediately prior to death's first strike, when fellow survivor Kevin (Ryan Merriman) presents her with his internet research on the survivors of *Final Destination*'s (2000) plane crash and their subsequent fates. The original characters therefore serve an expository purpose, expediting the process by which the new characters come to understand the nature of the threat they face, without presenting any causal connection between the two stories.

Many, perhaps most, sequels sit somewhere between these two extremes. In *Jaws 2* (1978), for example, the beach town of Amity is once again menaced by a Great White Shark, with Chief Brody (Roy Scheider) and his family once again at risk. Although the recurring characters' actions are certainly informed by their prior fictional history – Brody's belief that another Great White lurks nearby is dismissed by the mayor as the result of trauma experienced when defeating the original monster – the arrival of the new shark is not causally motivated by events from the first film (such a logic-defying explanation is reserved for *Jaws IV: The Revenge* [1987]) but is instead an unlucky 'coincidence'.

Similarly, *Beneath the Planet of the Apes* opens with a shot of the ocean, overlaid with a reading from the apes' Bible by their chief scientist Dr Zaius (Maurice Evans). It then segues into the penultimate scene from *Planet of the Apes* in which Zaius read the same passage to Taylor (Charlton Heston), the human interloper whose crash landing on the planet and subsequent capture by the apes was at the centre of that preceding film. This entire penultimate scene is replayed, followed by a truncated version of the final scene, in which Taylor sets off on horseback with mute slave-woman Nova (Linda Harrison) to explore the 'forbidden zone' and is confronted with the sight of the Statue of Liberty decaying on the shoreline, and the realisation that this nightmarish world is in fact Earth, many years in the future. Subsequently, a series of long shots follows Taylor and Nova as they journey further into the forbidden zone before the film cuts to a pair of newly arrived astronauts who have come in search of Taylor, only one of whom has survived their crash. Most of what follows concerns Brent (James Franciscus), the surviving explorer, in his quest to find Taylor, during which he encounters Nova, alone on Taylor's horse; is captured by the apes; escapes into the forbidden zone and subsequently discovers the remains of the New York subway system, which lead him to an enclave of highly evolved human survivors who communicate telepathically and worship a golden nuclear warhead. They are also, it transpires, holding Taylor captive, as Brent discovers when he too is jailed. Meanwhile, the newly emboldened apes, led by a belligerent faction of gorillas, have decided to venture into the forbidden zone, an act which ultimately provokes the human cult members to deploy their nuclear god. As this brief description indicates, the search for Taylor, while initially responsible for initiating this chain of events, is neither the cause of this devastating final effect nor much of what precedes it.

A side point, here, is the extent to which causal links become more or less important in relation to the number of sequels in any given series. Is a third or fourth film more or less likely than a second film to be closely knit to its predecessor(s)? There are few governing norms here, other than those specific to the series/franchise in question. It is quite possible that, as with Universal horror movies, the *Planet of the Apes*, *Friday the 13th* and *Final Destination* series, causal links will be weaker in later sequels than in earlier instalments. But it is equally possible that causality will be strongly maintained or even intensify over the course of a series so that, for example, *Return of the Jedi* has stronger and more direct causal links with *The Empire Strikes Back* than *Empire Strikes Back* has with *Star Wars*. As these divergent examples suggest, levels of causality will to some extent be dictated by the play of expectations surrounding a given sequel, expectations which are often the result of how earlier instalments deal with questions of causation. The *Saw* franchise (2004–10), for example, quickly established tight narrative integration from film to film as one of its defining characteristics, whereas no such expectations surrounded the *Die Hard* (1988–2013) or *Lethal Weapon* (1987–98) films. This incremental creation of series-specific conventions, of genres in miniature, extends far beyond issues of narrative causation and I shall return to it in the following chapter.

While the films discussed here are representative of particular points on the spectrum of causality, it is also worth noting that most Hollywood sequels, true to the classical norms outlined by Bordwell, Staiger and Thompson,[40] will include more than one line of action, meaning that the same film might combine a close-knit causal storyline with another which is either entirely new or only loosely linked to its predecessor. It is this delicate balancing act, which sees many sequels drawing on strategies from the broader pool of cinematic seriality, to which I shall now turn.

The episodic and the serial

Interweaving both a continuing plot strand (Taylor's journey, albeit briefly) and a new line of action, *Beneath the Planet of the Apes* is fairly typical of the Hollywood sequel's tendency to seek the middle ground between the episodic discontinuities of the series film and the narrative flow of the serial. As described in Chapter 1, the series-film format and the serial were already established when the feature-film sequel first appeared and, whether or not sequel producers were influenced by these other approaches, they remain useful categories against which the sequel can be defined.

Emerging as it did in the heyday of the B-grade film series, *The Thin Man* and its sequels exemplify the means by which episodic and continuous elements are frequently combined. As discussed in Chapter 2, the first sequel, *After the Thin Man*, is less causally motivated by earlier events than originally envisioned by producer Hunt Stromberg, but the opening scenes retain a clear sense of chronology, beginning with Nick and Nora Charles on the train they boarded at the end of the previous film, as it pulls into San Francisco on New Year's Eve. Much incidental business (including the reunion of the Charles' dog Asta with his female mate) passes before they receive a call from Nora's imperious Aunt Katherine (Jessie Ralph), summoning them to dinner that same evening, and a new chain of events is set in motion. At dinner it transpires that Aunt Katherine wants Nick, whom she holds in very low regard, to investigate the disappearance of Robert (Alan Marshall), husband to Katherine's daughter (and Nora's cousin) Selma (Elissa Landi). Although it seems that Nick's now-famous success in tracking the 'thin man' has prompted Aunt Katherine to enlist his help, the two mysteries are otherwise entirely unconnected, and the remainder of the story is devoted to this new case and its complications. With the case solved and the loose ends tied, an epilogue presents Nick and Nora once again on a train, in search of peace and quiet elsewhere. The film closes when Nora holds aloft a pair of knitting needles, on which hang the beginnings of a pair of baby booties, thus revealing to Nick that she is pregnant and setting up a development which may play out in future instalments.

The following film, *Another Thin Man*, elides the period of Nora's pregnancy and begins with the baby, Nick Jr, already several months old – but this development in the life of the Charles family has little bearing on the principal storyline, which, as Thin Man convention now dictates, involves Nick being coerced into taking on another case (again by an upper-class associate of Nora), entirely unrelated to prior events. Nick Jr becomes relevant when he is the victim of an attempted kidnapping by one of the key suspects, but otherwise Nick and Nora's new status as parents has little bearing on the central line of action. The remaining films in the series continue this pattern, introducing a new case while also, incidentally, charting the gradual development of the Charles family, primarily via the growth of Nick Jr, and Nick Sr's uneasy occupation of his paternal role. Development of the latter issue culminates in *Song of the Thin Man*, the final film of the series, when Nick puts his son over his knee but struggles to dole out the punishment Nora feels is required for the boy's disobedience.

The path taken by *The Thin Man* and its sequels is indicative not only because of its balance between discrete episodes and continuation, but because of the nature of what is continued. One of the two or more lines of action in the classical Hollywood film 'almost invariably', according to Bordwell, Staiger and Thompson, 'involves heterosexual romantic love',[41] and it is worth noting the frequency with which the serial element of any series of sequels involves, if not romantic love, then certainly interpersonal relationships. *The Thin Man* does this in a relatively low-key and lighthearted fashion, never bringing the solidity of Nick and Nora's marriage into question, instead generating comic friction from their respective foibles, most frequently Nora's haphazard (but often productive) involvement in Nick's detective work. If their relationship develops over the series, it is primarily in regard to their burgeoning roles as parents.

There are several sequels in which the interpersonal relationship strand is a source of film-to-film drama. These might be developed in a serial fashion over several films, as with the love triangles between Luke, Han and Leia in *Star Wars*, Peter Parker, Mary Jane Watson and Harry Osborn in the *Spider-Man* films (2002–7) and Edward (Robert Pattinson), Jacob (Taylor Lautner) and Bella (Kristen Stewart) in *The Twilight Saga*. More often, however, they will be of a more episodic nature, a common thread between films which provides a sense of continuity without necessarily being subject to the narrative attenuations or cliffhangers of the preceding examples: the marriages between George Banks and his wife in both versions of *Father of the Bride* and their sequels, and between Jack (Harrison Ford) and Caroline Ryan (Anne Archer) in *Patriot Games* (1992) and *Clear and Present Danger* (1994); and the ongoing professional and/or platonic relationships between Doc (Christopher Lloyd) and Marty McFly (Michael J. Fox) in the *Back to the Future* trilogy (1985–90) and Riggs (Mel Gibson) and Murtaugh (Danny Glover) in the *Lethal Weapon* films. As with the Thin Man, the progression from marriage to parenthood, or the arrival of an additional child, is a common developmental trope. This may either provide a secondary line of action, as in *Tarzan Finds a Son!*, *Brother Rat and a Baby* (1940) and *Addams Family Values* (1993), or, as identified earlier, could be the primary motivation for the new episode, usually in those films specifically orientated around family life, such as *Four Mothers*, *Look Who's Talking Too* (1990) and *Beethoven's 2nd* (1993). The extent to which any of the continuing or developing interpersonal relationships described above will be interwoven with another line of action will vary considerably, and is another means by which we can distinguish between those sequels which display tight film-to-film causality and those which do not.

Here we have further evidence that the majority of sequels, even those conceived in tandem with their originary film, seek to deliver some form of closure that is discrete to their micro-fabula, which is why episodic narrative elements are as common a presence as continuing ones. Such a strategy is familiar to us now not only from film but from television, particularly sitcoms, where the developments of certain interpersonal relationships (Niles [David Hyde Pierce] and Daphne [Jane Leeves] in *Frasier* [1993–2004], Dawn [Lucy Davis] and Tim [Martin Freeman] in *The Office* [2001–3]) are traced across multiple instalments, in tandem with other, episode-specific events, an observation which recalls one of Kristin Thompson's other hypotheses in *Storytelling in Film and Television*, that the supposed 'loosening of the notion of closure' is 'due, in large part, to television'.[42] In reality, of course, sequels were balancing the episodic and the serial many years before television became a household staple. Thompson's assertion that there is a contemporary tendency towards sequels, among other serialised forms, and that this is 'part of a general stretching and redefinition of narrative itself' simply doesn't hold up to historical examination, but it is worth noting that the above examples of serialised relationships (*Star Wars*, *Spider-Man*, *Twilight*) all come from the past thirty years.[43] With these films in mind, I propose a more nuanced version of Thompson's hypothesis: it is not the existence of sequels that indicates a shift towards seriality, but rather that the sequels themselves have, in the past thirty years, become more serial in their construction. Contributing significantly to this shift far more directly than television, I would argue, is an industrial trend towards the production of films whose sequels are deemed inevitabilities even before their release.

The macro-syuzhet and the saga

This leads us to a crucial distinction between subsequently conceived and pre-planned sequels: in both cases a macro-fabula will be constructed from a series of micro-fabula, but in the former this occurs incrementally, via discrete syuzhets, whereas in the latter we might effectively see a macro approach to the syuzhet, one which retards and holds back information and events from one film in order to reveal or play them out in the next. The aforementioned triangle between Peter (Tobey Maguire), Mary Jane (Kirsten Dunst) and Harry (James Franco) in *Spider-Man* and its two sequels is relevant here, in that future dramatic tensions – namely the budding romance between Peter and MJ, and the building conflict between Peter and Harry – are established in the first film, coming to fruition only in *Spider-Man 2* and *Spider-Man 3*. For example, the central antagonist in the first film is the Green Goblin, the psychotic alter ego of Norman Osborn (Willem Dafoe), father of Harry. Following the death of the Goblin in the film's climactic battle, Spider-Man returns Norman's body to the Osborn residence, and is caught in the act by Harry. The film's epilogue takes place at Norman's funeral, with all of the protagonists in attendance. Here it is established that Harry blames Spider-Man for his father's death ('One day Spider-Man will pay', he vows, before adding, in a moment of dramatic irony, 'Thank God for you Peter, you're the only family I have'), laying the groundwork for a conflict between Peter and Harry which only comes fully to a head in *Spider-Man 3*, when Harry, determined to avenge Norman's death, follows in his father's footsteps to become the Goblin. The full extent of Harry's role in the macro-fabula is thus not officially revealed until the third film, with the syuzhets of its two predecessors working to lay the groundwork for this development. Even here, however, much of what occurs is episodically specific, meaning that, while developing these attenuated elements, each syuzhet also has to cue story information which is discrete to a particular film, some of which (specifically that relating to each film's antagonist) is part of the primary storyline for that instalment. For this reason it is problematic to suggest that here we have a macro-syuzhet fully at work, a fact underlined by the series' production history. The Spider-Man franchise was always conceived as consisting of more than one film, with Maguire contracted for two films at the outset, but each of the screenplays was written separately and each film went into production only after the release of its predecessor.[44]

More truly indicative of how a macro-syyzhet might work is the self-contained saga, a series of films whose number of episodes is finite and defined from the outset (or close to it), a characteristic which immediately moves it closer in nature to the cinematic serials of the silent and studio eras. This, it seems, is another relatively contemporary development, beginning with the first *Star Wars* trilogy and latterly exemplified by the *Star Wars* prequel trilogy (1999, 2002, 2005), the *Harry Potter* series (2001–11), *Twilight* and of course *The Lord of the Rings* trilogy, consisting of *The Fellowship of the Ring* (2001), *The Two Towers* (2002) and *The Return of the King* (2003). The production context of the latter remains unprecedented in that all three films were shot back to back, whereas most instalments of *Harry Potter*, *Twilight* and most recently *The Hunger Games* were produced individually and in sequence – although in each of these latter three cases, the final two instalments were shot back to back, a luxury of an established franchise, as opposed to one in its infancy. It is therefore worth exploring further not only how Peter Jackson's three films operate simultaneously as individual entities and as a whole, providing one of the few examples of the macro-syuzhet in action, but also the manner in which they achieve this balance by reshaping J. R. R. Tolkien's source novels.

While not denying that there are some notable differences between the fabula of Tolkien's original three-part work and that of the cinematic trilogy it became, not least the increased prominence given to the female characters Arwen (Liv Tyler) and Eowyn (Miranda Otto), my focus here is primarily on the numerous alterations made at syuzhet level. In adapting the novels to the screen, Jackson, Fran Walsh and Philippa Boyens significantly restructured the delivery of fabula information in a manner which suggests a greater adherence to classical principles than might be assumed. Most of these structural alterations take on one of two forms: moving certain key events from one instalment to another; and skipping back and forth between the multiple story strands with far more frequency than Tolkien.

The former strategy is exemplified by the distinction between the conclusion of *The Fellowship of the Ring* on the page and that of its cinematic adaptation, specifically in their respective placements of the death of Boromir (Sean Bean), one of the band of men, dwarves, elves and hobbits (collectively known as 'the Fellowship') sworn to assist the hobbit Frodo Baggins (Elijah Wood) in his quest to destroy the 'One Ring' before it falls into the hands of the evil Sauron (Sala Baker) and jeopardises the future of Middle Earth. Towards the end of both the novel and the film, Boromir finds himself corrupted by the influence of the Ring, attempting to take it forcibly from Frodo and thus betraying his commitment to the Fellowship. In the film, as in the book, Frodo escapes Boromir by slipping the Ring onto his finger, a move which makes him invisible to human eyes but, hereafter, book and film diverge.

Tolkien has Frodo deciding to leave the Fellowship behind and journey to Mordor alone, attempting to slip away unnoticed while Boromir returns to the rest of the company and alerts them to Frodo's disappearance. The Fellowship scatter in search of Frodo and Tolkien follows Sam (played by Sean Astin in the film), Frodo's loyal servant, who finds his master and insists on joining him on the quest. The novel ends here, with Frodo and Sam setting off on the next phase of their journey and no further mention of the other characters. In the opening pages of Tolkien's *The Two Towers* we find Aragorn still in search of Frodo but instead discovering the mortally wounded Boromir. Explaining that he was attempting to protect the hobbits from a band of orcs, Boromir confesses to Aragorn his attempt to take the Ring from Frodo, and then, before he can clarify which of the hobbits have been taken, dies.

The film-makers structure these events rather differently. Aragorn (Viggo Mortensen) comes looking for Frodo without prompting from Boromir and the two have a brief exchange in which Aragorn reiterates his allegiance to the quest and Frodo explains that he must go it alone from hereon in, a brief farewell which is interrupted by the arrival of the orcs. Rather than have Boromir report the attack of the orcs only after the fact, the film plays it out at length and involves the other members of the Fellowship (aside from Frodo and Sam) in the conflict. As reported (but not shown) in the second book, we see Boromir die nobly in defence of Merry and Pippin (Frodo and Sam's hobbit friends, played by Dominic Monaghan and Billy Boyd), while Aragorn, Gimli the dwarf (John Rhys-Davies) and Legolas the elf (Orlando Bloom) come to his aid, albeit too late. After the orcs carry off Merry and Pippin, the final exchange between Boromir and Aragorn echoes that of the second book but is extended, allowing Boromir to inadvertently confirm that Frodo was not among the hobbits kidnapped. Several lines of dialogue follow, establishing the bond which has developed between the two men ('I would have followed you my brother', Boromir says. 'My captain. My King') and emphasising Boromir's heroism and honour over his flaws.

The inclusion and extension of the battle scene, the comparatively large amount of time devoted to Boromir's death, alongside its inclusion in the first rather than the second instalment, all imbue the first film with a greater sense of an ending than the first book. Although the principal line of action, the quest to destroy the Ring, remains unresolved, Boromir's character arc is brought to completion with a sense of ceremony and in a fashion which serves to underscore both Aragorn's heroism and the newly bolstered strength of the Fellowship. The latter is emphasised in the film's penultimate scene, in which Legolas and Gimli are persuaded by Aragorn that, rather than following Frodo and Sam, they should keep faith in the Fellowship and set out to rescue Merry and Pippin. 'Then it has all been in vain', decries Gimli, 'the Fellowship has failed.' 'Not if we hold true to each other', counters Aragorn, ending a rousing monologue with 'Let's go hunt some orc!' This scene represents merely an amplification of an equivalent scene in the first chapter of the second book, but, again, its appearance at the end of the first film demonstrates the extent to which the film-makers sought to create an emotionally satisfying conclusion, a closure effect in its truest sense, despite the absence of narrative resolution.

Following these modifications, the film-makers take a more radical approach to *The Two Towers*, presenting a far more dynamic syuzhet than that of its source novel. With the principal protagonists now divided into three groups – Frodo and Sam on the road to Mordor, Merry and Pippin in the clutches of the orcs, and the Fellowship in pursuit – Tolkien takes a rigidly systematic approach in presenting story information. Following the death of Boromir in the first chapter, the first half of the novel, entitled 'Book Three', follows Aragorn, Gimli and Legolas on the one hand and Merry and Pippin on the other, with Chapters 3 and 4 devoted to the latter strand. The second half of the novel, 'Book Four', returns to Sam and Frodo, presenting events in their journey seemingly concurrent to those depicted in 'Book Three', including their meeting with and taming of Gollum (Andy Serkis), bearer of the Ring before it fell into the hands of Bilbo (Ian Holm), Frodo's mentor. The film, conversely, skips constantly between the three story strands so that each unfolds simultaneously, while also interweaving additional scenes of Saruman (Christopher Lee) – once Gandalf's old mentor, now an evil ally of Sauron – building his army for the attack on Helm's Deep, information which is reported secondhand but never presented directly in the novel.

It would be easy to categorise these simply as necessary changes, the 'natural' result of transferring prose fiction to a medium in which crosscutting was seen as a key aesthetic development, but this reordering of fabula information significantly changes the dramatic arc as a whole, giving greater prominence to certain events, in particular the battle of Helm's Deep. Tolkien's two-book structure means that this confrontation between the armies of Saruman and the people of the human kingdom of Rohan, appears around a third of the way into the novel, before we know anything of the progress of Frodo and Sam. As a result of the film's dynamic interweaving of fabula information, the battle of Helm's Deep appears far later (after two and a half hours of screen time) and – because Jackson intercuts scenes featuring Merry and Pippin and Frodo and Sam (all of whom are elsewhere) – is not concluded for more than thirty minutes. The battle, then, becomes the dramatic focal point of this instalment, a clash between good and evil which serves (albeit on a grander scale) a similar purpose to that of the orc battle and death of Boromir in the first film, once again creating a climactic sense of an ending in place of narrative resolution.

Thus while the macro-fabula is certainly never forgotten, and the macro-syuzhet is never at rest, an episodic quality still creeps in. Gandalf's (Ian McKellen) final lines effectively summarise this balancing act: 'The battle for Helm's Deep is over. The battle for Middle Earth is about to begin. All our hopes now lie with two little hobbits, somewhere in the wilderness.' The scene which follows, the last of the film, sees Frodo and Sam following Gollum on a new route to Mordor. As Sam and Frodo talk among themselves, we watch as Gollum slips out of sight and debates with himself over his course of action: should he help the 'hobbitses' or take the Ring for himself? Hidden behind a tree, Gollum's evil self wins out. Realising it will be too difficult to kill them both, he declares: 'We could let Her do it. Yes, She could do it. Yes, Precious, she could. And then we takes it – once they're dead!' The 'She' in question is Shelob, a giant, spiderlike predator that lurks on the route to Mordor and, in the novel, Tolkien follows Frodo and Sam beyond the point reached in the film, until they have confronted Shelob. Jackson, on the other hand, chooses to end here, establishing a dangling cause, the effect of which shall not be seen until the third film. One might argue that this cliffhanger underlines the serial nature of The Lord of the Rings films, but it is still a rather less emphatic cliffhanger than that of the novel, which sees Frodo injured by Shelob and carried off to Mordor by a group of orcs as Sam looks helplessly on. Rather, coupled with Gandalf's monologue, the scene serves a dual purpose, first, as per the epilogue of the classical paradigm, reaffirming what has been achieved but then, conversely, indicating that there is more to come. Unlike the epilogues of those sequels described by Kristin Thompson, however, the dangling cause is not discrete from what has preceded: Gollum's mention of 'She' does create a narrative enigma, but one that is evidently the effect of his continued desire to take the Ring and Frodo and Sam's continuing quest to destroy it.

Unlike the Spider-Man films, here we have plotting on a grand scale: a macro-syuzhet that must almost constantly attend to and remind the audience of the larger story, the macro-fabula. And, unlike most sequels, The Two Towers and The Return of the King make few concessions to those who have not seen their respective predecessors: basic narrative comprehension is not a given for the uninitiated. Nonetheless, as I hope to have demonstrated, even in the close-knit narrative continuum of *The Lord of the Rings*, the macro-syuzhet attends as much to the structuring of its individual parts as to the shape of the whole to which they contribute. This is not a surprise, as such, if we acknowledge the nature of the market in which Jackson's films would circulate and the probable conditions of consumption that market dictates, with each instalment having to succeed commercially on its own terms: an economic reality reflected in their attempts to create three individually satisfying moviegoing experiences as well as a coherent saga.

Transmedia and classicism

This analysis of *The Lord of the Rings* leads us to an alternative model for understanding cinematic storytelling proposed by Henry Jenkins. In his account of 'convergence culture', Jenkins has suggested that there are signs that 'transmedia storytelling' is set to become more prevalent in Hollywood.[45] Although it uses cutting-edge media productions as its template, Jenkins's concept of transmedia is wedded to some very traditional aesthetic principles, specifically that of Aristotelian unity. But whereas Aristotle underscored the unified wholeness of a single artwork, Jenkins reformulates this as a unity played out across multiple platforms.

Using *The Matrix Reloaded* (2003), *The Matrix Revolutions* (2003) and a host of other *Matrix*-related media products as a case study, Jenkins notes that *Reloaded*:

> opens without a recap and assumes we have almost complete mastery over its complex mythology and ever-expanding cast of secondary characters. It ends abruptly with a promise that all will make sense when we see the third instalment ... . To truly appreciate what we are watching, we have to do our homework.[46]

Complicating things further, the Wachowski brothers dispersed narrative information across the animated shorts which comprised the DTV release of *The Animatrix* (2003) and the videogame *Enter the Matrix*. Some of the narrative information contained within these other manifestations of the franchise is sufficiently integral that it renders certain aspects of *The Matrix Reloaded* (specifically, the trajectory of the character Niobe [Jada Pinkett Smith], whose adventures are fleshed out only in the videogame) opaque. Here, Jenkins argues, 'is entertainment for the age of media convergence, integrating multiple texts to create a narrative so large that it cannot be contained within a single medium'.[47] Transmedia storytelling, then, adheres to classical principles but disperses them across several artworks: this is a new classicism for a new media age.

More a manifesto for future productions than a description of the status quo, Jenkins readily admits that 'Relatively few, if any, franchises achieve the full aesthetic potential of transmedia storytelling – yet', and that, thus far, 'the most successful transmedia franchises have emerged when a single creator or creative unit maintains control.'[48] We can only speculate on whether or not Hollywood might indeed adopt this approach in the coming years, but, as yet, there have been few subsequent instances of the kind of narrative interdependency Jenkins finds in *The Matrix* sequels. *The Lord of the Rings* certainly asks more of its audience than most, with Jackson reportedly refusing studio requests to include any kind of recap at the opening of the second or third films.[49] Nonetheless, even if some references and lines of dialogue are more likely to resonate with fans of Tolkien's novels than with complete newcomers, the basics of narrative comprehension are internal to the films themselves and not reliant on other texts on other platforms.

At present it seems that the kind of transmedia integration Jenkins espouses, will be stymied by the continued need for each individual film to reach as large an audience as possible. There are potentially huge commercial benefits to the release of any new entry in a franchise – boosting DVD, Blu-ray and digital sales and rentals for previous entries, television sales to broadcasters and sales of related consumer products – and Jenkins has correctly identified a corporate drive to extend properties into as many platforms as possible, but each film still needs to succeed in its own right. Whether or not we see them as standalone artworks, these mega-budget sequels are standalone business ventures which need, to some degree, to be individually profitable; it is ultimately this which discourages the kind of multi-platform narrative contingency that Jenkins's transmedia ideal requires. The kind of all-or-nothing attitude he perceives in the Wachowskis is a far riskier investment than the more traditional approach – what if no-one wants to enter your story world, however carefully integrated it is? – particularly when narrative integration isn't a prerequisite for the successful exploitation of that property on other platforms.

Perhaps the most radical implication of Jenkins's theory, then, is its inversion of traditional Aristotelian values. In positioning intimate narrative connections *between* works as an ideal, Jenkins is effectively prioritising the serial over the episodic, suggesting that sequels should not aspire to be discrete, closed narrative units. Nonetheless, despite assertions to the contrary, old-fashioned classical storytelling has yet to fully cede its place to a new model. And what better proof of its persistence than its continued influence on the cinematic sequel, a form which has previously been mistaken for a sign of classical narrative's demise?

To suggest this, of course, is not to deny that certain films have a relationship with products generated for other media, or that audiences might relate to a franchise via more than one of these platforms. In framing this chapter primarily in terms of syuzhet–fabula relations and the classical model, my focus has to an extent replicated Bordwell and Thompson's focus on narrative construction and the basics of narrative comprehension, largely to the exclusion of other elements. Thus I have not previously acknowledged either the broader field of extra and intertextual expectation which a viewer may bring to a sequel, some of which has little to do with narrative *per se*, or those references to a sequel's forebears which serve no direct narrative purpose. I am talking here primarily about the potentially amorphous issues of intertextuality, stardom and generic convention, all addressed in the chapters which follow.

6 | The McClane Principle: Intertextuality, stardom and character in the sequel

While the previous chapter elaborated upon the *narrative* connections between a sequel and its predecessor(s), the following two chapters will shift the focus to the interaction between narrative and non-narrative pleasures. 'Non-narrative' is perhaps too circumscriptive for what I mean here are those elements which either do not grow organically from the narrative and/or do not directly drive it forward. Those elements may include jokes, explosions, special effects, musical numbers, displays of physique and physicality, all of those pleasures, in other words, which have been posited as existing in opposition to classical narrative ideals by critics of Bordwell, Staiger and Thompson.[1] *The Classical Hollywood Cinema* does not entirely ignore such pleasures, in fact, bracketing them under the aforementioned rubric of 'intertextual motivation', whereby a framework of expectation (often orientated around particular genres or stars) guides the viewer's comprehension and 'justifies' certain fabula events or the syuzhet's presentation of those events.[2] While they argue (and have continued to argue) that intertextual elements do not fundamentally 'disunify' a film's narrative, Bordwell and Thompson do maintain a separation between the two. The sequel, however, recasts this model of intertextuality in particular ways, precisely because of its narrative relationship to an earlier film. This relationship, I shall argue, adds a layer of specificity to its sphere of intertextual reference which affects its interactions with both genre and star persona.

Chapter 8 will look at the role of generic conventions and expectations in sequel construction, while this chapter will examine the dynamic between star persona, character and narrative construction. But first I wish to contextualise this dynamic by situating it within the broader field of debates around intertextuality in cinema. The star/character relationship is commonly understood to be driven or informed by intertextual knowledge and conventions taken from other movies, but how does that dynamic shift when those other movies are direct narrative antecedents? And how is it altered again when the character has a persona that is as commonly known, or better known, than the actor embodying the role? As we shall see, the sequel's frequent recourse to intertextual reference – star-driven, character-driven or otherwise – is not automatically antithetical to classical notions of narrative unity and coherence and, in this sense, it is merely the most visible instance of the manner in which the invocation of earlier narrative events might itself be a source of, or springboard for, pleasure.

Use your allusions: narrativised intertextuality

Until now, I have ignored the wealth of writing on intertextuality, cinematic or literary, precisely because that writing has itself largely ignored or omitted mention of the sequel form; Gérard

Genette's concept of the hypertext, elaborated, as it is, in direct relation to the sequel, is far more useful in this regard. Even within this bracket, however, Genette reserves a special place for the sequel, observing that, unlike other hypertextual forms such as pastiche, the sequel 'must constantly remain continuous with its *hypotext*, which it must merely bring to its prescribed or appropriate conclusion while observing the congruity of places, chronological sequence, character consistency etc'.[3] Genette's assumption that a sequel is 'merely' bringing its predecessor to a close is obviously problematic, but his comments on the need to maintain consistency in chronology, character and so on, underscore the problem the sequel poses to most theories of intertextuality, based as they are in poststructuralist thinking which has tended to stress both the openness of the text and the textuality of the world outside.

Even though it appeared long after Julia Kristeva's original formulation of intertextuality, Genette's concept of hypertextuality, which describes a specific, prescribed relationship between one text and another, tends to be ignored. This is extremely unfortunate because, as Robert Stam has suggested, the concept is 'extremely suggestive for film analysis'.[4] Instead, writing on intertextuality in cinema, for example, that by Mikhail Iampolski, Umberto Eco, Barbara Klinger and Tom Gunning[5] tends to focus on the manner in which intertextuality undermines or undoes the coherent wholeness of the film text by forcing the viewer to move outside that text in order to make sense of its reference points. Iampolski explicitly separates this process from that of narrative comprehension, suggesting that intertextuality 'is particularly active in moments of narrative rupture, where the linear logic of the story breaks down',[6] although he also acknowledges that:

> Where the reader expends the effort required to draw on other texts and other codes, the quote [i.e. the intertextual reference] acquires its motivation, thereby not only imbuing the text with additional meanings but also restoring the mimesis it had violated. Intertextuality can thus be seen to enrich meaning and to salvage the very linearity of narrative that it had compromised.[7]

Here Iampolski is both echoing Bordwell's notion of transtextual motivation, via which the viewer can comprehend those moments in a film which seem to be in excess of narrative logic, and indicating the extent to which intertextuality tends to be conceptualised in opposition to narrative coherence. For writers such as Jim Collins, Umberto Eco and Fredric Jameson, a heightened level of intertextuality is one of the defining characteristics of contemporary 'postmodern' cinema.[8] Even Noel Carroll, who pointedly avoids reference to either postmodernity or intertextuality in his essay on a trend in 1970s Hollywood cinema he describes as 'allusion',[9] situates this form of intertextual referencing outside the realm of basic comprehension, suggesting that allusion-orientated film-making involves 'a two-tiered system of communication which sends an action/drama/fantasy-packed message to one segment of the audience and an additional hermetic, camouflaged, and recondite one to another.'[10] In Carroll's account, then, you don't need to get the reference, but doing so will give you a fuller, more rewarding viewing experience.

Barbara Klinger proposes an alternative, or rather additional, layer of intertextuality, one based not on reference to other fiction films, or even to references contained within the film itself, but rather to what she terms the 'promotional network' created by Hollywood's marketing and publicity machine, a network encompassing everything from above-the-line elements such as the poster and trailer to below-the-line elements such as star interviews and behind-the-scenes footage. By singling out certain elements (special effects, stars etc.) for promotion in any given film, this 'intertextual network' commodifies those elements, prying 'open the insularity of the text,' and, according to Klinger, producing 'economies of viewing that *fragment* rather than assemble the text, truly "man-handling" and "interrupting" it'.[11]

In each of these cases, then, intertextuality appears to be somewhat at odds with the more 'basic' functions of narrative. But what if the intertextual references within a film specifically invoke the narrative of its direct predecessor? Such is a formal characteristic of the Hollywood sequel, a characteristic which goes some way to explaining its absence from most writing on intertextuality.

The sequel provides not just another instance of the same intertextual practice which is either, dependent on your stance, characteristic of all texts throughout history, or a more recent sign of the postmodern or postclassical turn: it presents us instead with a highly particularised, narrativised form of intertextual reference. Even Klinger's consumerist account is problematised by the sequel given that here the promotional network surrounding it (unlike that for first instalments, or at least those based on lesser-known material) may well include speculation on narrative developments alongside other commodified elements. How will Ripley (Sigourney Weaver) return in *Alien: Resurrection* when we witnessed her death at the end of *Alien³* (1992)? Or, to give an example of a sequel based on a popular pre-existing source, how will the producers maximise the presence of Robert Pattinson in *The Twilight Saga: New Moon* (2009) when his character, Edward Cullen, has only a minor role in the corresponding novel? This version of intertextuality, then, encourages the viewer to venture outside the individual film to better appreciate or understand certain moments, but within prescribed limits, limits which designate a sequel's predecessor(s) as the first stop on the search for transtextual motivation.

This is not to deny that a sequel might reference films other than its predecessor, particularly when, as with the *Austin Powers* (1997–) and *Naked Gun* (1988–94) series, the original film was itself a parody of either a specific film or genre. But even these films refer back specifically to their predecessors, as well as a broader pool of parodic targets – albeit often in ways which have little or no direct relevance to narrative progression. Many of the gags in *Airplane II: The Sequel* (1982) and *Austin Powers: The Spy Who Shagged Me* rely as much on our recollection of similar gags from *Airplane!* (1980) and *Austin Powers: International Man of Mystery* as they do on our recollection of, respectively, the disaster movies and the James Bond series which they purportedly satirise. In *The Spy Who Shagged Me*, for example, Dr Evil's henchman Mustafa (Will Ferrell) falls over a cliff during a struggle with Austin (Mike Myers), appears to be dead but then, moments later, announces his survival in some off-screen dialogue – 'Hello up there. I seem to have fallen down a cliff. I'm still alive but I'm very badly injured!' Here we are being referred back not to Bond but to a very similar situation, in the previous *Austin Powers* film in which Ferrell delivers similar lines. In part these repetitions are governed by a set of generic expectations discussed further in Chapter 7, but such in-jokes and knowing winks are commonplace even in those Hollywood sequels for which comedy is a secondary concern.

Although the reiteration of a joke or humorous situation can be an end in itself, such references may simultaneously fulfil another, seemingly classical function. In *Die Hard 2*, when John McClane finds himself once again exploring the hidden spaces of a modern building (in this case Washington DC's Dulles airport) in pursuit of terrorists, his response, spoken aloud to no-one in particular, is: 'Man, I can't fucking believe this: another basement, another elevator. How can the same shit happen to the same guy twice?' On the one hand, this comment has no direct narrative purpose, it neither aids nor restricts our construction of the Die Hard 2 fabula and we might therefore dismiss it as an amusing diversion. On the other, in referring the viewer back to the events of Die Hard, it augments our understanding of McClane as a consistent character: a man who will foolhardily enter into a similar and similarly dangerous situation despite prior experience; a man whose mode of speech, as in the first film, is straightforward and foul-mouthed; and a man who, as in the first film, talks to himself in such intense situations, providing a running commentary on his own actions. Nonetheless, it should be stressed that while McClane's monologue creates a narrative bond between the two films, and deepens our understanding of his character, apprehending this reference to the earlier film is evidently not essential to our construction of a coherent fabula. As my analysis of Rambo's epilogue in Chapter 5 indicated, the viewer's ability to understand the connections between the micro-fabula of a sequel and the macro-fabula of the ongoing series to which it belongs is more luxury than necessity; while making those connections will facilitate a fuller appreciation and enjoyment, missing them will not leave us scratching our heads.[12]

The issue of the audience, its knowledge and reactions, is arguably one of film studies' principal and perpetual sources of contention, and, when discussing intertextual and extratextual references, the question of what the audience does and does not know simply cannot be avoided. Given that this book includes no audience research, one might well ask on what basis a discussion of intertextuality might proceed. In answer to such legitimate objections, I would counter that, while I have been at pains to illustrate that most Hollywood sequel narratives can be understood without prior viewing of their predecessors, it is nonetheless clear that, at an industrial level, sequel producers tend to assume that their primary audience is comprised of people who have seen its predecessor(s) and, at a textual level, that sequels tend to reward these returning audiences, not only with continuing narrative arcs but also with the other forms of self-referentiality.

What I am proposing, then, is that the sequel gives us a greater level of access to the assumed contract between audience and producer than a standalone work, even if that work is highly generic in form. A sequel's viewers have a firmer grasp of what they are paying to see and what pleasures to expect, just as its producers have a more particularised knowledge of what they are expected to provide. That the aforementioned in-jokes are such a common feature of the Hollywood sequel is evidence of this contract at work. We would be foolhardy to assume a monolithic reaction even among returning audiences, and my analysis of Rambo's closing moments suggests some of the ways in which prior knowledge might variably affect a viewer's response, but we can with greater confidence venture observations about what the audience is expected to know and to enjoy as a result of that knowledge. We might, in honour of Die Hard 2's foul-mouthed protagonist, call it the McClane Principle: not everyone might laugh at the thought of the same shit happening to the same guy twice, and some of those who do laugh might not have seen the first film, but laughing because one knows the source of the reference is one of the recurrent pleasures of the sequel form. The viewer who enjoys John McClane's comment because they remember the events of the first film is effectively a pared

'Another basement, another elevator …': John McClane (Bruce Willis) experiences a feeling of *déjà vu* in
Die Hard 2 (1990)

back version of Umberto Eco's model reader. Unlike the viewer able to decode the recondite
allusions to Hawks and Hitchcock in Carroll's account, however, the knowledge required of the
model sequel viewer is more self-evident: if you have seen *Die Hard*, you will be more likely to
appreciate the sequel's allusions because, for the most part, they are derived from that first film.
Of course there is more at play in this moment from *Die Hard 2* than simply the dialogue itself.
The mode in which that dialogue is delivered is also part of the potential pleasure on offer, and
so it is at this point, with the sound of Bruce Willis's weary, wise-ass New Jersey drawl echoing
in our ears, that we should turn to issues of character and star persona.

Intimidating Arnie: stars and character in the sequel

From its induction into the academy, primarily via Richard Dyer's *Stars*, writing about cinematic
stardom has rested to some degree on notions of intertextuality.[13] As Christine Geraghty has
observed, 'the model for work on stars and their audiences has been that of an unstable and
contradictory figure, constructed both intertextually (across different films) and extratextually
(across different types of material)'.[14] More recently, however, scholars of stardom have shown
a broader conception of their object of study, with Alan Lovell, Peter Krämer and Geraghty herself all arguing for a greater analytical emphasis on performance.[15] Furthermore, and perhaps
more radically, Jackie Stacey's landmark 1994 study *Star Gazing*, alongside aspects of Martin

Barker and Kate Brooks's work on the reception of *Judge Dredd* (1995) and Rachel Moseley's study of Audrey Hepburn have acknowledged the need to bring audiences into the equation.[16] These key works aside, relatively little in the way of audience-centred research about cinematic stardom has been published, seemingly leaving star studies at something of an impasse. One way out of this, Lovell has argued, is to shift focus away from the ideological readings that have dominated star studies and have attempted to inscribe coherent political meaning onto what he calls 'improbable candidates for carrying out the ideological task assigned to them'.[17] Extending this line of argument, I would suggest that this focus on stars' ideologica meanings has meant not only that too little has been written about their specific skillset (i.e. their abilities as performers, impersonators and so on), but also that too little attention has been paid to the manner in which their careers develop from film to film.[18] An actor's standing within the industry, dictated in part by their skill as a performer and in part by the financial success of their films, seems to me the most direct influence on their career path and for this reason I would suggest it as a key explanatory framework in the analysis of stardom. Here, star persona is a process rather than a fixed set of characteristics and what follows will look at stardom and sequelisation primarily through that lens.

What, then, are recurrent characteristics of the dynamic between star persona and character in the Hollywood sequel? I would suggest that this relationship tends to follow two broad patterns of development.

First, it can be observed that shifts in a star's persona, or in a star's career trajectory, are an influence on character development from one film to the next. Providing perhaps the most obvious example of this tendency are the alterations made to the character of Arnold Schwarzenegger's Terminator in the seven years between the release of *The Terminator* in 1984 and that of *Terminator 2: Judgment Day* in 1991. Schwarzenegger's choice of roles had diversified in the intervening years, seeing him move from the straightforward hardman characters that had previously populated his filmography into broad comedy with both *Twins* (1988) and *Kindergarten Cop* (1990). He had also made tentative steps into politics, appearing alongside George H. W. Bush at a presidential campaign rally in 1988 and been appointed as chairman of the President's Council on Physical Fitness and Sports in 1990. 'Conan the Republican', as Bush dubbed him, was therefore repositioning himself, both from within and without his film career, as a more approachable figure. Accordingly, *Terminator 2* rather ingeniously recasts Schwarzenegger's merciless killing machine as hero and protector to John Connor (Edward Furlong), the future leader of the human resistance whose mother Sarah (Linda Hamilton) had been his intended victim in the 1984 original. As director James Cameron commented at the time of the film's release:

> At the time when The Terminator came out … it was fine for Arnold to play an absolute lethal cold-blooded killer. Now … Arnold's role globally has changed and he is a great idol to children and people everywhere. I think it's very fortunate for me that the story that I came up with many years ago involved a change of the character of The Terminator to where he is now essentially the hero of the film.[19]

We might choose to remain sceptical about whether Cameron's original screenplay genuinely did reflect Schwarzenegger's career needs from the outset or whether, in fact, it was tailored

Edward Furlong and Arnold Schwarzenegger in *Terminator 2: Judgment Day* (1991)

accordingly closer to the time of production, but this nonetheless represents an open acknowl-edgment that the maintenance of this star's persona required a new approach to the character.

Yet there is more than one rationale at work here. The logic of the sequel, in which the same thing must be said differently, requires more than simple repetition; and the logic of the action-movie sequel requires an intensification of the generic pleasures with which it is associ-ated: more action, more explosions, more danger. Couched in these terms, repositioning Schwarzenegger as the hero, coupled with the introduction of another Terminator (a new model T-1000 played by Robert Patrick) as the aggressor answers this brief on multiple levels. The *New Yorker*'s Terence Rafferty, in his review of the film, comments on the 'insane conceit that Arnold Schwarzenegger is the *underdog*',[20] but it is precisely this which allows the film-makers to intensify the extent of the threat posed to the Connors by the T-1000. As Cameron put it, 'If I was going to put Arnold on the run … it had to be something that made us scared for him, so it obviously had to be something so outrageous.'[21] The shifts in Schwarzenegger's persona, therefore, dovetail with the need for the sequel to provide novelty as well as repeti-tion and to exceed its predecessor in generic terms, while also maintaining the original's the-matic concern with technology as a threat to humanity.

Second, the dynamic between star persona and character might also surface when a co-star or supporting character from the original film is promoted to a leading role in the sequel. This might play itself out purely at an extratextual level, as evidenced by the increased prominence and billing of Joe Pesci in the promotional artwork for *Lethal Weapon 3* (1992) compared with that for *Lethal Weapon 2* (1989). This promotion to above-the-title status reflects not the extent of Pesci's narrative role – his character Leo Getz is in fact less central to the narrative of the latter sequel – but rather an increase in his perceived commercial value due to his appearance in hit films in the intervening years: *Goodfellas* (1990), *Home Alone* and *My Cousin Vinny* (1992). More striking, however, are those films in which a star's extratextual value influences narrative form, as exemplified by *Speed 2: Cruise Control* (1997). After the huge success of its predecessor in the summer of 1994, Sandra Bullock, romantic support to Keanu Reeves's central protagonist, became a star in her own right, taking the lead in the romantic comedy *While You Were Sleeping* (1995) and cyber-thriller *The Net* (1995) – both of which performed well at the box office.[22] With Keanu Reeves unwilling or unable to participate in a sequel to *Speed*, the sequel was developed as a vehicle for Bullock, with Jason Patric cast as her new love interest. In other circumstances, the absence of Reeves might have forestalled *Speed 2* entirely, but Bullock's emergence as a financially viable star in her own right subsequent to *Speed* helped facilitate production of its sequel. Of course, given the success of its predecessor, it is possible that *Speed 2* would have been produced even without Bullock's involvement, but it seems unlikely that Fox would have been confident enough to invest to the extent that they did – with the production costs reported to be between $110 and $120 million – had she not agreed to return.

Speed 2 begins with Bullock's Annie taking a driving test, a reference to her situation in *Speed*, in which she has lost her licence for speeding and is resultantly a passenger on the bomb-rigged bus that Reeves's Jack Traven must defuse in that film's central sequence. As per sequel convention, *Speed 2*'s opening scene quickly fills us in on key events that have occurred in the ellipsis between the two films, while simultaneously establishing a new narrative strand: Annie has broken up with Jack because of his risk-taking approach to his police job, but has now taken up with Alex Shaw (Jason Patric), who is, unbeknown to Annie, another SWAT Team member and who, simultaneous to Annie's test, is on a motorbike in high-speed pursuit of a criminal suspect. Peter Krämer has suggested that, in *Speed 2*, Bullock is 'effectively reduced to the part of the helpless female bystander or victim', but this is only a partially accurate description of the manner in which her character is portrayed.[23] While it is true that, once kidnapped by the crazed John Geiger (Willem Dafoe), Annie is relegated to a position of relative helplessness, waiting to be saved by Alex, this occurs nearly seventy-five minutes into the film's two-hour running time. Prior to this, *Speed 2* is orientated around Annie's goals, the central predicament established in the opening minutes when she remarks to her driving instructor that neither she nor Alex has been in a relationship for more than seven months. When her driving test crosses paths with Alex's pursuit, revealing that, like Jack, he works in what she calls 'the suicide squad', Annie complains that 'I feel I don't even know you.' It is her desire for stability which motivates Alex to woo her with a romantic cruise, thus providing the pretext for the remainder of the action. With the exception of a few short scenes establishing Geiger's dastardly intentions, the first thirty minutes are principally concerned with this relationship drama and on Alex's faltering attempts to propose to Annie: scuppered initially by her persistently negative comments about commitment and latterly, thirty-five minutes in, by the onset of Geiger's hijack attempt. Between this moment and her kidnap, Annie and Alex are both directly involved in the unfolding action. Although shown to be less adept at heroics than her boyfriend, Annie is nonetheless involved in rescuing fellow passengers and, subsequent to his entrapment by Geiger, Alex himself. Thus while it may be appropriate to note the retrogressive gender roles, it is also clear that Bullock's status as a box-office draw (and Patric's lack thereof) has dictated that she is not simply damsel in distress – not, at least, for the film's first half, which, as the *Variety* reviewer remarked, is characterised by attempts at screwball comedy which seem mismatched to the action which later dominates.[24] Furthermore, Annie's put-upon, 'unlucky-in-love' situation is similar to that of Bullock's characters in *The Net* and *While You Were Sleeping*, suggesting an attempt to incorporate the qualities of a 'Sandra Bullock movie' into the template established by *Speed*.

Annie's relative centrality is explicable not only in the extratextual terms of Bullock's stardom, but also because, intertextually, she supplies the principal narrative link between the two films. Aside from a brief appearance by Glenn Plummer, the disgruntled Jaguar owner in the first film, only Annie carries the memory and direct experience of the events represented in *Speed* – and with them the prime justification for *Speed 2* to trade on the memory of that earlier success. We are reminded of this privileged narrative status throughout, with Annie as much a commentator on the action as she is a participant in it. When Geiger's plan finally begins to take effect, Annie's reaction is one of exasperation rather than fear: 'No! This is my vacation, damnit!' she moans, as the ship begins to quake and the lights to fall down around them; 'I swear I am never leaving the house again', she cracks, as dangerous gas escapes through the air vents. Her previous exposure to terrorist threat may have left her comically world-weary but it has also given her a greater facility to cope, as underlined by her comment to a group of terrified fellow passengers as she leads them to safety: 'I've been in worse situations than this and panicking does not help, trust me.' These acts of knowing, McClane-esque, commentary resurface in the film's epilogue. Having safely returned to Los Angeles, Annie is once again taking her driving test, with the same examiner, when she narrowly avoids pulling out in front of a bus, causing her to remark 'that bus was going way too fast'. Reminding us that the same shit can happen to the same girl twice, especially if that girl is played by Sandra Bullock, this parting shot once again reinforces her central status as the extratextual and intertextual justification for this sequel's existence.

One final variation on this interplay between star and character worthy of note occurs when an already established star is introduced into a sequel as a new, previously unseen character. Such was the case when director Leo McCarey cast Ingrid Bergman as Sister Mary Benedict in *The Bells of St. Mary's* in 1945. As detailed in Chapter 2, David O. Selznick, who had Bergman under exclusive contract at the time, drove a hard bargain with McCarey for her services. According to accounts by both Bergman and her press agent, Joe Steele, Selznick was opposed to sequels because they were never as successful as their predecessors and he warned Bergman that she 'would just be a stooge for Bing Crosby's singing'.[25] On the evidence of *Going My Way*, this would seem to have been a fair assumption on Selznick's part. After MGM refused to loan him Spencer Tracy, McCarey had subsequently crafted the role of Father O'Malley specifically for his longtime friend Crosby, most notably by incorporating no less than seven musical numbers (eight, if one counts the reprise of the title song) into the film. Despite running for approximately the same duration, *The Bells of St. Mary's* includes only four such numbers for Crosby, the first of which ('Aren't You Glad You're You?') does not appear until

forty minutes of screen time have elapsed. There could, of course, be any number of explanations for this disparity, but one of them is evidently that far more screen time is dedicated to
Bergman's character than was granted to any of the supporting cast in *Going My Way*. She is
effectively Crosby's equal in terms of story development, with Sister Mary Benedict's efforts to
relate to her students being parallelled with those of O'Malley, and her subsequent illness (a
case of TB of which she is unaware) being central to the progression of the narrative. Benedict
is even granted her own musical moment, singing in Swedish to her fellow nuns in celebration
of their acquisition of a new building in which to house their school.

Again, this shift in the balance of character is explicable at both a textual and industrial level.
At the time of her casting, following *Casablanca* (1942), *For Whom the Bell Tolls* (1943) and
Gaslight (1944), the latter of which earned her an Academy Award for Best Actress, Bergman
was a major star and perceived as a significant commercial asset, as indicated by the considerable fee negotiated by Selznick. Given how much he had invested in her casting, and its perceived potential benefits, it seems unlikely that McCarey would have relegated Bergman to the
position of Crosby's stooge. Equally, in narrative terms, her prominence works to generate new
drama and create new obstacles for O'Malley. Although *Bells* ultimately repeats the scenario
presented in *Going My Way*, in that O'Malley must convince Sister Mary to give up her post and
take leave for the good of her health, much as he was tasked to do with Father Fitzgibbon
(Barry Fitzgerald) in that first film, this element is not the specific motivation for O'Malley's
arrival and it is only introduced in the final third of the sequel, when he is made aware of her
illness. Until this point, Sister Mary is a far more formidable opponent (albeit in the gentlest,
kindest sense) to O'Malley than the befuddled, frequently bedridden Father Fitzgibbon, and so
represents a far greater challenge – and therefore another instance of the intensification which
the logic of the sequel form encourages, about which more in Chapter 7.

One further example worth considering here, particularly insofar as she represents a different kind of star, is Sigourney Weaver in her recurring role as Ripley in *Alien* and its three
sequels. While *Alien* was her breakout film, and while Ripley is without question her signature
role, what has followed is a career based not on similar roles in similar films but instead on
demonstrations of her ability and versatility as an actress, an emphasis borne out by the manner
in which, unlike the academic writing on *T2*, which frequently addresses Schwarzenegger's persona, most analyses of the *Alien* franchise, including those discussing Ripley's character in detail,
pay little attention to Weaver's extratextual meaning in a way that suggests it is of negligible
importance.[25] Weaver emerged from *Alien* as a star – or, at very least, a star-in-the-making –
much as Ripley had emerged as the unlikely survivor of the alien's rampage through the
Nostromo. Stardom in the traditional sense, however, was something she claimed to have no
interest in, for example complaining in a 1981 interview that 'there are so many good supporting roles that I'll never be considered for'.[27] Her subsequent roles, including a romantic
lead in *The Year of Living Dangerously* (1981), comic turns in William Friedkin's anarchic *Deal of
the Century* (1983) and *A Woman or Two* (1985) and a combination of both in *Ghostbusters*
(1984), confirmed Weaver's lack of interest in developing a consistent, recognisable persona.
Nonetheless, her association with Ripley, and the centrality of that character to the appeal of
Alien, came to the fore when James Cameron was asked to write a sequel and, he claimed, had
to argue for Weaver to be involved:

> It turned out that everybody but us thought that the film could be made without Sigourney Weaver
> … as far as we were concerned, we started with Ripley from the end of the last film, and it was her
> story … .We had to fight very hard for Sigourney to be in the picture, which to me was crazy.[28]

The success of *Aliens* in 1986 ensured that Weaver would continue to be perceived as an essential to the series, to the extent that she could command not only hugely inflated fees but also a co-producer credit on both *Alien³* and *Alien: Resurrection*. The years immediately following *Aliens* saw her take on the commercial and industrial status of star, arguably peaking in 1988 with two Academy Award nominations for her dramatic lead in the acclaimed *Gorillas in the Mist* (1988) and her comic supporting role in the box-office hit *Working Girl* (1988). Nonetheless, as indicated by the differences between these two roles, and the further distinction between these roles and that of Ripley, Weaver's fame and popularity continued to be orientated around her versatility as a performer, a pattern suggesting that her career can usefully be understood in terms of the distinction made by Christine Geraghty between 'star-as-professional' and 'star-as-performer', the former being characterised by a consistency across roles, whereas in the latter 'attention is deliberately drawn to the work of the acting so that … it is the performance and work which are emphasised, not leisure and the private sphere'.[29] Of note here is that Weaver's 'star-as-performer' status comes across not only via the variety of her filmography but also in relation to her multiple portrayals of Ripley. Shortly after the release of *Aliens*, Weaver talked about the changes between the 1979 and 1986 versions of Ripley as 'important' to her and reflected on what attracted her to the sequel:

> If I see my role as a Chinese warrior, a Valkyrie, or as the Henry V-I'll-never-get-to-play, then I'm
> interested in it. It's a chance to do a classic male part. If I see it as gun play, I'm not interested.[30]

She has commented similarly on shaving her head for *Alien³* and of the 'kinky' and 'sensual' elements of *Alien: Resurrection*.[31] According to Weaver, then, reprising the role revolves around professional development of her craft rather than a return to the familiar. The evolution of Ripley, the character, presents a challenge to Sigourney Weaver, the performer, and one that is cast in terms that explicitly invoke her background in the theatre.

For an actor to discuss their work in this manner is of course not unusual, but it does suggest how a sequel might satisfy the career needs of a star-as-performer such as Weaver, much as it might similarly benefit a star-as-professional such as Sylvester Stallone. One might argue, further, that here again sequel logic dovetails with the star's needs, in that both actor and film require and/or are tasked with providing novelty as well as repetition. In this scenario, then, a sequel becomes preferable to a similar role in a generically similar film, precisely because it allows for development and experimentation within limits, as opposed to the repetition by stealth required by the latter.

One final variation on this star-as-performer dynamic comes when a new actor takes on the role of a well-known character with a pre-existing set of conventions and expectations. While the industry's reliance on such characters has always been considerable, the scale and economic role of the films in which they appear have visibly changed over time, as have the preferred sources for the presold properties in question – from detective fiction in the 1930s

Director James Cameron and Sigourney Weaver as Ellen Ripley on the set of *Aliens* (1986)

to Broadway musicals in the 60s and comic books in the 2000s – a change which has impacted on the dynamic between stardom and character. Because comic-book characters, for example, come with not only a considerable amount of narrative baggage but also with a pre-existing set of visual iconography, they present a quite different challenge to actors and film-makers than, say, the Biblical figures which were a common source of spectacular drama in the Hollywood cinema of the 1950s. Despite this shift, one consistent trend is that there are very few examples of stars taking on such roles from any period: Valentino as the Sheik, Douglas Fairbanks as Zorro and D'Artagnan, Ronald Colman as Bulldog Drummond and Warner Baxter as the Cisco Kid are some of the few examples pre-1955, while Harrison Ford as Jack Ryan in *Patriot Games* and *Clear and Present Danger*, Matt Damon as Jason Bourne, Tom Hanks as Robert Langdon in *The Da Vinci Code* (2006) and *Angels and Demons* (2009) and Robert Downey Jr in *Sherlock Holmes* (2009) and *Sherlock Holmes: A Game of Shadows* (2011) are their more recent equivalents. One might also argue the case for Basil Rathbone and Christian Bale, both of whom were well known by the time they donned the deerstalker and cowl to play Sherlock Holmes in *The Hound of the Baskervilles* (1939) and Batman in *Batman Begins* respectively, but neither of whom were stars so much as they were respected actors.

Indeed, Rathbone and Bale are arguably more representative of the second and more common tendency: pre-existing characters played by actors who are either relative unknowns or what Richard deCordova has termed 'picture personalities', known and recognised to a degree but with little or no established and distinct star persona at the time of their casting.[32] From the studio era we might cite Peter Lorre as Mr Moto, Warner Oland as Fu Manchu,

Sidney Toler as Charlie Chan, Johnny Weissmuller as Tarzan, George Sanders as The Saint and The Falcon, Bonita Granville as Nancy Drew, Penny Singleton as 'Blondie' Bumstead and Warner Baxter as the 'Crime Doctor'. This pattern has continued in the post-studio era with Christopher Reeve as Superman, Tobey Maguire as Spider-Man, Angelina Jolie as Lara Croft in *Lara Croft: Tomb Raider* (2001), Eric Bana as the title character in *Hulk* (2003) and Sean Connery, Timothy Dalton, Pierce Brosnan and Daniel Craig as James Bond (Roger Moore is an exception here, having had significant starring roles in both *The Saint* [1962–9] and *The Persuaders* [1971–2] television series immediately prior to his stint as 007).

These two lists reveal much about the changing status of recurrent, pre-existing characters in Hollywood's output before and after the breakdown of the studio system. For while the studio-era films are almost invariably B-grade productions destined to fill out the bottom half of a double bill, their post-studio equivalents are all big-budget event movies intended to lead the way at the box office. Crucially, whereas the commercial status of the films themselves has changed dramatically, the industrial and commercial status of the actors playing the characters has not, meaning in turn that many of the highest-grossing films since the late 1970s have not been star vehicles, a trend which has led to pronouncements of the death or waning power of the movie star.[33] Yet, while it is a commonplace to note contemporary Hollywood's increased reliance on sequels, spin-offs and franchises, and to remark on the increased prominence of directors and special effects, one implication of this apparent shift has been left relatively unexamined: that we might understand the characters themselves as the principal stars of these films.

Of course, a star is not necessarily the only source of a film's appeal and success, and the same is true of a character, but it is worth noting that a star-character might usefully be understood similarly to a star-actor, bringing with it a set of consistent character traits, intertextually established audience expectations and generic conventions, and even a particular look or style. The rigidity of those traits, conventions and expectations is somewhat dependent on the ubiquity of the character and the extent of its prior audiovisual history. William Uricchio and Roberta Pearson have discussed the nature of these conventions in relation to Batman, noting that 'character, that is, a set of key components, becomes the primary market of Batman texts'.[34] Their analysis helpfully highlights the manner in which a pre-existing character and a star might be similarly understood, as indicated by the fact that the five key components they identify as constituting Batman's character – traits/attributes, events, recurrent characters (by which they mean his regular adversaries and allies), setting and iconography – might all, with the exception perhaps of recurrent characters, be usefully applied to a description of star persona.

What, then, is the actor's role in portraying a star character? Surprisingly little has been written about this type of interaction, perhaps in part because star studies has tended to focus on those stars whose personas, intertextual by their very nature, seem to transcend any single film or character.[35] In these cases, I would posit, we might best understand the role of the actor as involving some combination of both impersonation and interpretation, attempting to physically embody the character in a manner which is recognisable and conforms to expectation, while simultaneously distinguishing one's own performance from prior interpretations.

The extent to which the act of interpretation is evident may in part rely on the star status of the actor in question. Jack Nicholson's performance as The Joker in *Batman* draws overtly on pre-existing elements of his persona – an anarchic streak and maniacal tendencies, for example – but in a manner well suited to the pre-existing components of the character; the grandstanding, inappropriate joke-telling and over-the-top gestures all central to earlier representations of The Joker, not only in the camp environment of the 1960s TV series but also in Alan Moore's serious-minded take on the character in the graphic novel *The Killing Joke*.[36] Even when faced with an established star persona, then, the star-character can hold its own. In general, however, such matching between star-character and star-actor is neither common nor requisite, primarily because most actors do not carry the baggage of such a well-established persona. This is where the act of impersonation comes to the fore. Christian Bale's intense, serious portrayal of Bruce Wayne/Batman does not overtly invoke a pre-existing star persona, but it does, on the other hand, feed back into our general understanding of Bale as an intense and serious actor with a Method-like approach to his roles.[37]

If we concur with Geraghty's notion that the star-as-performer has become the dominant model for contemporary film stardom, then it becomes clear that the rise of the star-character allows actors to foreground their skills as performers and impersonators rather than their extratextual personas. Thus we might talk about Christian Bale's Batman in the same manner that we might discuss Olivier's Hamlet, as the embodiment of an enduring character by a skilled, well-known performer who will deliver their own interpretation of the role. This approach to casting, it should be noted, can become a promotional motor for both sequel and actor, in that announcements about such actor-character combinations have the potential to generate considerable advance publicity.

Character and narrative: a delicate balance

Whether orientated around star persona, pre-existing property or some combination thereof, the extension of a character's fictional life over multiple instalments leads us to consider another challenge the sequel poses to the classical paradigm. The narrative model proposed in *The Classical Hollywood Cinema*, after all, rests on an almost organic unity between character and narrative. We come to know a protagonist through their goals and actions, and it is those goals and actions which drive the narrative forward. Although we might be invited to make certain assumptions based on generic knowledge or the persona of the star playing the role, most of what we need to know about that character can be derived from this one narrative (although of course this does not preclude us knowing or assuming more than narrative comprehension requires).[38] This holds true even when that character and narrative are derived from another source: whichever production or film version we may have seen, we know Hamlet principally in terms of one set of actions (or inactions) from one particular narrative.

In the classical ideal, then, character drives narrative and narrative defines character. But when a character returns in a sequel or a series of sequels, or if the character comes from a serialised source, then the balance between character and narrative shifts. What we can potentially know about that character explicitly stems from more than the narrative at hand, and so the role of the later narrative(s) in defining character becomes, if not secondary, then certainly less central. Much as the bulk of A-grade production in the studio era was motivated by the need to maximise investment on the stars under contract, initiating the need to seek out or create specific vehicles for those stars, so we might understand sequel or series production as revolving around a need to find stories to continue the cinematic life of the characters (whether or not they are played by stars or are star vehicles) who form part of a studio's intellectual property. Hence the recurrent practice, as with the *What Price Glory?* series, *Die Hard with a Vengeance* and so on, of remodelling script material to suit the needs of an existing series or franchise. We might couch this shift in the balance between character and narrative in screenwriting terms. Whereas the challenge for the screenwriter of *Alien* might be 'How will we come to learn about the character of Ripley as she defeats the alien?', the challenge for the screenwriter of *Alien³* becomes 'How will Ripley defeat the aliens on a planet without guns?' We can encapsulate many sequels in these terms. What will Harry Callahan (Clint Eastwood) do when faced, in *Sudden Impact* (1983), with a female vigilante? How will Andy Hardy, in *Love Finds Andy Hardy*, balance the affections of not one but two girls? Or, in *Batman Returns*, how will Batman outsmart both The Penguin and Catwoman? And so on. This is not to shut off the possibility that a sequel might forge character and action such that the former continues to develop or change via the latter, but rather to indicate the manner in which its narrative construction might again differ from classical norms if its protagonist is already a known quantity.

As I have previously remarked, this balance in part depends upon the type of characters involved, and how they are defined. Detectives and crimefighters such as Sherlock Holmes, Mr Moto and Batman are defined primarily in terms of their work, their crimefighting activity being more central than their personal lives. Because this work will never be done, and because narrative variation comes in the form of new cases or master-criminals, their characters tend to remain relatively static in story after story. The same can be said, to some degree, of spies such as James Bond and cops such as John McClane and Harry Callahan. Importantly, these characters are already full-formed adults. If one of a character's central traits is that they are yet to reach full maturity, as with Frodo Baggins, Harry Potter, Luke Skywalker and Andy Hardy, then growth and development are part of the process of variation which the sequel demands.

To assume that these factors are either simply coincidental or the organic product of these characters' situations would of course be to ignore the possibility that generic determinants might to some degree dictate the nature of the characters. Writing on the role of genre in relation to the star vehicle, Andrew Britton has argued that 'the existence of a genre, *and a relation between the genres*, is a prior condition of the vehicle: vehicles constitute a distinct sub-set, more or less highly individuated, of conventional relations which always precede the star'.[39] While I would take issue with the suggestion that genre necessarily precedes the star, especially given that studios organised production around the talent under contract as much as around specific genres, it is true that many of the characters discussed here were born into a pre-existing, industrially defined generic context, whether it be the growing market for detective stories in the early twentieth century into which Moto, Chan and Perry Mason were introduced, or the increased demand for platform games which led to the creation of Lara Croft in the 1990s. Genre, like stardom, is central to Bordwell and Thompson's discussion of 'intertextual motivation', but, as I shall argue in the following chapter, the role of genre convention within the sequel, centred as it is on recurrent and specific combinations of character, star and story type, is far from straightforward.

7 | A formula of formula: Genre and the sequel

In a memo dated 7 May 1942, writer Harry Kurnitz gave notes to producer Everett Riskinn on 'The Thin Man's Rival', a script which eventually became the basis for *The Thin Man Goes Home*. Kurnitz pointed to a scene in which Nick Charles interviews a man suspected of murder and suggested that William Powell's freewheeling sleuth would 'appear more of a detective' if the suspect is 'tripped' into admitting his hatred for the victim. Connecting this observation to a broader set of compositional rules, Kurnitz added that 'A reluctant witness is a better suspect than a man seemingly bent on involving himself – "The Art of the Mystery Story by Professor Wolfgang Kurnitz".' Later, when discussing the script's closing pages, Kurnitz criticised the implication that Nick knew the identity of the murderer prior to the climactic interrogation scene. This revelation, he noted, ran counter to the equivalent scenes of past Thin Man instalments, in which Nick brought 'the characters together in the hope of igniting a spark which will illuminate the dark niches of the minds with which he is confronted [...] If Nick knows who killed who, it is not considered cricket.'[1]

These two observations tell us much about the relationship between genre and the sequel. Kurnitz approached this Thin Man instalment not only in relation to the conventions and compositional techniques of a 'genre-at-large' ('the Mystery Story') but also in relation to another, more finely tuned set of conventions specifically associated with and internal to the Thin Man series, conventions established by their repetition in the four films preceding *The Thin Man Goes Home*. Nick Charles must fulfil certain generic requirements relating to his profession (i.e. the solving of mysterious crimes), but he also has certain features which distinguish him from his peers. Unlike Charlie Chan, his thought processes are not inscrutable and, unlike Sherlock Holmes, his methods are not scientific; instead, his knowledge only briefly exceeds that of the audience, and only then in the final moments. Although, unlike Chan *et al.*, he has an ongoing romantic relationship (with his wife, Nora) which allows for development and change in his personal life, for Nick to alter his professional approach as a detective would undermine the unspoken contract of obligation and expectation between the Thin Man series' producers and its assumed audience, the metaphorical 'cricket' to which Kurnitz refers. Here, then, we see a sequel negotiating two sets of conventions and expectations: at a macro level, those relating to the detective or mystery genre, with which the film and its predecessor(s) are generally associated; and, at a micro level, those belonging to what we might simply call the Thin Man genre. Illuminating the manner in which these two sets of conventions are established, and the manner in which they interact and inform one another, is one of this chapter's principal concerns.

More broadly, my intention here is to shed further light on the poetics of the Hollywood sequel by considering the parallels between the role of the sequel form and the role of genre within the industry. It is not uncommon for genre theorists to assume that the generic nature of Hollywood output is the result of the need for producers to simultaneously replicate previous successes while also differentiating their product; to offer audiences (or at least to appear to be offering them) something both new and familiar.[2] Nonetheless, it is important to recognise that a strategy of product differentiation takes on a different quality if the elements originally distinguishing a film are extended into a sequel or a film series. Here, then, what initially differentiated *The Thin Man* from other detective films becomes standardised in its sequels, the novel becoming familiar. As such formulas develop, so the act of differentiation is guided by a different set of criteria. While Hollywood sequels are almost invariably generic, therefore, their similarities cannot be understood on strictly the same terms as those between films within a genre, because the interaction between standardisation and differentiation from sequel to sequel takes place within a narrower, more particularised sphere.

Divided into five parts, this chapter will go on to further scrutinise the repetitive nature of the sequel at a formal and narrative level, identifying the tendency for sequels to amplify certain recurring elements, delivering more of the same with an emphasis on 'more'. It will also consider the manner in which industrial forces come to bear on the nature of what a sequel carries over from its predecessor and what is discarded. As this suggests, while much of this chapter is dedicated to discussion of how the generic dynamic between a first film and its sequel might develop at a formal level, it remains mindful of the fact that this dynamic is principally determined not by a hermetically sealed textual process, but also by extratextual factors. Before we can address these issues, however, we must first consider how film genre theory has tended to conceptualise the formulaic nature of Hollywood's output, particularly in relation to genre cycles. 'Formula' is the key word here, because this is a chapter more concerned with repetition than continuation, or, rather, with the sequel's need to repeat set against its need to move a continuing narrative forward in time.

Genre and the sequel

The awkward fit between existing genre theory and the sequel form is immediately apparent when we note that a greater degree of formal similarity characterises the relationship between the first film of a series and its sequel(s) than the relationships between constituent films of a given genre. Films in the same genre might originate from the same gene pool, so to speak, but sequels ostensibly inherit DNA from their predecessors, along with the family name, a relationship which, as observed in previous chapters, occasionally finds itself reflected in narrative terms, as in the numerous 'Son of' films, and the many sequels dramatising some form of genetic, psychological or economic inheritance from one protagonist to the next. Nonetheless, some principles governing genre still seemingly apply to the antecedent–sequel relationship: sequels usually share at least some formal characteristics with their predecessors; and, at an industrial level, such films provide a variation on what Barry Langford terms 'the generic "contract" of familiarity leavened by novelty', offering variations on familiar situations featuring recurrent characters.[3]

Given these conceptual similarities, it follows that genre theory should in some part be extendable to a poetics of the sequel. Might we not, after all, transpose models of generic change, transformation and cyclicism to a study of those same shifts between original and sequel(s)? Unfortunately, although notions of generic fixity have long since been modified or abandoned by film scholars in favour of genre as a historically dynamic process, and despite the prevalence of evolutionary terminology, there have been surprisingly few attempts to describe how genre as process might actually function.[4] It is a curious tendency of writing on genre that, while the existence of production cycles and genre's cyclical nature is now something of a given, relatively few studies actively engage with understanding the cycle itself as a process.[5] Even those studies which stress the non-linear, stop-start nature of genre cycles, rather than a smooth evolutionary path, rarely engage directly with the full implications of such an acknowledgment. Barry Grant, for example, concedes that genre history is shaped by cycles, defining them as 'intense periods of production of a similar group of genre movies', but does not consider how such periods impact on the broader generic sphere.[6] In this account, cycles are something that occasionally happen to a genre, rather than being part of the process of genre formation itself.

In an exception to the above tendency, Rick Altman has proposed the notion of 'The Producer's Game' – an attempt to describe more accurately the industry's role in genre formation. In this account, producers identify box-office successes, analyse them in order to identify which elements made them successful, and make another film utilising those elements in conjunction with elements drawn from other hits.[7] The Producer's Game, Altman argues, 'puts studio personnel in the place of the critic', insofar as it requires industry insiders to isolate those elements of a hit which can be replicated in subsequent films.[8] Altman's approach does convincingly stress the dynamic nature of the process: producers might not identify the correct elements, for example, meaning that it may take time before whatever appealed to the audience finds its way into a new film. Furthermore, given that different producers will be looking at the same hit, there is every possibility that certain key elements (be they common themes or character types) will find their way into very different types of film, as is reflected in Tino Balio's survey of production trends in the 1930s.[9] Altman's attempt to position producers as critics, however, somewhat flattens crucial distinctions between the activities of these two groups. Producers, after all, are looking to isolate the specific ingredients from a recent hit which attracted audiences, whereas critics are retrospectively looking at both the first film and what followed so as to isolate formal similarities. Producers are also, unlike critics, not simply looking for what can be (or has been) replicated but, rather, what they are able to replicate with the resources available, resources which may differ in scale (particularly in terms of production budgets) and type (in terms of the creative talent at their disposal, for example) to the producers of the hit under scrutiny.

More recently, Richard Nowell has made a concerted effort to describe the cycle as an industrial process. Nowell first distinguishes the cycle from shorter-term trends he terms 'fads' (in which similar themes, settings or character types recur across different types of film over a particular period) and 'clusters' (a very shortlived surge in production of a particular type) and longer-term 'staples', a term which describes the regular production over many years.[10] He then identifies the chronologically distinct stages which together constitute a cycle, beginning with what he terms a 'trailblazer hit', defined as a commercially successful film 'that differs from contemporaneous hits'.[11] Thereafter follow two distinct phases: a first wave of imitative films, or 'prospector cash-ins', from which emerges at least one further success, termed a 'reinforc-ing hit'; and a second wave in which a larger quantity of imitators ('carpetbagger cash-ins') is produced, after which the cycle winds down, and the number of similar films being produced drops to what Nowell calls 'base level'.[12]

Although Nowell does not discuss the sequel directly, his model does enable us to better ascertain the parallels and intersections between genre as a cycle and sequelisation as a process. After all, the sequel is almost invariably perceived as a form of cash-in, following in the wake of a hit and modelled closely on its predecessor. And, as the historical account in Part 1 has demonstrated, sequels are a regular feature of cyclical production, representing a form of legitimised carpetbagging. Such carpetbagging takes place because, as Altman has observed, stu-dios have always preferred to emphasise their films' 'proprietary characteristics (star, director and other related films from the same studio) over sharable determinants like genre'.[13] Despite these points of intersection, it is important to understand that the cyclical process of initiation and imitation Nowell describes cannot capture fully the nuances involved in the process of sequelisation. From an industrial perspective, there are subtly different issues at stake when a producer seeks to cash in on his or her own success; a distinction I will discuss in more detail in the following sections.

While most genre theory comes up short when applied to the process of sequelisation, many of the issues which have to date plagued genre theory are less contentious when con-sidered in relation to the sequel form. Whereas it is difficult to establish how the content of one film may or may not have influenced subsequent films within the same genre, one can be reasonably confident that a significant influence on the makers of a sequel is exerted by the sequel's predecessor. Similarly, by using a title which invokes a direct relationship to an earlier film, sequel producers can anticipate audience expectations in ways that even the most imita-tive, non-sequel genre films cannot. Moreover, because of the transparency of the aforemen-tioned 'contract' between audience and producer, it is possible for critics and historians to surmise more of what audiences might know of and expect from a sequel. While it is prob-lematic to assume that audiences for *Swing Time* (1936) were well schooled in the conventions of Astaire and Rogers musicals, for example, it is safer to conclude that the majority of the audi-ence for *The Twilight Saga: Breaking Dawn – Part 1* (2011) had already viewed *The Twilight Saga: Eclipse* (2010), and therefore held concrete expectations about its sequel. Convention and expectation, in other words, are more easily isolatable and identifiable in sequels than they are in a given genre film. As the Thin Man example which opened this chapter suggests, the makers of sequels or series establish highly particularised sets of conventions and unique miniature ecosystems in which take place the interplay between audience expectation and the balance of differentiation/replication. Like any ecosystem, these conventions are subject to external and internal influences and, in order better to understand both the nature of these influences and the changes they might affect, it is necessary not only to consider which kinds of conventions are established from one film to the next, but how those conventions persist or change over time. Given the flaws of early film genre criticism, flaws which frequently stemmed from ahis-torical assumptions about the rigidity of genres, I should make it clear that, in using the term 'convention', I am not suggesting that a circumscribed set of characteristics necessarily govern each and every series or franchise. On the contrary, in examining the manner in which certain qualities of a first film are either reiterated or discarded by its sequel, I seek to describe the process by which formulas are created, stressing all the while that, because it is a process, when I speak of convention I am referring to a loose rubric rather than a set of inflexible rules.

Family resemblances: the genericity of the sequel

Just as film genres are defined by divergent sets of criteria (the topographical specificities of the Western, for example, having little bearing on our definition of a comedy or musical), so the formal traits a sequel inherits from its predecessor vary wildly in both scale and type. Pre-existing genre norms evidently have a role to play here, insofar as they will partially govern the nature of that inheritance. Thus The Thin Man sequels, operating within the same master genre as the original, carry over the narrative conventions of the detective genre, but are quite flexible in terms of their topographic and iconographic features. The Thin Man Goes Home, for example, differentiates itself from its predecessors precisely by moving the action from the cityscapes of previous instalments to the small town where Nick Charles grew up, leaving behind the nightclubs and dive bars that have been the series' regular stomping ground for picket fences and country shacks. Convention dictates that the Charleses must always be solving a murder, but they can and will do that anywhere. By the same token, while True Grit has various qualities identifying it as a Western, including its narrative concerns with vengeance and vigilantism, it is also evident that its sequel, Rooster Cogburn, could not take place in an urban setting. Of course we might imagine an alternative scenario in which Rooster (Wayne) finds himself in New York City, but that would run counter to some part of the original film's appeal, which was to see its star once again riding a horse, toting a Winchester, protecting the innocent and confronting outlaws in Old West locales – 'This was the essence of Wayne, the distillation', wrote Roger Ebert.[14] A sequel, in other words, is unlikely to stray in any fundamental sense from the broad generic territory (narrative, iconographic or otherwise) inhabited by its predecessor – so unlikely, in fact, that it is a struggle to identify clear-cut exceptions to this rule. One might argue that Gremlins 2 is more overtly comic than its predecessor, or point to the darker tone of The Empire Strikes Back relative to that of Star Wars, but these are gradations rather than wholesale shifts. The differences in kind between Alien and Aliens are often remarked upon, the latter often described as belonging more to the action genre than the horror category, and yet, while grander in the scale of both threat and response (as its pluralised title indicates), Aliens still draws from the same broad generic pool in order to provide many of the same pleasures: there is horror derived from the alien form and its invasion/ destruction of the human body; thrills generated by the alien's hunting of a small group of characters in a series of dark, dank locations; and the film again builds to a one-on-one confrontation between Ripley and the monster.[15] I am belabouring this rather obvious point precisely because its seeming obviousness, stemming from the unlikelihood that Aliens might have instead been a romantic comedy or The Empire Strikes Back a musical, indicates the extent to which generic patrimony is a given, a 'natural fact' of the sequel form.

But of course this is only part of the picture. Even before we consider explicit continuities of narrative and character, Rooster Cogburn, for example, has more in common with True Grit than simply its surface participation in the Western genre. It is also tonally consistent with its predecessor, at turns comic and elegiac in its continued acknowledgment that Rooster is a little too old to be carrying on as he is. This tonal consistency is in turn the product of the sequel's narrative, in which Rooster is again called upon to uphold the rights of an innocent third party (in this case Katharine Hepburn's staunchly religious Eula Goodnight rather than Kim Darby's recently orphaned and vengeful Mattie Ross) against a band of younger outlaws and, resultantly, once again forms an emotional bond (this time romantic rather than paternal) with his protégé. The basic narrative these films share is common in the Hollywood Western, but the sheer strength of the likeness – as opposed to, say, a film in which Rooster is called upon to protect or avenge *himself*, or in which he moves to another frontier town – is not explicable solely by the fact of their belonging to the same genre. *True Grit* and *Rooster Cogburn* are both Westerns, but to categorise them as such only hints at the extent of their formal similarities.

At the same time, we cannot automatically assume a straightforward hierarchy of influence, in which *Rooster Cogburn*'s relationship to *True Grit* is necessarily of greater relevance than its relationship to the Western genre. *Rooster Cogburn* is a Western because *True Grit* was a Western, but it is a sequel to *True Grit* not because of that shared generic affiliation but because it again follows the character of Rooster, depicting events in his life which chronologically follow those of its predecessor; and yet, in turn, it is that character and those events which contribute to the film's status as a Western. The circularity of this relationship, and the indeterminate play of influence therein, suggests the difficulties inherent in attempting to remove any sequel from its full generic context. *Rooster Cogburn*'s participation in the Western genre is necessary because it seeks not only to continue *True Grit*'s story, but also to replicate the manner in which that first film entertained us. The concept of genre is relevant, then, because, alongside those continuities of character and narrative which are its defining characteristic, the Hollywood sequel also strives (with wildly varying levels of success) to offer a continuity of pleasure.

Once more with feeling: character continuity, intensified repetition and conventionality

How, then, is such continuity achieved? As the *Rooster Cogburn* example suggests, one of the commonest strategies, and arguably the commonest source of the sequel's poor critical standing, is to initiate a thinly veiled re-enactment of the original narrative. Such a tactic is the stock in trade of conceptual series such as Gold Diggers and Broadway Melody and the extent to which it is employed tends to be inversely proportional to the number of returning characters. Avoiding any pretence of narrative continuity, the aforementioned studio musical series recast many of the same performers as new characters, enabling it to replay many of the same scenarios. *Airport* and its three sequels have only one recurrent character, aviation engineer/specialist/pilot Joe Patroni (George Kennedy), and are therefore free to centre on a similar dramatic situation involving a similar set of characters. Crucial here is that Patroni's profession legitimises his continued presence in the series: it would be incredibly poor fortune to be a passenger or stewardess on four doomed airliners within the space of a decade, but if you are paid to avert such disasters it's all in a day's work. Historically, Hollywood has tended to rely on recurring characters in mission- or case-based employment (including spies, detectives, superheroes and doctors), thereby ensuring a steady supply of situations capable of being contained within discrete narrative episodes, and thus facilitating the repetition of a basic story arc from film to film. With the exception of the detective genre, such narrative repetition is rarely an end in itself; it is rather a means by which other pleasures (laughter, thrills and the like) may be generated. The fact that *Airport 1975* (1974), the first *Airport* sequel, deals not with the aftermath of the original crash and its survivors, but instead with another airborne crisis, underscores the extent to which the disaster itself, rather than the characters, is the key to its appeal.

The recycling of familiar plots and character types is of course central to the emergence, maintenance and development of genres: without such repetitions the very notion of cinematic types and the discursive function of such categories would be largely redundant. For the sequel, however, the act of repetition is more fraught, complicated as it is by the fact of past (fictional) events and the effect of those events on recurrent characters. A new film seeking to capitalise on a pre-existing success, but with no official connection to that success, can be openly imitative; *Friday the 13th* can be created in the image of *Halloween*, blatantly recycling its narrative structure, character types and source of terror, in the process contributing to the formation of what came to be known as the slasher film, without fear of legal recrimination. A sequel, on the other hand, cannot operate with such freedom. Its paratextual affiliation to its predecessor promises a reprise of certain pleasures, but, if it features recurring characters, its repetitions cannot be actual; the characters cannot literally re-enact or re-experience those same events anew. Laurie Strode might be stalked once again by Michael Myers in *Halloween II*, but this does not reverse the events of the previous film: Laurie's friends are still dead and she and Michael cannot meet again for the first time. To respond to John McClane's rhetorical question: the same shit cannot literally happen to the same guy twice, only the same *kind* of shit.

As suggested, this challenge is lessened if the recurrent character has a legitimate reason to repeat themselves, particularly if their profession is the source of, or the rationale for, their involvement in a new (but similar) set of dramatic events. The challenge, and therefore the connection between films, is lessened still further if (as with the majority of series films of the 1930s) the recurrent character is a fully formed expert in their chosen field. In *Airport*, Joe Patroni is already an experienced technician, just as Sherlock Holmes is always already a master detective, meaning that there is nothing any given case can teach him that will be identifiably utilised in future instalments. Often, however, a sequel is obliged to acknowledge its recurrent protagonist's memory of prior events and/or their acquisition of knowledge and expertise – in other words, their development as characters. This, arguably, is one of the central challenges facing any film-maker seeking to create a sequel: how to develop characters without losing or compromising the generic appeal of previous instalments? Umberto Eco has noted how the *Superman* comic books sidestep this issue by downplaying any sense of chronology, and by presenting stories which 'develop in a kind of oneiric climate … where what has happened before and what has happened after appear extremely hazy'.[16] He suggests that these comics avoid chronological or temporal progression because 'each general modification would draw the world, and Superman with it, toward final consumption', thus bringing about an end to the commercial returns which can be generated.[17] Although this observation may be applicable to the instalment-heavy world of comics, and, to some extent, to the series films of the 1930s and 40s, there are more pressing issues for most Hollywood sequels than their characters' eventual progression towards death. More problematic is the extent to which the protagonist's experiences in previous films might affect their actions in the sequel(s); the limited probability that such extraordinary experiences might occur more than once in a lifetime; and how this flouting of the laws of probability challenges the verisimilitude of such repetitions.

Such developments need not, as such, be barriers to the supply of repetitious pleasures; in fact they might provide the impetus for repetition. It is a trope of the superhero genre (whether on page or the screen) that the hero's true identity is always under threat of discovery, with the potential for such revelations being a frequent source of drama – but it is rare that the effects of such knowledge are fully felt, as with *The Dark Knight* (2008), in which The Joker (Heath Ledger) threatens to publicly announce Batman's identity only to decide that he enjoys their costumed antagonism too much to destroy it, or *Superman II*, in which Lois Lane convinces Clark Kent to divulge his secret, only to have her memory of this admission wiped by the Man of Steel (using his telepathic powers) in the closing moments. Similarly, the *Back to the Future* trilogy ingeniously dramatises the manner in which the knowledge Marty McFly acquires through dramatic experience might later be reapplied to positively affect the outcome of the very same past events.

Generally, however, the fact of the character's acquired knowledge and experience, coupled with the need to provide a similar form of entertainment, leads to two tendencies in Hollywood sequels featuring key recurrent protagonists. First, the original central character might be relegated to a more peripheral, advisory role – their experience used to assist a new set of protagonists – as with Clear Rivers (Ali Larter) in *Final Destination 2* (2003), Nancy in *A Nightmare on Elm Street 3: Dream Warriors* or Ollie Reed (Kent Smith) in *Curse of the Cat People* (1944), the focus of which is Ollie's daughter, Amy (Ann Carter). Second, and more common, the character will confront an intensified set of the same type of challenges or obstacles which are usually the result of (or additionally complicated by) one of the six types of disruptive force that motivate sequel narratives outlined in Chapter 6.[18]

With regard to the first of these two tendencies, the horror genre again proves interesting, because its sequels so frequently feature recurrent characters who are not professionally engaged in an activity which motivates the film's central generic pleasures. It seems no coincidence, then, that there are many horror sequels in which the original protagonist is relegated to a subsidiary role (including the aforementioned examples, but also *Hellbound: Hellraiser II* [1988]), or in which the only recurrent character is the monster/psychopath himself.

The second tendency, this amplified or intensified version of the established formula – more of the same, with an emphasis on 'more' – is one of the commonest of sequel tropes. Thus we have multiple *Aliens* rather than one *Alien*; a liquid-metal Terminator able to withstand all standard forms of firepower; an imperious Ingrid Bergman rather than an ineffectual Barry Fitzgerald in *The Bells of St. Marys*; multiplying numbers of adversaries for Batman and Superman in *Batman Returns* and *Superman II*, and ever-more-intimidating contenders for Rocky to face off against in the boxing ring. This process of intensification can manifest itself in an even more modular fashion. Thus in *Any Which Way You Can* (1980), more screen time is dedicated to Clyde, pet orangutan of mechanic-cum-bare-knuckle fighter Philo (Clint Eastwood), whose presence was one of the distinguishing features of its predecessor, *Every Which Way but Loose* (1978) – an intensification epitomised by a montage, thirty minutes into the film, showing Clyde shooting basketball, playing in a hammock and generally enjoying himself to a song entitled 'The Orangutang Hall of Fame'. The montage appears without explanation, and is neither motivated by prior events nor related to the following action, so we must assume that the rationale for its inclusion was to give an expanded showcase to one of the original film's key pleasures. Similarly, in *Crank 2: High Voltage* (2009), Chev Chelios (Jason Statham) once again has sex with his girlfriend in public, but this time in a more spectacular setting in front of an ever larger audience (at a racetrack rather than in a parking lot). Lastly, in *Indiana Jones and the Temple of Doom* (1985), Indiana (Harrison Ford) pulls his gun in response to a hoard of men wielding swords, an intensified repetition of the moment in which he draws his gun on a single sword-wielding adversary in *Raiders of the Lost Ark* (1981), with humour derived from the fact that, contrary to audience expectation, Indiana's gun doesn't work on this occasion. That *Temple of Doom* is a prequel rather than a sequel merely underlines the extent to which, in terms of repetition and intensification, diegetic chronology is often a secondary concern relative to the extra-textual chronology of production and reception.

As these examples suggest, this tendency towards intensified repetition may have no meaningful relationship with character development *per se* – and yet there are a few instances in which the two elements are elegantly combined. One such example is the *Scream* series (1996–), that rare horror franchise in which the victims rather than the killer are recurrent, and in which the protagonist's acquisition of knowledge and accretion of past experience is played out in the service of recurrent, generic thrills. Given its overt engagement with the genre in which it participates, the *Scream* series has unsurprisingly attracted considerable academic attention relating to its self-reflexive qualities and debates around postmodernism.[19] Space does not allow for a full engagement with the latter, but it is relevant here in that the development of the character of Sidney (Neve Campbell) through the acquisition of knowledge and experience over the course of *Scream* (1996) and its first two sequels (1997, 2000) is directly informed by what might usefully be understood as a development of her generic competence. *Scream* establishes Sidney as a character already affected by experiences prior to its own story, haunted by the murder of her mother and with attendant 'intimacy issues', which, although the film avoids making an explicit psychological connection, are seen to be the cause of her disdain towards 'scary movies'. When asked by the masked killer (in one of his trademark anonymous phone calls) why she doesn't watch them, she explains that 'they're all the same. Some stupid killer stalking some big breasted girl who can't act, who's always running up the stairs when she should be running out the front door.' What follows immediately thereafter is a confrontation with the killer in which Sidney is herself forced to run upstairs because the front door is bolted shut, trapped, as it were, not only within the house but within the conventions of a genre she dislikes. As the film progresses and the violence escalates, however, we witness her gradual appropriation of the rules of this particular game. In choosing to shed her virginity, she flouts one of the rules for horror-movie survival proffered by film geek Randy (Jamie Kennedy). Later, in the climactic confrontation with the killers (one of whom, it transpires, is her boyfriend Billy [Skeet Ulrich]), she shoots Billy in the head as he is about to 'rise from the dead for one last scare' – another genre convention described by Randy. This inversion of the rules is underscored by her follow-up line: 'Not in my movie.' *Scream* thus represents Sidney's development, and ultimate victory, in terms of her ability to repurpose and reject the rules of the horror genre as suits her need for survival.

How, then, do *Scream 2* (1997) and *Scream 3* (2000) negotiate between the need to acknowledge their returning protagonists' prior experiences and the need to provide a similar set of pleasures? Centrally, I would suggest, in four ways: first, in a trope familiar to the horror genre, by introducing new characters who are unaware of the pre-existing rules; second, by establishing situations in which a different set of rules apply, meaning that new lessons must be learnt before the threat can be overcome; third, by turning Sidney's knowledge into one of the obstacles; and, last, by intensifying the level of potential threat. The first of these needs little explanation: transferring the main site of the action to a university campus in *Scream 2*, and then to Hollywood in *Scream 3*, ensures a ready supply of new and therefore unwitting (if still cine-literate) victims, from the class of college film students in the former, to the group of film-makers involved in the production of *Stab 3* in the latter. The second is in many ways equally straightforward, although it is bound up with the third in that Sidney's increased preparedness necessitates that the killer resort to ever more ingenious tactics to hunt her down. Thus, in *Scream 2* her dorm-room telephone has call-tracing capability, making the first film's anonymous phone calls impossible, and in *Scream 3* she is living as a recluse in a secluded, rural locale, working from home under a pseudonym. At the same time, this preparedness, this product of prior experience, becomes an obstacle in itself. The intimacy issues, one of Sidney's defining characteristics in *Scream*, have mutated into a broader lack of trust which impedes her progress in its sequels: in the second film, despite his pleas, she is wary of her boyfriend Derek (Jerry O'Connell) and will not untie him from the stage rigging in the climactic scene, leaving both of them at the mercy of one of the true killers, Mickey (Timothy Olyphant); in *Scream 3*, again in the climactic scene, her hesitation in trusting Detective Kincaid (Patrick Dempsey) grants the killer time to strike. Sidney's paranoia is repeatedly proven to be entirely justified, and in this respect it is an example of the manner in which the *Scream* sequels utilise self-perpetuating cycles of behaviour to generate repetitive pleasures: Sidney's experiences reinforce her paranoia, which in turn (inadvertently) initiates a process of stalking, the deaths of her associates and her resultant inability to trust those who can help, ensuring that she must ultimately use her own initiative to overcome her antagonist(s).

Such repetitions drive not only the development of the fabula across *Scream 2* and *3*, but also create individual moments of surprise and suspense. This is exemplified by the scene in *Scream 3* in which Sidney is stalked around the studio backlot, ultimately finding herself trapped in a set replicating her old family home in Woodsboro. Entering the house, Sidney first revisits a simulacrum of her old bedroom,[20] in which excerpts of dialogue from her first bedroom scene with Billy in *Scream* ('Would you settle for a PG-13 relationship?') infiltrate the soundtrack, connoting the return of old memories. She turns to look out of the window and then, suspecting she may be in danger, blocks herself in using the door of her closet, a move which recalls her actions in two scenes from the first film: the first in which she prevents her father entering so that he won't see Billy hiding behind the bed; the second during her first confrontation with the killer in which she is forced to run upstairs rather than out of the front door. At this point in *Scream 3*, she backs towards the window, warily staring at the blocked bedroom door, at which point the killer suddenly appears behind the window and grabs her from behind. Once again, the film suggests, Sidney's accreted experience can only protect her for so long. Crucially, too, this moment specifically exploits our own knowledge of Sidney's past

'Not in my movie …': Sidney Prescott (Neve Campbell) is front and centre of the official UK
poster for *Scream 3* (2000)

and even the specifics of her prior actions, in order not only to generate a greater resonance
but also to facilitate a surprising variation on familiar events; the killer's appearance through the
window rather than from behind the door. While this scene overtly displays the machinations
of the film-making process, at the same time its primary reference point is not the broader
family of slasher movies but rather the 'real' events of its predecessor. On the one hand, this
counterpointing between the real and the cinematic lends the sequels a surface similarity with
their originary film, steeping events in ever-thickening layers of self-reflexivity. On the other, it
motivates the recurrent presence of both Sidney and her two fellow protagonists, reporter
Gale Weathers (Courtney Cox) and Woodsboro police deputy Dewey (David Arquette), by
creating a connection between the current crimes and past events. Defeating masked psycho-
paths is not Sidney's profession, but the media industry's continual publicising and fictionalising
of her past provides a plausible context in which that past can (both literally and metaphori-
cally) come back to haunt her again and again, thus ensuring repetitive, generic thrills.

This brings us to two observations about the generic nature of the Hollywood sequel. First,
while it is clear that most Hollywood sequels conform to Christopher Richards's notion of the
'consolidatory', in that they seek 'to reinforce the set patterns, tropes and formulaic tendencies
of the first part', it is important to acknowledge that the process of sequelisation culminates in
a paradoxical situation in which, as observed in relation to *The Thin Man*, the elements that distinguished the original film from others within its genre are the very elements most likely to be
repeated by its successor(s).[21] Thus *Home Alone* sequels (1992–2002) invariably pit a young
boy against adult criminals; each Hardy family film features at least one father–son talk between
Andy and his father the Judge; and Detective Axel Foley always ignores his superiors' strict

instructions not to investigate the central mystery in *Beverly Hills Cop* and its two sequels (1987, 1994). In the sequel form, then, there is a tendency for what was previously novel to become formulaic, for variation to become repetition. *Scream* is both an exemplar and an exception in this regard, representing a particularly sophisticated instance of a sequel turning these repetitions to its narrative advantage.

Formation and fluctuation: extratextual influence

While thus far I have discussed genre formation in the sequel primarily as a formal process, it is important to acknowledge that this process is not taking place in a vacuum, and is always subject to the influence of extratextual factors. Hollywood sequels tend to be influenced by two sets of intersecting extratextual forces: those commercial factors specific to a given production, which guide the nature of a sequel's repetitions; and developments in the broader genre with which a sequel or series is associated, resulting in that sequel evincing noticeable shifts in presentation, tone or structure from those of its predecessor.

It is here that the role of the first sequel in this process of formula formation comes into view, a role that is, unsurprisingly, mitigated by its commercial performance relative to that of the first film. *Rambo: First Blood Part II* (1985) was a huge box-office hit, out-grossing *First Blood* by more than three to one.[22] It is unsurprising therefore that *Part II* effectively served as a blueprint for subsequent sequels: *Rambo III* and *Rambo*. It was the sparkling commercial success of the second film, rather than the solid results of the first film, that the makers of subsequent sequels wished to emulate. Thus, while many sequels are modelled closely on the first film, sometimes a second film does usurp its predecessor to become the principal template for subsequent instalments. Consequently, although the makers of *Rambo: First Blood Part II* retained some similarities to the first film, they largely forwent the mournful tone of *First Blood* in favour of an overtly patriotic triumphalism and an emphasis on mechanised combat and explosive action. Moreover, whereas *First Blood* pitted army vet and combat expert John Rambo against United States law enforcement and the military, the principal adversaries in the second film were Vietnamese soldiers and the Soviet military. *Part II* thus establishes a more easily repeatable template; centring on a single mission, which is introduced and resolved within a relatively discrete narrative unit, concluding with the hero free to repeat these actions in subsequent instalments.

One might identify a teleological bent to this account, in that the influence of the first sequel and/or the original film on subsequent instalments can only be fully grasped in retrospect, forcing us to read earlier instalments in the light of their successors. And yet to identify that influence is not to suggest it persists either without specific acts of maintenance or free of varying levels of modification. For all of their structural similarities, *Rambo* is quite different in tone to *Rambo III*, and it is precisely because the sequel must provide some form of novelty that the conventions of any given series, like those of any genre, will always be in a state of flux.

Other extratextual influences on the sequel can come from developments within its category and from the broader commercial context of mainstream cinema. Technological developments, of which the shifting standards in special effects are perhaps the most obvious example, can affect the development of presentational conventions across sequels. The representation of Yoda, ancient Jedi master, in the two *Star Wars* trilogies is a locus for such shifts. In *The Empire Strikes Back* and *Return of the Jedi* the character is embodied by a puppet, voiced and controlled by Frank Oz. In *Star Wars Episode I: The Phantom Menace* (1999) he appears in both puppet form and as a computer-generated image, while in *Star Wars Episode II: Attack of the Clones* (2002) and *Star Wars Episode III: Revenge of the Sith* (2005) he is solely a CGI creation. Because these films depict events chronologically prior to the first trilogy, Yoda's changing appearance might be understood in terms of his relative youth, but, however closely the CGI is modelled upon the original puppet, the difference remains perceptible.

Exemplifying the confluence of multiple forms of extratextual influence is *Belles on Their Toes*, sequel to *Cheaper by the Dozen*. Based on the family memoirs of the same name of Frank B. Gilbreth Jr and Ernestine Gilbreth, *Cheaper by the Dozen* follows the exploits of eccentric industrial engineer Frank Gilbreth (Clifton Webb), his wife Lillian (Myrna Loy) and their twelve children, as narrated by eldest daughter Ann (Jeanne Crain). Largely episodic in structure and light in tone, the film shifts gear in its final minutes when Frank collapses suddenly and dies on his way to speak at a conference in Europe – all of which occurs off screen. In the final scene, Lillian announces that she will go to the conference and speak on Frank's behalf. As she then climbs the family staircase, pausing to look at the family photograph hanging halfway up, Ann's voiceover returns to explain that the family will survive, and that, after the conference, Lillian will follow in Frank's footsteps to 'become the foremost woman industrial engineer in the world'. The absence of Frank, and therefore Clifton Webb, inevitably meant that any cinematic adaptation of *Belles on Their Toes* could not exactly replicate the format of its predecessor, whose action was driven largely by his eccentricities. Frank's decisions are not only the primary motor for events (beginning with his announcement in the opening scene that they must move from Providence to Mont Clair) but also the central source of comedy, as exemplified by the scene in which he aims to demonstrate to his children the benefits of having one's tonsils removed by undergoing the operation himself, without general anaesthetic. It is no surprise, therefore, that Daryl F. Zanuck and producer Samuel Engel looked beyond the original film for inspiration when planning the sequel. Their approach is summarised by a memo from Zanuck to Engel in which the production head explains that 'The whole idea is to make this semi-musical for a price no more than the cost of TAKE CARE OF MY LITTLE GIRL. The ingredients are very similar,' while cautioning that 'The present script is at least 20 pages too long allowing for the musical numbers.'[23] *Take Care* was still a few months from release at the time of Zanuck's memo, but would prove a modest hit in July 1951 and, crucially, starred Jeanne Crain – at that time one of the studio's most popular contract players.[24] Although her vocals were usually dubbed, Crain's association with musical numbers had begun with an early role in *State Fair* (1945), and Zanuck's instructions reflect the need to reposition *Belles* as a star vehicle for Crain in Webb's absence, as indicated by his request that Engels 'place more emphasis' on the role of Ann as he developed the screenplay.[25] Subsequently, *Belles* not only sees Ann take on greater prominence, but also devotes far more time to music and musical numbers than its predecessor. The first of these, 'Being Lazy', appears within the first five minutes and sets the predominant template for the subsequent numbers in that it is sung communally by the family. This use of music is not a complete departure from *Cheaper by the Dozen*, but rather expands upon a key moment from that film, in which the family sing 'When You Wore a Tulip (and I Wore a Big Red Rose)' on their road trip to Mont Clair; a moment whose significance is retrospectively heightened in *Belles* when it appears in flashback, as one of Lillian's happiest memories, in the film's closing scene. Nonetheless, the prevalence of musical numbers, alongside the absence of Clifton Webb, means that *Belles* has less screen time in which to recount fabula events and that it places less emphasis on comedy. Here, then, we can see how narrative developments (Frank's death) intersect with film-specific extratextual concerns (the subsequent need to transform the sequel into a suitable vehicle for Jeanne Crain) and broader production trends (the contemporary popularity of the musical) to affect the development of a sequel.

A more recent extratextual influence on sequel formation is the trend towards the 'reboot', which seeks to attract new audiences while also enticing pre-existing fans with the promise of a revisionist, or at least more contemporary, approach to a familiar character or fictional world. As earlier chapters have indicated, the practice of rebooting is not new, with casting changes from one series film to the next a commonplace in the studio era, particularly when the property was losing its commercial lustre. The James Bond series (1962–) has regularly rebooted, albeit primarily in relation to different actors being cast as Bond, but its most recent transformation represents one of the best examples of the influence of extratextual forces on structure, tone and presentation. At the presentational level, both *Casino Royale* (2006) and *Quantum of Solace* draw heavily on their generic peers, in particular the Bourne films (2002–), featuring kinetic action sequences shot with handheld cameras, while the action itself includes 'parkour' in *Casino* and, in *Quantum*, a rooftop chase much like that featured in *The Bourne Ultimatum*. Tonally, the film is darker than most of its predecessors, with a greater focus on violence and its consequences and with Bond conducting himself in a less gentlemanly and more brutish fashion – exemplified by *Casino Royale*'s opening flashbacks, in which Bond is shown killing an adversary in cold blood. Perhaps the most striking departure, however, is the manner in which *Quantum*'s narrative is structured in relation to its predecessor. Previously, the Bond films had largely adhered to a traditional series format, with each instalment functioning as a discrete episode and, with a few exceptions, little attempt to acknowledge any chronological relationship between events over the course

James Bond (Daniel Craig) gets caught up in a rooftop chase in *Quantum of Solace* (2008) which recalls *The Bourne Ultimatum* (2007)

of the series. Recalling Umberto Eco's description of Superman, the Bond stories generally marked a 'withdrawal from the tension of past-present-future',[26] with the episode-specific mission completed by the film's conclusion. *Casino Royale*, by contrast, concludes on a more open-ended and uncertain note. Bond's romantic interest, Vesper Lynd (Eva Green), is dead and the film's final scene depicts Bond walking towards a mysterious figure we presume to be Mr White the man he believes responsible for her death. *Quantum of Solace* picks up moments later, with Bond taking Mr White back to MI6 headquarters for interrogation and subsequently follows 007's attempts to avenge Vesper. This transforms the conventional Bond narrative from one revolving around a mission of international importance to one driven by its protagonist's personal vendetta. Perhaps inevitably, the latter ultimately evolves into a variation on the former, with the trail that began with Mr White leading Bond to foil the plans of Mr Greene (Mathieu Amalric) to steal and trade on Bolivia's water supply. Such narrative continuities mean that *Quantum* is the first instance of a fully fledged sequel in the long history of the Bond series, moving it away from the series format and so away from what has in the past twenty years become a largely disused mode of seriality.[27] Instances such as this are rare indeed, but then Bond itself is exceptional, its longevity meaning that it is one of the most enduring bellwethers of trends which are external to the logic of its fictional world, but which resonate there, nonetheless.

The sequel as conventional

The heightened level of continuity between *Casino Royale* and *Quantum of Solace* is indicative of not only the long-running series' particular susceptibility to exterior generic trends, but also the manner in which the Hollywood sequel has its own form of genericity. As I hope this chapter has made clear, this is not to suggest that we should conceptualise the sequel in the same manner as we do the horror, Western or musical genres – but we must also acknowledge that sequelisation is itself governed by a historically fluid set of conventions or compositional norms which may influence, or indeed be influenced by, the construction of any given instance of the form; and that these norms are subject to developments and trends which cut across all genres and subgenres of Hollywood film-making.

As with the changes which take place within the traditionally recognised genres, these trends are often highly superficial. Surveying the list of sequels in the appendix, for example, it quickly becomes apparent that conventions in titling have shifted over time. Early and studio-era sequel titles tended towards the descriptive, using linguistic and grammatical echoes of the original (*Four Wives* following *Four Daughters*, *Whistling in Dixie* following *Whistling in the Dark*, *Dear Brat* [1951] following *Dear Ruth* [1947] and *Dear Wife* [1949]) which often also hinted at the nature of the continuation (*The Son of the Sheik*, *Bride of Frankenstein*, *Tarzan's New York Adventure*, *Andy Hardy Meets Debutante* [1940], *Gidget Goes to Rome* [1963], *Beneath the Planet of the Apes*) or simply made clear that continuation was in order (*Topper Returns* [1941], *The Return of Frank James* [1940], *Jolson Sings Again* and so on) and tended (as with the series film) to anchor their titles around the name of the central protagonist. It was not until the 1970s that numbering began to take hold, explicitly denoting a sequel's chronological relationship with its predecessor. While the first such film from a major studio was *The Godfather: Part II* in 1974, the independent production *Deep Throat: Part II* (1974), sequel to the hugely successful adult film starring Linda Lovelace, had also played in American cinemas earlier that same year. Shortly thereafter, *French Connection II* (1975) simplified further by removing 'Part', although on some advertising the Roman numerals were replaced with '2', making this the first Hollywood film to advertise itself with the numeric marker that would later become so prevalent. Labelling a sequel 'Part II' or 'Part 2' remained common practice throughout the 1970s and early 80s, although sequels increasingly followed the pared down *French Connection* example. Later in the 1970s, *The Exorcist II: The Heretic* (1977) was the first film to pair a number with a descriptive subtitle, a move subsequently followed by other horror sequels, including *Damien: Omen II* (1978), *Piranha II: The Spawning* (1981) and *Amityville II: The Possession* (1982). Despite being satirised by *Airplane II: The Sequel* (1982), this particular trend persisted in the horror field (*Halloween III: Season of the Witch*, *Friday the 13th Part IV: The Final Chapter*) and spread to other genres, as indicated by *Porky's II: The Next Day*, *Star Trek II: The Wrath of Khan*, *The Care Bears Movie II: The Next Generation* (1985) and *Superman IV: The Quest for Peace* (1987) among others. In the early 2000s, there was a move away from the use of numbers or numerals, with some of the most successful sequels (including those in the *Matrix*, *Harry Potter*, *Bourne* and *Lord of the Rings* franchises) and even some lesser ones (*Bring It On: All or Nothing* [2006], *Dirty Dancing: Havana Nights* [2004]) shunning them altogether, opting instead for the more descriptive titling of the studio era; a trend prefigured by the self-conscious homage to that earlier paratextual format paid by the Indiana Jones titles. Most of these standard title formations have coexisted since the 1970s, with *Sex and the City 2* (2010) and *Iron Man 2* (2010) more recently foregoing a descriptive subtitle, thus underscoring the fact that these are tendencies rather than absolutes.

These paratextual shifts arguably reflect more significant developments in the sequel's formal characteristics; developments touched upon throughout the historical account in the first four chapters. As I hope has become clear, the sequel form has tended to inhabit the space between the episodic, discrete units of the series-film format and the more closely intertwined segments of the later silent serials. While many of the same narrative strategies have persisted throughout its century-long history, it is also evident that at certain historical moments it has tended to gravitate closer to one or the other of these points on the spectrum. These shifts are the result of an interlocking set of historical, commercial and aesthetic circumstances. Thus we can ascribe Hollywood's moves towards or away from multi-part storytelling (by which I mean sequels, series films and serials), along with trends towards or away from narrative continuity within the sequel itself, as being a result of pre-existing tendencies within those genres popular at a given historical moment; tendencies in the nature of their source material (the popularity of the highly reiterative detective, horror and comic-book genres in the 1930s, 70s and 2000s respectively, set against the dominance of the standalone musical and historical epic in the 1950s and 60s); the industrial circumstances which encouraged particular modes of serial production, from the demand for B-movies in the 1930s to the boom in direct-to-video sequels created by the DVD market in the early 2000s; and, last, to storytelling trends in other media. All of these factors may come to bear on trends within sequelisation at any given time. The recent shift towards narrative continuity in the James Bond series is a case in point, in that it is reflective of each of these factors. While it seems clear that the *Bourne* films have influenced both the respective compositions of *Casino Royale* and *Quantum of Solace* and the level of narrative inter-connection between them, it is also evident that the latter has become more prevalent not only within this particular genre but also throughout contemporary Hollywood sequel pro-duction, particularly in those films designated as blockbusters.

In Chapter 7 I argued that, even within an intricately connected series such as *The Lord of the Rings*, individual episodes still maintained a discrete coherence that allowed for, if not a full appreciation, then at least a degree of standalone comprehensibility. This does not diminish, however, the prevailing evidence that there has been a move towards the introduction of the 'dangling cause' in the final moments of the Hollywood blockbuster,[28] pointing the way to future narrative events that might be played out in a sequel. In part this relates to the source material for much blockbuster cinema since the 1990s, material which has pre-established sequel potential in that it is part of a preordained saga or series (the *Bourne, Harry Potter, Da Vinci Code* and *Twilight* novels) or derives from a traditionally serialised format such as the comic book, video game or television series. More broadly, we might say that this shift is reflective of similar changes taking place across the entertainment landscape. Recent critical writing on tel-evision and comic books indicates that ongoing narratives rather than discrete episodes have, since the 1970s, become increasingly prevalent in both media,[29] while the rather younger video-game industry has incorporated such strategies almost since its inception.[30] Have the movies been influenced by television, comic books and video games, or vice versa? We can only speculate on patterns of influence, but the fact that this development has been largely syn-chronic across media suggests that it would be unwise to assume, as Kristin Thompson does, that film has been influenced by television – not least because it was from cinema and radio that television first inherited the serial format.

The enhanced seriality of *Quantum* emerges, then, as representative of generic shifts at both a micro and macro level: shifts in the spy and action-thriller genre as represented by the *Bourne* series; shifts in the construction of the Hollywood sequel which place increasing stress on narrative integration; and shifts across entertainment media towards serialisation. As with any genre, these shifts are not convincingly explained in purely formal or aesthetic terms, the bigger picture becoming visible only if we acknowledge that, from the choice of suitable source material onwards, they are reflective of contemporary Hollywood's industrial drive to create not single films but franchises; ventures which build on a pre-existing audience and which lay the ground not only for future films, but also for adaptations of those films in other media and related consumer products.[31] One might question the unique contemporaneity of this indus-trial mindset, but it is clear that the sequel's current compositional norms, its generic conven-tions, are as intrinsically linked to this particular historical context as the series film was to the studio system in the 1930s.

This focus on the franchise is just another iteration of the proprietary impulses which have governed film production in Hollywood since the 1910s, impulses which are both a reac-tion against and a spur to the development of genres, driving the practice of product differ-entiation but also inspiring cinematic imitation from competing producers. As I hope this chapter has demonstrated, while the process of sequelisation is subject to many of the same extratextual forces as the process of genre formation, the sequel itself resists straightforward comparisons to the broader workings of genre. It must walk a tightrope between these two modes, differentiating itself from while also imitating its predecessor, developing its characters while also ensuring they are involved in similar situations, and moving its narrative forward in time without moving away from the pleasures which the original provided.

As a result of these distinguishing features, the Hollywood sequel affords a glimpse into the formation of generic conventions which is both enlightening and misleading. It is enlightening because it facilitates identification of the process of genrification across a growing family of films, and allows us to speak with some confidence about the patterns of influence, creative personnel and audience expectations informing that process. It is misleading, however, because we must remember that this process is skewed by the sequel's need to evince some level of narrative continuity with a prior film. Rooted as it is in the temporality of narrative fiction, the Hollywood sequel must be like its predecessor, but, with time both real and fictional marching on, it can never be quite the same.

Conclusion
The Hollywood sequel:
A story complete in itself

In its review of *The Romance of Tarzan* in 1918, *Wids Daily* advised its readership of theatre owners that they 'lay particular stress on the fact that this takes up the story where the other film left off', while also making plain to their customers 'that it is not necessary that they saw the first film in order to understand and enjoy this, which is a story complete in itself'.[1] The previous year, the floundering Kalem Company had announced intentions to produce films which would be 'a combination of a series and a serial … a serial inasmuch as there will be a continued thread of interest, and a series inasmuch as each episode will be a complete story in itself'.[2] Echoing the words of the subtitle which introduced *His Trust* and *His Trust Fulfilled* back in 1911, these two reports underscore a central conundrum in the development of the sequel in Hollywood: how to create, market and exhibit a film which continued the narrative and traded on the popularity of its predecessor(s), but which would also successfully function as both a standalone artwork and, crucially, a standalone commercial enterprise?

This question had particular pertinence during the 1910s, before the feature film had overtaken other narrative formats to become the cornerstone of Hollywood's output, thus necessitating the kind of clarification for audiences advised by *Wids*. One underlying thrust of this book, however, has been that in many ways the Hollywood sequel has continued to be shaped by such intertwined formal and economic concerns – and that understanding it as an artwork demands that we simultaneously understand it as the commercial product of an ever-changing industry. This understanding, furthermore, must be rooted in the knowledge that the sequel is defined as such by a bipartite temporal relationship: on the one hand, between the fictional present and its fictional past; and on the other hand, between the sequel as it is produced and consumed in the material world, and the production and consumption of its predecessor. In approaching the form of the Hollywood sequel, I have attempted to address these two relationships, first, between narrative artwork and commercial product and second, between fictional chronology and 'real-world' chronology, and further to understand the various ways in which they might intersect with and impact upon each other. In conclusion, therefore, I want to briefly recount some key points of intersection, while also indicating how this study of the sequel might be fruitfully continued.

Cause and effect: narrative comprehension and the sequel form

A long time ago I said that a film is an answer and a TV show is a question, because on a TV show you are constantly looking for more, and finding more. On a movie you've got to take everything out and distil it to its finest essence. When you're into the sequel of a movie you're sort of in a little bit of both worlds. You are expecting that people know something about what's going on, but you have to assume that some don't.

Joss Whedon, writer/director of The Avengers and The Avengers 2[3]

If we can say that a defining characteristic of the Hollywood sequel is its attempt to achieve a standalone coherence, it is clear that this stems directly from the same artful inclusiveness underlying the Wids reviewer's comments on Tarzan, which in turn derives from an opportunistic imperative to address two sets of hypothetical viewers: those who have either not seen the previous film, or do not fully remember the story it told; and those who are returning having seen and enjoyed the sequel's antecedent(s). As I demonstrated in Chapter 5, the perceived need to accommodate uninitiated viewers has encouraged attempts to maintain a discrete level of basic narrative comprehensibility, and a tendency towards the kind of open-door chronology which ensures that we are almost invariably made aware (or reminded) of those events from the previous film relevant to story developments in its sequel. More broadly, it has also ensured that the majority of Hollywood sequels concern themselves as much with initiating new plotlines as with developing those from an earlier film, offering a micro-fabula which maintains a largely autonomous coherence, even when it contributes to the macro-fabula of an ongoing series such as Rambo, and thus rendering them more episodic than their chronological relationship with an earlier film would suggest.

While the above results in part from the need to remain accessible to new viewers, which in turn derives from the need to maximise commercial returns, the Hollywood sequel can be characterised by its simultaneous attentiveness to an audience who are better acquainted with its predecessor. Hence the recurrence of what I have termed the 'McClane Principle', as outlined in Chapter 6, which dictates that sequels will frequently address a returning audience in a parenthetical and often humorous fashion, referring back to earlier events but with only minimal effect on the progression of the micro-fabula at hand. In a broader sense, as discussed in Chapter 7, the McLane Principle points to the challenges inherent in producing an artwork which must both take story and characters forward, but must also replicate the pleasures of its predecessor in a manner which can best be described as generic. Different sequels resort to different methods to justify their echoing of earlier events, a task made necessary because the need to furnish a similar set of pleasures tends to necessitate the provision of a similar set of narrative situations: another basement, another elevator and yet more terrorists. When character arcs, situations, lines of dialogue or jokes recur over two or more films, so it is that those films become micro-generic, developing tropes and conventions specific to the series of which they are part, while also contributing to the broader pool of generic tropes at a macro level.

In serving two audiences, one cognisant of past fictional events, the other less so, the sequel is perennially faced with the challenge of delivering familiar pleasures in a new guise, while telling a story that is at once serial and episodic, picking up where a previous film left off and yet complete in itself. That this central division between audiences has not changed provides some explanation as to why the form of the Hollywood sequel appears to have undergone only modest changes in the past century and why in turn my poetics has tended to stress its transhistorical qualities, rather than to trace a modulating aesthetic history. One major development has been a general drift, beginning in the 1970s and intensifying since the 90s, towards greater film-to-film continuity, with the feature-film sequel edging slightly further in the direction of the serial and away from the discrete episodic mode. Just as Jason Mittell has posited in relation to a similar development in contemporary American television, it seems probable that this shift has in part been facilitated by the growth of an on-demand viewing culture since the advent of video in the early 1980s, with prerecorded technology enabling a greater potential recall of past fictional events.[4] There is clearly more to be said about this development in the sphere of feature film – not least about the industry's economic incentives for encouraging such a culture, via, for example, DVD and Blu-ray boxset sales and VOD transactions– and I point to it here as indication of how future critical enquiry into the sequel form might develop.

Effects and cause: the industry and the sequel

Although the formal characteristics of the Hollywood sequel can usefully be understood in relation to the needs of its two intended audiences, this does not so fully explain why it has been an enduring feature of the industry's output for the best part of a century. In the broad historical sweep of Chapters 1 through 4, I have sought to trace the fluctuating impact of industrial change upon sequel production, while also teasing out some recurrent tendencies and continuities – the latter serving as a corrective to the contemporaneous slant which has characterised much prior academic and popular critical engagement with the form. Perhaps most notably among these, when demand for feature film has outweighed supply – with the growth of the double bill in the 1930s, the video boom of the mid-80s, and the DVD boom of the early 2000s – there has been a concomitant increase in the production of one or more forms of low-budget seriality. Something similar occurs whenever a new audience sector is identified via an unexpected, cheaply produced hit, as was briefly the case with the 'Blaxploitation' cycle in the early 1970s, and the 'slasher' cycle in the early 80s.

As these patterns suggest, there is more than one industrial context from which a sequel might emerge, and, while every sequel will in some sense be seeking to exploit the success of its predecessor, success cannot always be measured solely in terms of box-office returns. While we can assume that sequel production is almost invariably commercially motivated, there are often additional factors in play. Economies of scale, via the recycling of sets, props and costumes (or their digital equivalent), might make it more commercially viable to sequelise than to create a new fictional environment. Particularly in the studio era, but also more recently with DTV production, a sequel might be an expedient way of ensuring that contract staff are kept at work or that studio facilities are continually in use. And, while for some studios a sequel may be one among many production options, for a fledgling or financially insecure film company, such as Universal in the 1930s or New Line, Cannon and Carolco in the 80s, a sequel may be more of an economic necessity, a means by which to establish itself or simply to survive within a highly competitive marketplace. Equally, for the creative talent involved, although it may well represent a chance to secure a higher fee, there are other, less fiscally tangible enticements: in the case of Leo McCarey and The Bell's of St. Marys, for example, the ability to dictate the terms of one's contract with a studio; for Rudolph Valentino with The Son of the Sheik and Sylvester Stallone with Rambo, the opportunity to revive one's flagging career and reputation within the industry; or, with James Whale and *Bride of Frankenstein* and Joe Dante and *Gremlins 2: The New Batch*, the opportunity to exercise complete creative control with minimal studio interference.

Just as I have distinguished the sequel from other narrative formats while acknowledging the porous, historically specific nature of the boundaries between them, so, in this chronological survey, I have sought to situate the sequel within a succession of other histories: that of the serial and series in the early 1900s; of the rise of double bill and B-movie production in the 30s; of the studio era's vertical integration and long-term contract system; of the preference for standalone, roadshown epics in response to the rise of television in the 50s and 60s; the rise of video and the pre-sale in the 80s; the absorption of the Hollywood studios into large multimedia conglomerates in the 90s and so forth. While it is a story complete in itself, therefore, the history of the Hollywood sequel as both an aesthetic object and a commercial product can be fully appreciated only in relation to its industrial context.

The end is just the beginning

As the question with which I began suggests, this study has concerned itself primarily with the 'how' of the sequel. How have film-makers approached the various challenges inherent in creating a sequel? How has the form of the sequel been a response to the industrial conditions in which it is produced and consumed? How do sequels differ from other forms of extended storytelling in cinema and elsewhere? And how do they address viewers with differing levels of access to fabula information? We might usefully build from the account provided here to consider some other 'how' questions. How might the form of the cinematic sequel differ or have differed in other national, historical and industrial contexts, for example? And how applicable is the poetics I have developed in this book to the sequel in other narrative art-forms? Addressing such questions would enable us to distinguish between a set of transnational and transhistorical norms and those characteristics specific to Hollywood.

Because answers to 'how' questions have dominated, it has not been within the scope of this book to fully consider the 'why' of the sequel, particularly in relation to issues of consumption. Chapters 1 through 4 provide at least some indication of why the *industry* has turned to sequel production on a regular basis, but, of course this does not explain why *audiences* would want to watch them – often in very large numbers. I would like to draw this book to a close, therefore, by forwarding two modest hypotheses in response to the why of the sequel's popularity, which might form the basis for future study:

1 Just as the sequel reduces the perceived risks for the producer-financier, so it reduces risk for the viewer: the risk that what is being paid for will not be worth our money or time. The producer's rationale, 'the last one made money, so will this', thus finds itself echoed in the consumer's rationale, 'I enjoyed the last one, I should also enjoy this.'
2 That, while its potential to offer repetitive pleasures should not be ignored or undervalued, the sequel also has the potential, as with multi-part narratives in other media, to comment on characters' lived experience over time, and to create a more nuanced and richer engagement between audience and character than is within the remit of a single feature film; not

least because it has the option to synchronise the amount of time which has passed in our lives with that of the characters.

While the first of these hypotheses suggests the transactional nature of the sequel as a commodity within a marketplace, the second assumes that the sequel can and occasionally does offer audiences something beyond reliability, and so demonstrates another explanation for the form's popularity with audiences. Reliability is as worthy a quality in entertainment as it might be in any other product or service, and I do not wish to denigrate either the aesthetic value in the repetitious pleasures offered by the Hollywood sequel, nor the audience's right to seek the same. What I would like to propose, however, is that narrative continuation is not only the sequel's defining characteristic but also one of its main springboards for pleasure, even when those pleasures recall its predecessor.

Consider this moment from *Toy Story 3* (2010), in which college-bound teenager Andy has placed all of his old toys, bar Woody the cowboy, in a refuse bag. As he is about to take the bag up to the attic, Andy is distracted by his sister and so leaves it on the landing, only for his mother to appear and, assuming the bag is 'trash', take it down to the street in preparation for an imminent refuse collection. Determined to rescue his friends from the dumpster, Woody attempts to hail Andy's pet dog, whistling loudly and calling out 'Buster, come 'ere boy, come 'ere!' As he does so the film cuts to a wider shot, leaving an area of anticipatory space, and there is an accompanying flourish on the musical score, suggesting a heroic entrance. Our expectation is undercut when Buster lumbers slowly into the frame, his fur flecked with grey and stomach hanging down, panting exhaustedly at the effort involved in mustering even this small burst of motion. Woody leaps on Buster's back, yelling 'Okay boy, to the kerb!' – at which point his putative canine steed yawns and rolls over, crushing Woody in the process. This action recalls an equivalent moment in *Toy Story 2*, in which toy penguin Wheezy is plucked from the shelf by Andy's mother for inclusion in a yard sale taking place outside. Woody whistles for Buster, who comes bounding in. Woody jumps from his place on the bookshelf, lands on the dog's back, and cries, 'Okay boy, to the yard sale!' With Woody in tow, Buster then gallops heroically down the stairs, drops him off at the yard sale, and then carries Wheezy to safety as instructed.

Toy Story 3 is full of vignettes such as this, which encapsulate much about the potential pleasures a sequel might offer, and also indicate why we cannot simply describe such pleasures as repetitious. Clearly there is more than one manner in which this scene might be enjoyed and, as ever, one need not have seen *Toy Story 2* in order to take something from it. Yet the full effect of this moment, its humour and poignancy, rely on the viewer having some memory of the equivalent scene in that earlier film. It is humorous because it defies our expectations – we expect youthful, energetic Buster, we get instead his lethargic, older self – and poignant because it does so in a manner which underscores the passage of time, and the inescapable physiological progression that brings. What is particularly to be enjoyed here, then, is not repetition *per se*, but rather a variation on familiar events – a variation perceivable precisely because it occurs against a backdrop of familiarity. This symbiosis between repetition and variation, whereby the latter is rendered both visible and dramatically or comically effective because of its juxtaposition with the former, is not unique to the sequel but is nonetheless a sleight of hand which the form is particularly well placed to pull off. Taken collectively, furthermore, the manner in which the three *Toy Story* films have incrementally dramatised both the passing of childhood and the act of saying goodbye to old friends is an exemplar of the sequel form's potential to comment on human life experience via means less readily available to a single artwork.

While I am not suggesting that this is the only criteria against which we might measure a sequel's value as an art-form, it is noteworthy that many of the sequels which have attracted widespread critical praise either address issues of maturation and ageing, as with *The Son of the Sheik*, *The Godfather: Part II*, *The Empire Strikes Back*, *Before Sunset* (2004) and *Spider-Man 2*, and/or find elegant means by which to make the play of repetition and variation integral to a continuing story, as in *Terminator 2: Judgment Day* and the *Back to the Future* trilogy, whose time-travel narratives necessitate that certain past events be re-enacted in order to bring about an alternate present or future.

It seems appropriate to note at this juncture that both the sequel's challenge to Aristotelian aesthetic principles *and* its ability to comment (implicitly or explicitly) on our lived experience, derive in part from its complicating effect on matters of closure. We might say, as past critics of the sequel have often done, that this unravelling of closure is the result of nostalgic, conservative wish-fulfilment, allowing us to re-experience fondly remembered pleasures. This it might well be. But moving beyond an original happy ending also means acknowledging that life does not resolve itself so neatly: new problems arise and old ones recur, people and situations change, life goes on. That sequels tacitly attest to these realities may have more to do with the industry's ongoing attempt to capitalise on prior successes than with any noble artistic attempt to capture the stuff of life, but this does not diminish the form's capacity to affect and engage by reminding us of the affinities between past and present, and of the proximity between an ending and a beginning.

Appendix:
Explanatory note: A statistical survey of sequels, series films, prequels and spin-offs, 1910–2009

The sequel and series-film production statistics referred to throughout this book are drawn from a survey in which I have compiled an alphabetical list of more than 1,800 sequels, prequels, series films and spin-offs – any film, in other words, which carries over characters and/or whose narrative exhibits an acknowledged chronological relationship with that of a previous film – produced and released in North America between 1911 and 2009. Also listed are the films which inspired those sequels, or which led to a series. For reasons of space, it was not possible to include the database within the finished book, but it is available for review at http://thehollywoodsequel.wordpress.com/.

This survey was compiled using various sources, primarily the Internet Movie Database (www.imdb.com), the American Film Institute Catalogue and a selection of published, encyclopaedic reference guides to cinematic seriality: Bernard Drew, *Motion Picture Series and Sequels: A Reference Guide* (New York: Garland, 1990); Robert A. Nowlan and Gwendolyn Wright Nolan, *Cinema Sequels and Remakes, 1903–87* (Jefferson, NC: McFarland, 1989); and James L. Limbacher, *Haven't I Seen You Somewhere Before? Remakes, Sequels, and Series in Motion Pictures, Video and Television, 1896–1990* (New York: Pierian, 1992).

The database incorporates various information for each entry, organised as follows:

1 TITLE – This is the title used for original release in North America.
2 YEAR OF RELEASE – The year in which it was first released in North America.
3 STUDIO – Here I have given as accurate an indication as possible as to which company financed the film's production. Where possible, I have also included the distributor, in particular when that role has been taken by a major studio. The inclusion of the latter is relevant because, particularly since the 1970s, the majors have increasingly funded independent film production via an upfront investment in distribution rights.
4 TV/DTV – This column indicates if the film first appeared on and/or was made to be broadcast on pay television (TV) or released on home video or DVD (DTV).
5 RELATED TO – If the film is not first in a series, this column indicates the film from which it originates.
6 DIRECTOR(S) – Only the officially credited director is listed.
7 STARRING – This lists the first-billed cast members. Where possible, I have included recurring actors from previous films in the series, even if their role in the sequel is relatively minor.

8 TYPE – This is divided into 'sequel', 'series', 'prequel', 'conceptual sequel', 'conceptual series', 'spin-off' and 'first film', the latter indicating the film which has been followed either by a sequel or series.

9 ORIGINARY SOURCE – This indicates the type of source material on which the first film in the series was based.

Using the information gathered here, I have been able to calculate a statistical breakdown of sequels by decade, which is summarised in Figures A.1 and A.2 on the following pages.

Inevitably, the information included is not exhaustive. There are no doubt certain films which have not been captured by my research, particularly in the period between 1911 and 1929, where the available records are unlikely to be complete. Nonetheless, I believe this represents a relatively comprehensive and representative set of data, which gives a reasonably accurate impression of the levels of sequel and series production over the past century, and the broad range of films which might be bracketed under those terms.

Summary statistics

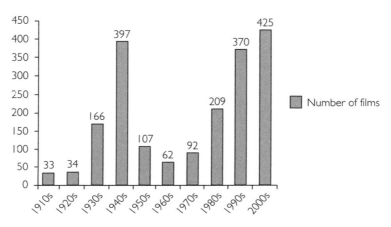

Figure A.1 Sequel and series film releases by decade

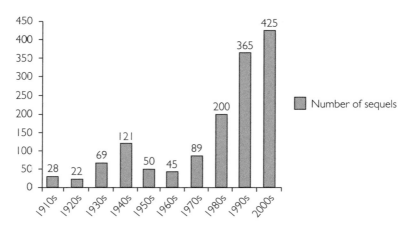

Figure A.2 Sequels only by decade

Notes

'Here we go again … again'

1. Thomas Schatz, 'The New Hollywood', in J. Collins, H. Radner and A. P. Collins (eds), *Film Theory Goes to the Movies* (New York: Routledge, 1993), p. 20.

2. Timothy Corrigan, *A Cinema without Walls: Movies and Culture after Vietnam* (New York: Rutgers University Press, 1991), pp. 167, 169.

3. Vincent Canby, 'Jaws II – Or "Did You Ever See a Shark Dancing?"', *New York Times*, 8 May 1977; Vincent Canby, 'Sequels Are a Sign of Fear', *New York Times*, 25 May 1975; Richard Corliss, 'Sequels Aren't Equals', *Time*, 20 December 1993 (http://www.time.com/time/magazine/article/ 0,9171,979869,00.html); Julie Salamon, 'The Return of Nearly Everybody', *Wall Street Journal*, 15 July 1983; Janet Maslin, 'Is It a Happy Ending if a Movie Breeds No Sequel?', *New York Times*, 6 February 1983; James Monaco, *American Film Now* (New York: New American Library, 1979); Peter Rainer, 'Sequelmania: Is It Throttling Hollywood?', *L.A. Herald-Examiner*, 8 July 1983, p. D7; Stephen M. Silverman, 'Hollywood Cloning: Sequels, Prequels, Remakes and Spin-offs', *American Film* vol. 3 no. 9 (July–August 1978), pp. 24–30; J. Hoberman, 'Ten Years That Shook the World', *American Film* vol. 10 no. 8 (June 1985), pp. 34–59.

4. Roger Hagedorn, 'Technology and Economic Exploitation: The Serial as a Form of Narrative Presentation', *Wide Angle* vol. 10 no. 4 (1988), p. 11. Hagedorn has published a revised version of this essay, in which he slightly modifies this statement, noting that

   > People may no longer flock to the cinema on Saturdays to see the latest episode of their favourite serial, but the current inundation of sequels (*Rocky I, II, III* and *IV*) and films such as *Back to the Future* illustrate this industry's renewed interest in profiting from successful narratives through continued elaboration.

   The added nuance certainly helps avoid the earlier essay's more direct conflation of serials and sequels, but it does nothing to positively distinguish these two forms and as such remains problematic. See Hagedorn, 'Doubtless to Be Continued: A Brief History of Serial Narrative', in Robert C. Allen (ed.), *To Be Continued: Soap Operas around the World* (London: Routledge, 1995), p. 40.

5. Peter Krämer, *The New Hollywood: From Bonnie and Clyde to Star Wars* (London: Wallflower, 2005), p. 92; Steve Neale, *Genre and Hollywood* (London: Routledge, 2000), pp. 247–8; Sheldon Hall and Steve Neale, *Epics, Spectacles and Blockbusters: A Hollywood History* (Detroit, MI: Wayne State University Press, 2010).

6. Thomas Simonet, 'Conglomerates and Content: Remakes, Sequels, and Series in the New Hollywood', in B. A. Austin (ed.), *Current Research in Film: Audiences, Economics, and Law*, Vol. 3 (Norwood, NJ: Ablex, 1987), pp. 154–62.

7. Simonet, 'Conglomerates and Content', p. 157.

8. Justin Wyatt, *High Concept* (Austin: University of Texas Press, 1991); Winston Wheeler Dixon, *Film Genre 2000* (New York: State University of New York Press, 2000), pp. 7–8; Kristin Thompson, *Storytelling in Film and Television* (London: Harvard University Press, 2003), pp. 75, 105; Michael Allen, *Contemporary U.S. Cinema* (London: Longman, 2003), p. 183.

9. Thompson, *Storytelling in Film and Television*, pp. 101–2; Allen, *Contemporary U.S. Cinema* pp. 187–9; Simonet, 'Conglomerates and Content', pp. 156–7; Carolyn Jess-Cooke, *Film Sequels* (Edinburgh: Edinburgh University Press, 2009), pp. 3–6.

10. For more on *Pauline*, see Ben Singer, 'Serial Melodrama and the Narrative *Gesellschaft*', *Velvet Light Trap* no. 37 (Spring 1996), pp. 72–80.

11. Jess-Cooke, *Film Sequels*, p. 5. A similar confusion is in evidence in certain essays in Constantine Verevis and Carolyn Jess-Cooke (eds), *Second Takes: Critical Approaches to the Film Sequel* (Albany: State University of New York Press, 2010). For a more detailed review of both, see Stuart Henderson, 'Review of *Film Sequels* and *Second Takes*', *Scope* 21 (October 2011) (http://www.scope. nottingham.ac.uk/bookreview.php?issue=21&id=1329).

12. Jennifer Forrest (ed.), *The Legend Returns and Dies Harder Another Day: Essays on Film Series* (Jefferson, NC: McFarland, 2008); Claire Perkins and Constantine Verevis (eds), *Film Trilogies: New Critical Approaches* (Basingstoke: Palgrave Macmillan, 2012).

13. Exemplary in this respect is Terry Castle's disquisition on Richardson's sequel to *Pamela*, from which she briefly diverts to ruminate on the nature of the form itself. Grafting Lacanian theory onto the sequel and its audiences, she suggests that readers are 'motivated by a deep unconscious nostalgia for a past reading pleasure, positioning the "charismatic original" as that which its sequel lacks, that which "it cannot literally reconstitute"'. Terry Castle, *Masquerade and Civilization: Carnivalesque in Eighteenth-century English Culture and Fiction* (London: Methuen, 1986), pp. 133–4. See also Heidi Ganner Rauth, '"To Be Continued?" Sequels and Continuations of Nineteenth Century Novels and Novel Fragments', *English Studies* vol. 64 (1983), pp. 129–43; E. C. Riley, *Don Quixote* (London: Allen & Unwin, 1986); John M. Picker, 'George Eliot and the Sequel Question', *New Literary History* vol. 37 (2006), pp. 361–88; and Michael Austin, 'The Figural Logic of the Sequel and the Unity of *Pilgrim's Progress*, *Studies in Philology* vol. 102 no. 4 (2005), pp. 485–509.

14. Gérard Genette, *Palimpsests: Literature in the Second Degree* (Lincoln: University of Nebraska Press, 1997); Christopher Paul Richards, *The Idea of the Sequel: A Theoretically Orientated Study of Literary Sequels with Special Emphasis on Three Examples from the First Half of the Eighteenth Century* (Unpublished Thesis, University of Leeds, 1989), p. 57; Umberto Eco, 'Innovation and Repetition: Between Modern and Post-Modern Aesthetics', *Daedalus* vol. 114 no. 4 (Fall 1985), pp. 161–84.

15. Eco, 'Innovation and Repetition', p. 167.

16. Forrest, *The Legend Returns and Dies Harder Another Day*, p. 7.

17. Stuart Jeffries, 'Netflix's Ted Sarandos: The "Evil Genius" behind a TV Revolution', *Guardian*, 30 December 2013 (accessed 5 January 2014: http://www.theguardian.com/media/2013/cec/30/ netflix-evil-genius-tv-revolution-ted-sarandos).

18. Perkins and Verevis, *Film Trilogies*, p. 1.

19. Distinguishing a spin-off from a sequel proper is often a matter of context. *Ma and Pa Kettle* (1949), for example, was advertised by Universal as 'the hilarious sequel to *The Egg and I*', despite the fact

that it centred on that film's supporting characters. *The Scorpion King* (2002), on the other hand, is more clearly a spin-off because the story it tells derives from *The Mummy Returns* (2001), and has no direct impact on the progression of the series' ongoing narrative, as evidenced by the arrival of *The Mummy: The Tomb of the Dragon Emperor* (2008), which picks up after *The Mummy Returns* and has no need to reference either *The Scorpion King* or its direct-to-video sequel, *The Scorpion King 2: Rise of a Warrior* (2008).

20. In this respect, one might describe my approach here as being broadly aligned with the tradition of 'historical poetics', as propounded primarily by David Bordwell, Kristin Thompson and Henry Jenkins. If not quite in line with all aspects of that tradition, I would nonetheless propose that this book is 'problem-and-question-centred' in a manner commensurate with Bordwell's definition of historical poetics, and that it represents an attempt to approach certain research questions from the bottom up, formulating responses to those questions in response to my findings, rather than a top-down attempt to mould those findings to fit a set of pre-existing historical and theoretical assumptions. See David Bordwell, 'Historical Poetics of Cinema', in Barton Palmer (ed.), *The Cinematic Text: Methods and Approaches* (Atlanta: Georgia State University Press, 1988), pp. 369–98; Henry Jenkins, 'Historical Poetics', in Joanne Hollows and Mark Jancovich (eds), *Approaches to Popular Film* (Manchester: Manchester University Press, 1995), pp. 99–122.

21. It should be noted that I am following common practice here by using the term 'Hollywood' throughout this book as a shorthand to refer to all commercial film-making in North America. Geographically, of course, this is largely inaccurate, but the vast majority of the films discussed hereafter were to some degree funded, produced and/or distributed by companies with a base in Los Angeles County.

22. For more about the methodology employed, see the accompanying note in the Appendix. To access the full database, visit http://thehollywoodsequel.wordpress.com/.

Chapter 1

1. Charles Musser, 'Moving towards Fictional Narratives: Story Films Become the Dominant Product, 1903–1904', in Lee Grieveson and Peter Krämer (eds), *The Silent Cinema Reader* (London: Routledge, 2004), pp. 87–102; Tom Gunning, 'Cinema of Attractions', in Thomas Elsaesser (ed.), *Early Cinema: Space, Frame, Narrative* (London: BFI, 1990), pp. 56–7.

2. Gérard Genette, *Palimpsests: Literature in the Second Degree* (Lincoln: University of Nebraska Press, 1997).

3. Vaudeville was certainly a common venue, but Charles Musser has identified a range of additional sites and circumstances: in churches and opera houses, by travelling exhibitors at carnivals and between acts at the theatre. See Ben Brewster, 'Periodization of Early Cinema', in Charlie Keil and Shelley Stamp (eds), *American Cinema's Transitional Era: Audiences, Institutions, Practices* (Berkeley: University of California Press, 2004), p. 69; Richard deCordova, *Picture Personalities: The Emergence of the Star System in America* (Urbana: University of Illinois Press, 1990), p. 24; Charles Musser, *The Emergence of Cinema: The American Screen to 1907* (New York: Charles Scribner's Sons, 1990), p. 9

4. Eileen Bowser, *The Transformation of Cinema 1907–1915* (New York: Charles Scribner's Sons, 1990), p. 6.

5. Musser, 'Moving towards Fictional Narratives, p. 99.

6. Ibid., p. 89.

7. Charles Musser, *Before the Nickelodeon: Edwin S. Porter and the Edison Manufacturing Company* (Berkeley: University of California Press, 1991), pp. 274–5.

8. Musser, *The Emergence of Cinema*, pp. 257–9.

9. Although produced by Vitagraph, these first eight films were distributed by the Edison Manufacturing Co.; the remainder were produced by Edison and subsequently American Mutoscope and Biograph. See Anthony Slide, *The Big V: A History of the Vitagraph Company* (London: Scarecrow Press, 1987), p. 10; Musser, *The Emergence of Cinema*, p. 283.

10. Kemp R. Niver, *Biograph Bulletins 1896–1908* (Los Angeles, CA: Locare Research Group, 1971), p. 75.

11. De Cordova, *Picture Personalities*, pp. 23–4.

12. Bowser, *The Transformation of Cinema*, pp. 106–8.

13. David Kiehn, *Broncho Billy and the Essanay Film Company* (Berkeley, CA: Farwell Books, 2003), p. 63.

14. Tom Gunning, *D. W. Griffith and the Origins of American Narrative Film: The Early Years at Biograph* (Urbana: University of Illinois Press, 1991), p. 141.

15. Eileen Bowser, *Biograph Bulletins 1908–1912* (New York: Octagon Books, 1973), p. 117.

16. The system of trade between the film exchanges and exhibitors was founded on the single reel as a basic unit of currency, while many nickelodeons had only one projector, meaning lengthy intervals between reels. See Bowser, *The Transformation of Cinema*, p. 199.

17. Robert M. Henderson, *D. W. Griffith: The Years at Biograph* (New York: Farrar, Straus and Giroux, 1970), pp. 109–10; Kemp R. Niver, *D. W. Griffith: His Biograph Films in Perspective* (New York: Renovare Co., 1974), pp. 158–95.

18. *Moving Picture World*, 4 February 1911.

19. 'Two Notable Films', *Motion Picture News*, 4 February 1911.

20. Jess-Cooke, *Film Sequels*, p. 16.

21. Ben Singer, 'Serial Melodrama and the Narrative *Gesellschaft*', *Velvet Light Trap* no. 37 (Spring 1996), p. 73.

22. Ben Singer, 'Serials', in G. Nowell Smith (ed.), *The Oxford History of World Cinema* (Oxford: Oxford University Press, 1997), p. 110; Francis Lacassin, 'The Eclair Company and European Popular Literature from 1908–1919', *Griffithiana* vol. 16 no. 47 (May 1993), pp. 61–87.

23. For more on the increasing symbiosis between the motion picture industry and the publishers of magazines and newspapers, see Richard Abel, 'Trash Twins', in *Americanizing the Movies and "Movie-Mad" Audiences, 1910–1914* (Berkeley: University of California Press, 2006), pp. 220–6.

24. Singer, 'Serial Melodrama and the Narrative *Gesellschaft*', p. 73.

25. Ibid., p. 73; Kalton C. Lahue, *Bound and Gagged: The Story of the Silent Serials* (New York: A. S. Barnes, 1968), pp. 18–19; Anthony Slide, *Early American Cinema* (New York: A. S. Barnes, 1970), pp. 158–9; Bowser, *The Transformation of Cinema*, p. 206.

26. A related point has been made by Josh Lambert, in an excellent piece on intertextuality and cliffhangers in Harry Hershfeld's 'Desperate Desmond' comic strip and its related adaptations in theatre and film. Lambert notes that the adoption of the cliffhanger mode in cinema was not so much the result of film producers taking inspiration from comic strips, but rather facilitated by the successful synchronisation of distribution networks and 'intertextual supplements', such as the recapping of earlier events at the start of each episode, which would enable viewers to successfully follow the story in the correct order. See Josh Lambert, '"Wait for the Next Pictures":

Intertextuality and Cliffhanger Continuity in Early Cinema and Comic Strips', *Cinema Journal* vol. 48 no. 2 (Winter 2009), pp. 16–20.

27 Singer, 'Serial Melodrama and the Narrative *Gesellschaft*', p. 74.

28 Janet Staiger, 'Combination and Litigation: Structures of US Film Distribution, 1896–1917', in Elsaesser, *Early Cinema*, p. 201.

29. Anthony Slide, *Early American Cinema* (rev. edn) (New York: A. S. Barnes, 1994), pp. 69–70; Bowser, *The Transformation of Cinema*, p. 206.

30. Slide, *Early American Cinema*, p. 69.

31. Bowser, *The Transformation of Cinema*, p. 196.

32. Ben Singer, *Melodrama and Modernity: Early Sensational Cinema and Its Contexts* (New York: Columbia University Press, 2001), pp. 263–5.

33. See Abel, *Americanizing the Movies and "Movie-Mad" Audiences, 1910–1914*, p. 195; Slide, *Early American Cinema*, pp. 191–2.

34. Anthony Slide, *American Racist: The Life and Films of Thomas Dixon* (Lexington: University of Kentucky Press, 2004), p. 92.

35. 'America Is Invaded Again in the Films', *New York Times*, 7 June 1916, p. 11.

36. '"The Fall of a Nation" Rises to Dramatic Heights', *Motion Picture News*, 24 June 1916, p. 66; *Moving Picture World*, 24 June 1916, p. 115; *Variety*, 9 June 1916, p. 23; *Wids*, 15 June 1915, p. 11.

37. Jesse L. Lasky, *I Blow My Own Horn* (London: Victor Gollancz, 1957), p. 92.

38. *Variety*, 3 August, 1917, p. 24.

39. *Wids*, 2 August 1917, p. 5.

40. Ben Singer, 'Feature Films, Variety Programs, and the Crisis of the Small Exhibitor', in Keil and Stamp, *American Cinema's Transitional Era*, pp. 87–8.

41. Ibid., p. 99.

42. Lasky, *I Blow My Own Horn*, p. 103.

43. *New York Times*, 6 June 1921, p. 4.

44. *Variety*, 26 March 1920, p. 51.

45. *Motion Picture News*. 18 June 1921, p. 124.

46. *Photoplay*, June 1920, p. 68.

47. 'National Ready to Film "Tarzan of the Apes"', *Motion Picture News*, 4 August 1917, p. 100.

48. Robert W. Fenton, *Big Swingers: Edgar Rice Burroughs 1875–1950; Tarzan 1912–* (Englewood Cliffs, NJ: Prentice Hall, 1967), p. 76; Gabe Essoe, *Tarzan of the Movies* (New York: Citadel Press, 1968), p. 13.

49. 'National Ready to Film "Tarzan of the Apes"', p. 100.

50. Richard Koszarski, *An Evening's Entertainment: The Age of the Silent Feature Picture 1915–1928* (New York: Charles Scribner's Sons, 1990), pp. 72–3.

51. 'First National Gets Two Big Productions', *Moving Picture World*, 9 March 1918.

52. 'Many First Run Houses Book "Tarzan of the Apes"', *Moving Picture World*, 9 March 1918.

53. *Variety*, 1 February 1918.

54. Distribution agreement between First National and National Film Corporation of America dated 18 July 1918, 'Romance of Tarzan' Production File, First National Files, Warner Bros. Archives, USC. See also 'First National Takes "Tarzan" Sequel, *Moving Picture World*, 3 August 1918.

55. See Fenton, *Big Swingers*, p. 89; and Essoe, *Tarzan of the Movies*, p. 20. Letter from Burroughs to First National Exhibitors' Circuit, dated 5 August 1918, First National Files, Warner Bros. Archives.

56. '"The Romance of Tarzan" Opens at New York Strand', *Moving Picture World*, 26 October 1918.

57. '"Tarzan" Shown at Strand' *New York Times*, 14 October 1918, p. 15.

58. Peter Decherney, *Hollywood's Copyright Wars: From Edison to the Internet* (New York: Columbia University Press, 2012), pp. 54–5.

59. After this ill-fated formative experience with Parsons, Burroughs was both savvier and more wary, a stance which would eventually lead to his own disastrous attempts to adapt his own work to the screen in the late 1930s. See Tino Balio, *Grand Design: Hollywood as a Modern Business Enterprise, 1930–1939* (New York: Charles Scribner's Sons, 1995), pp. 328–9.

60. Tino Balio, *United Artists: The Company Built by the Stars* (Madison: University of Wisconsin Press, 1976), pp. 24–9.

61. Tino Balio, *United Artists: The Company That Changed the Film Industry* (Madison: University of Wisconsin Press, 1987), p. 10.

62. Balio, *United Artists: The Company Built by the Stars*, p. 28.

63. The *Paramount* decree refers to the US Supreme Court ruling in 1948 against Paramount studios in an antitrust case, forcing Paramount, and ultimately the other major studios, to divest themselves of the theatres they owned across the United States.

64. Ibid., pp. 45–51.

65. Koszarski, *An Evening's Entertainment*, p. 349.

66. Jeffrey Vance, *Douglas Fairbanks* (Berkeley: University of California Press, 2008), p. 183.

67. Ibid., p. 187.

68. Ibid., p. 97.

69. Ibid., p. 183.

70. *Variety*. 17 June 1925, p. 35.

71. *Photoplay*, August 1925, p. 51.

72. Koszarski, *An Evening's Entertainment*, p. 33.

73. The first, after a brief reconciliation with Lasky, was box-office disappointment *Monsieur Beaucaire* (1924).

74. Emily Leider, *Dark Lover: The Life and Death of Rudolph Valentino* (London: Faber and Faber, 2003), p. 334.

75. Ibid., pp. 148–50, p. 334.

76. Balio, *United Artists: The Company Built by the Stars*, p. 56.

77. Leider, *Dark Lover*, pp. 334–5.

78. According to *Variety*'s box-office reports, *The Eagle* was 'the biggest draw on Broadway' in its first week at the Strand theatre, opening 'bigger than either "Beaucaire" [*Monsieur Beaucaire* (1924)] or "The Sainted Devil" [1924]', and was the 'Best boxoffice bet in town', when it opened at the Loew's State in Los Angeles. The film opened poorly at the Loew's State in Boston, however, just as *Cobra* was premiering to poor results in other cities, for example in New York, where its Broadway first run at the Rivoli 'opened fairly well, but fell away to almost nothing'. See 'Strand and "Eagle" Ahead on B'way Last Week, $49,600', *Variety*, 18 November 1925; '"Eagle" $30,000 Leads L.A. Grosses', *Variety*, 25 November 1925, p. 30; 'Pre-Xmas Slump Hits All B'way Pictures Except "Big Parade"', *Variety*, 16 December 1925, p. 35; 'New Orleans Turns on Cobra for $4,600', *Variety*, 16 December 1925, p. 35.

79. Leider, *Dark Lover*, p. 170.

80. Figure taken from a copy of Hull's contract, E. M. Hull Collection at the Woman's Library. Leider has pointed out the wild variations between the accounts of Zukor, Lasky and *Variety* in terms of the amount paid for the movie rights to Hull's original novel, with Zukor claiming $50,000, Lasky $12,500 and *Variety* $7,500. See Leider, *Dark Lover*, p. 153. Given the amount Hull accepted for the sequel, and the $5,000 she was paid by Fox for 'The Shadow of the East' in 1922, it seems highly unlikely that she was paid anything near the figure quoted by Zukor.

81. Leider, *Dark Lover*, p. 367.

82. Ibid., p. 168.

83. Balio, *United Artists: The Company Built by the Stars*, p. 47.

84. Leider, *Dark Lover*, p. 370; '"Son of Sheik" as "Long Run Preview"', *Variety*, 14 July 1926, p. 8.

85. *Variety*, 4 August 1926, p. 7.

86. See ibid., p. 6; *Variety*, 18 August 1926, p. 44.

87. Ibid.

88. Balio, *United Artists: The Company Built by the Stars*, p. 56.

89. Gaylyn Studlar, '"THE PERFECT LOVER"? Valentino and Ethnic Masculinity in the 1920s', in Lee Grieveson and Peter Krämer (eds), *Silent Cinema Reader* (London: Routledge, 2004), pp. 300–1.

Chapter 2

1. Frank S. Nugent, 'Consider the Sequel', *New York Times*, 31 May 1936.

2. John T. McManus, 'Thumbs Down on Doubles', *New York Times*, 31 May 1936.

3. D.W.C., 'Small Profits Feed Poverty Row', *New York Times*, 31 May 1936.

4. More than 360 series films were released between 1929 and 1955, versus approximately 239 serials and 197 sequels. For more figures, see Figures A.1 and A.2 in Summary Statistics.

5. Peter Lev, *Transforming the Screen 1950–1959* (London: University of California Press, 2003), p. 198.

6. Tino Balio, *Grand Design: Hollywood as a Modern Business Enterprise, 1930–1939* (Berkeley: University of California Press, 1995), pp. 13–14.

7. Don Miller, *The B Movies: An Informal Survey of the American Low-budget Film, 1933–45* (New York: Curtis Books, 1973), p. 35; Balio, *Grand Design*, p. 28.

8. Sheldon Hall and Steve Neale, *Epics, Spectacles and Blockbusters: A Hollywood History* (Detroit, MI: Wayne State University Press, 2010), p. 95.

9. Balio, *Grand Design*, p. 29.

10. Ten years later, *Variety* would report that close to 65 per cent of US theatres still played double bills on a part-time basis. 'Certain sections of Kentucky, Missouri, Indiana, Nebraska and Kansas are still pretty much single bill', the report claimed, but 'dualing' was still 'firmly intrenched' in most other areas of the country (*Variety*, 6 December 1944, p. 7).

11. Brian Taves, 'The B Film: Hollywood's Other Half', in Balio, *Grand Design*, pp. 317–25; Don Miller, *The B Movies*, pp. 36–7.

12. Todd McCarthy and Charles Flynn (eds), *Kings of the Bs: Working within the Hollywood System* (New York: E. P. Dutton and Co., 1975), p. 17; Robin Cross, *The Big Book of B Movies, or How Low Was My Budget* (London: Frederick Muller Ltd, 1981), p. 7; Balio, *Grand Design*, pp. 29–30.

13. Richard B. Jewell, 'RKO Film Grosses, 1929–1951: The C. J. Tevlin Ledger', *Historical Journal of Film, Radio and Television* vol. 14 no. 1 (1994), p. 41.

14. Ulf Jonas Bjork, 'Double Features and B Movies: Exhibition Patterns in Seattle, 1938', *Journal of Film and Video* vol. 41 no. 3 (1989), p. 47.

15. Balio, *Grand Design*, p. 102.

16. Most histories of the B-movie have rightly focused on studios such as Republic, Producers Releasing Corporation and Monogram, alongside the smaller independent, 'Poverty Row' producers who devoted themselves (largely because they could not afford to do otherwise) to B-level production. My focus here, however, is on the eight major studios, because it was their changing attitudes and approaches to B-movie production which ultimately signalled the direction in which the industry would move.

17. Research notes in the George B. Seitz Collection held at the AFI refer to a full screenplay dated 3 September 1937. See also Memo from Ostrow to Knopf, 26 August 1937, MGM Collection, USC Cinematic Arts Library.

18. The Eddie Mannix Ledger is held as part of the permanent collection at the Margaret Herrick Library. In it, Mannix, who was an administrative vice-president at MGM from 1925 until his death in 1963, documents the negative cost, domestic gross and foreign gross for each film released by the studio between 1924 and 1962. For further details and a broader interpretation of these figures, see H. Mark Glancy, 'MGM Film Grosses, 1924–1948: The Eddie Mannix Ledger', *Historical Journal of Film, Radio and Television* vol. 12 no. 2 (1992), pp. 127–44.

19. Although its domestic earnings were marginally lower at $363,000, *You're Only Young Once* outstripped the earnings of its predecessor abroad, earning $309,000 versus $129,000. *Judge Hardy's Children*, meanwhile, performed better on both counts: domestic earnings were hugely up at $578,000, while foreign earnings increased slightly to $323,000. All figures from the Eddie Mannix Ledger, Margaret Herrick Library.

20. The exhibitor reports of the film's first-run showings are almost invariably negative, with Loew's Indianapolis expecting a 'poor' result, Baltimore's Century Theater reporting a 'bare' trade, the United Artists Theater in Los Angeles suggesting trade was 'pretty brutal' and the Fox in Philadelphia suggesting it was 'not so hot' (*Variety*, 17 March 1937, pp. 8–10; *Variety*, 24 March 1937, pp. 8–10; *Variety*, 31 March 1937, pp. 8–9; *Variety*, 7 April 1937, pp. 9–11). Little commercial progress was made on the following two Hardy films. In most key locations, *You're Only Young Once* played as part of a double bill, for example with MGM's Edward G. Robinson-starrer *Last Gangster* (1937) at Grauman's Chinese Theatre in Los Angeles, the Met Theatre in Brooklyn and at the Orpheum in Boston, with the studio's Myrna Loy-led *Man-Proof* (1938) at the Capitol in Montreal and the Carlton in Providence, and with Warner's *Hollywood Hotel* (1937) at the Fox Theatre in San Francisco. Most reports from exhibitors during its first-run period from December 1937 through to January 1938 were discouraging at best. The one true bright spot, and perhaps a partial explanation for the studio's persistence with the series, was in Chicago where

> Outstanding among the pictures is 'Judge Hardy' at the Roosevelt, which has a built-up audience from previous 'Hardy Family' pictures … . Series has a big following locally, and click of current release indicates that Metro has a b.o. idea in the family group.

See 'Everything Considered Chi's H.O.'s Fine', and report on Broadway figures in *Variety*, 13 April 1938, p. 9. For *You're Only Young Once*, see *Variety*, 29 December 1937, p. 10; 12 January 1938, p. 8; 19 January 1938, pp. 7–8; and 26 January 1938, p. 10.

21. Agreement between Erle Stanley Gardner and Warner Bros., 9 April 1934, Perry Mason Legal Files, Warner Bros. Archive, USC.

22. Robert Gustafson, *The Buying of Ideas: Source Acquisition at Warner Brothers 1930–1949* (PhD dissertation, University of Wisconsin, 1993), p. 60.

23. Pressbook held at Warner Bros. Archive, USC.

24. In an agreement dating to 25 April 1931, Fox contracted with Biggers for an option on his next, as yet unpublished Charlie Chan story, to be submitted no later than 15 January 1932, with options on a second and third story in January of 1933 and 1934 respectively, along with an option to purchase two previously published stories: *The Chinese Parrot* and *The House without a Key*. See Memo from J. H. Tracy to Robert Yost, 27 January 1932, UCLA Performing Arts Library, Fox Legal Files Collection.

25. Thomas Schatz, *Boom and Bust: American Cinema in the 1940s* (Berkeley: University of California Press, 1999), p. 173.

26. Glancy, 'MGM Film Grosses, 1924–1948, pp. 136–7.

27. Howard Sharpe, 'The Star Creators of Hollywood (Third in a Series)', *Photoplay*, December 1936.

28. See, for example, the scholarly discussion about B-movies documented on David Bordwell's blog, entitled 'Bs in Their Bonnets: A Three-day Conversation Well Worth the Reading', 22 February 2007, http://www.davidbordwell.net/blog/?p=438, accessed 25 September 2009.

29. This is reflected in *Variety*'s annual end-of-year breakdown of star rankings by studio where, for 1933, Loy ranked fifth in the list of MGM's 'Featured Players', which was itself billed below its list of the studio's eleven 'Stars'.

30. 'Leading Film Names of 1933', *Variety*, 2 January 1934, p. 27; 'Leading Film Names', *Variety*, 1 January 1935, p. 26.

31. Figures from the Eddie Mannix Ledger.

32. Hunt Stromberg, 'Notes on The Thin Man Sequel', 29 August 1934, Hunt Stromberg Papers, Margaret Herrick Library.

33. W. S. Van Dyke, '"Rx for a Thin Man"', *Stage*, January 1937.

34. Jeanine Basinger, *The Star Machine* (New York: Vintage, 2009), p. 404.

35. Figures from the Eddie Mannix Ledger.

36. Charles Francisco, *Gentleman: The William Powell Story* (New York: St Martin's Press, 1985), pp. 189–95; James Kotsilibas-Davis, *Myrna Loy: Being and Becoming* (London: Bloomsbury, 1987).

37. Glancy, 'MGM Film Grosses, 1924–1948, p. 136.

38. The Eddie Mannix Ledger.

39. Rudy Behlmer, 'Tarzan: Hollywood's Greatest Jungle Hero: Part 1', *American Cinematographer* vol. 68 (January 1987), p. 44.

40. Thomas Schatz, *The Genius of the System: Hollywood Filmmaking in the Studio Era* (New York: Pantheon, 1988), p. 170.

41. Behlmer, 'Tarzan', pp. 44–6.

42. Figures from the Eddie Mannix Ledger.

43. 'Goldstone Handling MG Third 'Tarzan'', *Variety*, 29 January 1935, p. 6.

44. Richard Koszarski, *An Evening's Entertainment: The Age of the Silent Feature Picture 1915–1928* (New York: Charles Scribner's Sons, 1990), pp. 86–7; Balio, *Grand Design*, p. 17; Douglas Gomery, *The Hollywood Studio System: A History* (London: BFI Publishing, 2005), p. 60; Bernard F. Dick, *City of Dreams: The Making and Remaking of Universal Pictures* (Lexington: University Press of Kentucky, 1997), p. 57.

45. Schatz, *The Genius of the System*, pp. 85–7; Dick, *City of Dreams*, p. 74.

46. Ian Conrich, 'Before Sound: Universal, Silent Cinema, and the Last of the Horror-Spectaculars', in Stephen Prince (ed.), *The Horror Film* (London: Rutgers University Press, 2004), pp. 40–2.

47. See for example, Phillip J. Riley, *Dracula, Production Background* (Chesterfield, NJ: MagicImage Filmbooks, 1990), pp. 41–2; Michael Brunas, *Universal Horrors: The Studio's Classic Films, 1931–1946* (Jefferson, NC: McFarland, 1990), p. 11.

48. It has been suggested that Laemmle had already closed the deal for *Frankenstein* some weeks before *Dracula's* release, so confident was he of that film's success. There is no direct evidence of this, however, and the date of the deal suggests otherwise. See Schatz, *The Genius of the System*, p. 91; Mark Gatiss, *James Whale: A Biography, or the Would-be Gentleman* (London: Cassell, 1995), pp. 67–8; Bruce Dettman, *The Horror Factory: The Horror Films of Universal, 1931–1955* (New York: Gordon Press, 1976), p. 14.

49. Lugosi maintained that he decided the role was not for him, but Junior later claimed that Lugosi's screen test as the monster was so bad it made him laugh 'like a hyena'. See Rudy Behlmer, *America's Favorite Movies: Behind the Scenes* (New York: Frederick Ungar, 1982), p. 8; Rick Atkins, *Let's Scare 'Em!: Grand Interviews and a Filmography of Horrific Proportions, 1930–1961* (London: McFarland, 1997), p. 18.

50. James Curtis, *James Whale: A New World of Gods and Monsters* (London: Faber and Faber, 1998), p. 234; Behlmer, *America's Favorite Movies*, p. 18.

51. Similarly, Robert Florey, who had originally been scheduled to write and direct *Frankenstein* before being replaced by Whale, claimed that he had wished to avoid killing off Frankenstein at the film's climax, because he was 'thinking of a follow-up in case of success'. See Curtis, *James Whale*, pp. 129, 234; Schatz, *The Genius of the System*, p. 94.

52. Curtis, *James Whale*, p. 234.

53. Ibid., p. 324.

54. 'Karloff Again Set at U after Freelancing', *Variety*, 11 July 1933, p. 29.

55. Curtis, *James Whale*, pp. 234–5.

56. '6 Laemmle, Jr., Pix to Cost $4,000,000', *Variety*, 15 January 1935, p. 5.

57. Schatz, *The Genius of the System*, pp. 234–5; Balio, *Grand Design*, p. 17; Dick, *City of Dreams*, pp. 103–5.

58. David J. Skal, *The Monster Show: A Cultural History of Horror* (New York: Norton, 1994), pp. 197–8.

59. Dick, *City of Dreams*, pp. 108–9.

60. *The House of Dracula* (1945), was, according to *Variety*, set to become a 'super-horror', having been budgeted at $750,000, almost twice the amount spent on predecessor *The House of Frankenstein* (1944). See 'U Boosting Coin for Monster Monster Pic', *Variety*, 21 March 1945, p. 3.

61. Helmut G. Asper and Jan-Christopher Horak, 'Three Smart Guys: How a Few Penniless German Emigrés Saved Universal Studios', *Film History* vol. 11 no. 2 (1999), pp. 135–42.

62. Unlike Asper and Horak's account, Bernard F. Dick accords Rogers some credit in the development of Durbin as a star, pointing out that during his previous tenure at Paramount he had overseen the

development of the studio's musical comedy roster and had sought to carry that tradition over to Universal (Dick, *City of Dreams*, pp. 111–12).

63. Asper and Horak, 'Three Smart Guys', p. 146; Dick, *City of Dreams*, p. 115.

64. Asper and Horak, 'Three Smart Guys', p. 135.

65. 'Deanna Joins Up', *Variety*, 25 March 1942, p. 22.

66. As Peter Lev has suggested, 'the closer one looks at the film industry during the 1940s, the more evident it becomes that World War II marked an extended, dramatic, and most welcome interval in a decade-long period of industry decline' (Lev, *Transforming the Screen*, p. 2).

67. Staiger in David Bordwell, Janet Staiger and Kristin Thompson, *The Classical Hollywood Cinema: Film Style and Mode of Production to 1960* (London: Routledge: 1985), p. 332.

68. Schatz, *Boom and Bust*, p. 181; Janet Wasko, *Movies and Money: Financing the American Film Industry* (Norwood, NJ: Ablex Publishing, 1982), pp. 107–8.

69. Schatz, *Boom and Bust*, pp. 79, 179–82.

70. Studio figures are difficult to come by, but according to a *Variety* countdown of 'rental champs', *Bells* had rentals of $8 million whereas rentals for *Going My Way* were $6.5 million. See 'All-time Film Rental Champs (of U.S.–Canada Market)', *Variety*, 16 January 1985, pp. 60, 66. Furthermore, when *Bells*' reported gross of $21.333 million is adjusted for inflation, it ranks among the highest-grossing films of all time in North America – and, at the time of writing, the tenth highest-grossing sequel on the list. See http://www.boxofficemojo.com/alltime/adjusted.htm.

71. For more on this see Matthew Bernstein, 'Hollywood's Semi-independent Production', *Cinema Journal* vol. 32 no. 3 (Spring 1993), pp. 41–54.

72. The contract summary for Crosby lists a 30 December 1940 agreement with Paramount, committing him to make eleven films for Paramount. McCarey's four-film deal with RKO is referred back to in a later agreement between the director's Rainbow Productions and the studio. See Paramount Contract Summaries, Margaret Herrick Library; McCarey Collection, Louis B. Mayer Library, American Film Institute.

73. McCarey purchased Frank Cavett's screenplay from RKO in an agreement dated May, 1943. On 3 May 1943, McCarey signed his agreement with Paramount and Crosby signed his agreement with RKO (McCarey Collection, Louis B. Mayer Library, AFI).

74. Agreement between McCarey and Paramount Pictures, 3 May 1943.

75. Mae Tinée, 'Movie "Going My Way" Is a Rare Treat', *Chicago Tribune*, 10 June 1944; 'McCarey's 'Way Deal May Net Him $1,000,000', *Variety*, 16 August 1944, p. 1.

76. McCarey's files, in fact, indicate that in February 1944 – after the completion of *Going My Way* but before its premiere in May 1944 – work had begun on a screenplay called *Fiesta*, to be written by Frank Partos and mooted as the next Crosby–McCarey collaboration. This is evidenced by a memo from RKO's Joe Nolan to Sid Lipsitch, in which he states: 'He [Partos] is writing on a story entitled FIESTA which Leo McCarey is preparing. This is in connection with Bing Crosby.' See Memo from Nolan to Lipsitch, 15 Feburary 1944, McCarey Collection, Louis B. Mayer Library.

77. Wes D. Gehring, *Leo McCarey: From Marx to McCarthy* (Lanham, MD: Scarecrow Press 2004), pp. 193–4. This is borne out by the preview cards for *Going My Way* held in the McCarey Collection at the AFI, one of which explicitly requests 'Give us more Bing The priest'. See also Peter Bogdanovich, *Who the Devil Made It* (Alfred A. Knopf: New York 1997), p. 423, in which McCarey claims that he effectively produced *Bells* 'somewhat on demand'.

78. The second of McCarey's contractually required pictures for Rainbow was *Good Sam* (1948). See Agreement between McCarey and Rainbow, 2 January 1945; Distribution agreement between Rainbow and RKO, 13 January 1945, McCarey Collection, AFI.

79. Fred Stanley, 'On Hollywood', *New York Times*, 4 March 1945. See also Memo from Earl Rettig to McCarey, 'RE: Bergman Picture Deal', 29 October 1945, McCarey Collection, AFI.

80. Steve Neale, *Genre and Hollywood* (London: Routledge, 2000), p. 239.

81. Memo from Jack Warner to Hal Wallis, 7 September 1939, Production Files, Warner Bros. Archive, USC.

82. Agreement between Dunne and Twentieth Century-Fox, 4 December 1952, Fox Production Files, USC Cinematic Arts Library.

83. Barbara Berch Jamison, 'And Now Super-colossal Headaches', *New York Times*, 10 January 1954.

84. '"Demetrius" Biz Tops "Millionaire"', *Hollywood Reporter*, 22 June 1954, p. 6; Aubrey Solomon, *Twentieth Century-Fox: A Corporate and Financial History* (London: Metuchen, 1988), pp. 225, 249.

85. *Love Finds Andy Hardy* file, MGM Production Records, USC Cinematic Arts Library.

86. As observed by Tino Balio, this cycle of family films coincided with the decline of screwball comedy in the late 1930s, producing films which were the ancestors of television sitcoms, 'domestic comedies' which 'focused on minor incidents in a supposedly typical American family' (Balio, *Grand Design*, p. 279). H. Mark Glancy's cataloguing of the William Schaefer Ledger indicates that *Four Daughters* was the studio's sixth highest-grossing film for the 1938–9 season, with domestic earnings of $1.332 million and foreign earnings of $465,000. The ledger is held as part of the William Schaefer Collection at the University of Southern California. In it, Schaefer, who was Jack Warner's executive secretary from 1933 until Warner's death in 1979, documents the negative cost, domestic gross and foreign gross for each film released by the studio through to 1967. For further details see H. Mark Glancy, 'Warner Bros Film Grosses, 1921–51: The William Schaefer Ledger', *Historical Journal of Film, Radio and Television* vol. 15 no.1 (1995), Appendix 1, p. 19.

87. Memo from Jacob Wilk to Jack Warner, reporting on the findings of Morris Ebenstein in Warner's New York Legal Department, 15 September 1938, *Four Wives* Production Files, Warner Bros. Archive, USC. See also signed contract between Warner Bros. Pictures and Fannie Hurst for 'Sister Act', 19 November 1936, Warner Bros. Archive.

88. As reported by Steve Trilling in a memo to Hal Wallis, dated 9 August 1939, *Four Wives* Production Files, Warner Bros. Archive.

89. 'WB-Metro Pix Series Inspires Authors to Use Negotiator for Story Deals', *Variety*, 13 December 1939, p. 6.

90. Premiering in the week before Christmas 1939, *Four Wives* held its own at the box office, earning $1.195 million domestically and $282,000 abroad, placing it ninth on Warner's seasonal chart. In his *New York Times* review, Frank S. Nugent declared that 'Sequels so rarely even approximate the quality of their originals that the Warners deserve a special commendation this morning for their "Four Wives"', and suggested that its quality 'reconciles us tranquilly to the vista it has opened of a "Four Mothers" … , a "Four Grandmothers" and possibly a "Four Granddaughters"'.

91. Letter from Jacob Wilk to J. L. Warner, 20 February 1940, *Four Wives* Legal and Story Files, Warner Bros. Archive.

92. Memo from Wilk to Ebenstein on 6 March 1940, *Four Wives* Legal and Story Files, Warner Bros. Archive.

93.	'Author's Balk at M-G's Idea to Perpetually Use Same Characters', *Variety*, 22 November 1939, p. 1.

94.	Warner Bros. eventually settled with Tarkington on 8 August 1941, with the studio given the rights

>	to use the names of the characters appearing in said Writings or the names of any of them as the names of characters appearing in any photoplay or photoplays produced by Purchaser [W.B.], whether or not such photoplays are in whole or in part based on, taken from or in any way suggested by said Writings or any part thereof'.

>	For each new film produced 'running over four thousand feet' the studio would have to pay Tarkington $1,000, with a $200 payment for each film produced at a shorter length. This still applied a decade later, after Tarkington's death, when the studio produced *On Moonlight Bay* (1951) and its sequel *By The Light of the Silvery Moon* (1953).

95.	'WB-Metro Pix Series Inspires Authors to Use Negotiator for Story Deals', p. 6.

96.	Universal, for example, had evidently not built such a clause into its agreement with David Stern, author of the novel *Francis*, which became a film of the same name in 1950. On the evidence of a *Variety* report, it appears that it was only after the film's considerable success that the studio negotiated for additional rights, striking a deal with Stern to write an original screenplay for a sequel entitled *Francis Goes to the Races* (1951). The deal also gave Universal the film rights to the already published *Francis Goes to Washington*, any future novels, and TV, radio and commercial rights for any 'tie-up' featuring the comically sentient mule. See 'Francis to See How the Other Half Lives', *Variety*, 17 May 1950.

97.	Agreement between Fox and Gilbreth-Careys, 4 May 1949, Twentieth Century-Fox Legal Files, UCLA.

98.	'Jolson Calls Off Deal for Metro Biog Sequel', *Variety*, 6 April 1948, p. 3.

99.	'Inside Stuff – Pictures', *Variety*, 22 February 1950, p. 16.

100.	Jonathan Latimer, 'Thin Man Story', Twentieth Century-Fox Production Files, USC Cinematic Arts Library.

101.	'Hell to Pay', uncredited treatment, 1 September 1932; 'Hell To Pay' draft screenplay, Dudley Nichols and Henry Johnson, 12 September 1932; 'Hell To Pay' revised draft screenplay, 8 October 1932; Twentieth Century-Fox Script Files, USC Cinematic Arts Library.

102.	Sometimes this material derived from outside Hollywood, as with *Love Finds Andy Hardy*. That film borrows its central set-up (in which a boy dates a girl he doesn't like as a favour to a friend, causing distress to the girl he actually prefers) from a short story by Vivian Bretherton published two years earlier in *Cosmopolitan* and bearing no relation to the Hardy family.

103.	The film went on to earn $4.036 million in the US alone against relatively inexpensive costs of $1.215 million. Figures from the Eddie Mannix Ledger.

104.	'Sequel to Father of the Bride', Frances Goodrich and Albert Hackett, 7 March 1950, Turner/MGM Script Files, Margaret Herrick Library.

105.	'Sequel to Father of the Bride' treatment, 30 March–27 April 1950; 'FATHER'S LITTLE DIVIDEND' screenplay, 15 April–14 July 1950, Turner/MGM Script Files.

106.	'It is not very often that the sequel to a successful film turns out to be even half as successful or rewarding as the original picture was', wrote Bosley Crowther in the *New York Times*, 'But we've got to hand it to Metro: its sequel to 'Father of the Bride' is so close that we'll willingly concede it to the humor and charm of that former film' (13 April 1951), p. 18. Domestic earnings reached $3.122 million, against costs of just $941,000 – a significant saving on the cost of the original.

107. Lev, *Transforming the Screen*, pp. 12–19.

Chapter 3

1. Whereas the majors produced 253.3 films per year on average in the 1950s, for example, that figure had dropped to 160.3 for the 1960s and then again to 107.6 per year during the 70s. These figures are based on statistics derived from Joel Finler, *The Hollywood Story* (London: Wallflower, 2003), pp. 364–6.

2. Figures taken from Stuart Henderson, 'The Hollywood Sequel Database', http://thehollywood sequel.wordpress.com/.

3. Joseph R. Dominick, 'Film Economics and Film Content: 1964–1983', *Current Research in Film* vol. 3 (1987), pp. 137–53.

4. As both Murray Smith and Peter Krämer have observed, the term 'New Hollywood' has been used inconsistently by different writers to refer not only to this period but also to earlier years and everything thereafter. See Murray Smith, 'Theses on the Philosophy of Hollywood History', in Steve Neale and Murray Smith (eds), *Contemporary Hollywood Cinema* (London: Routledge, 1998), pp. 3–20; Peter Krämer, *The New Hollywood: From Bonnie and Clyde to Star Wars* (London: Wallflower, 2005), p. 2.

5. U.S. Bureau of the Census, *Housing and Construction Reports*, series H-121, numbers 1–5, quoted in Frederic Stuart, *The Effects of Television on the Motion Picture and Radio Industries* (New York: Arno Press, 1976), p. 23. From 1949 to 1954, the number of television sets in US homes grew from 1 million to 32 million. See Tino Balio, 'Introduction to Part One', in Tino Balio (ed.), *Hollywood in the Age of Television* (Boston, MA: Unwin Hyman, 1990), p. 15.

6. Ibid., pp. 22–31.

7. See Balio, 'Introduction to Part One', pp. 21–3; Richard Maltby, 'Post-classical Historiographies and Consolidated Entertainment,' in Neale and Smith, *Contemporary Hollywood Cinema*, pp. 28–30; and for a full account of why these initiatives faltered, see Douglas Gomery, 'Failed Opportunities: The Integration of the U.S. Motion Picture and Television Industries', *Quarterly Review of Film Studies* vol. 9, no. 3 (Summer 1984), pp. 220–3.

8. This sentiment is echoed by Richard Maltby's assertion that 'an overview of Hollywood's post-war industrial history must emphasize convergence, consolidation and synergy among the audio-visual entertainment industries.' Janet Wasko in Peter Lev, *The Fifties: Transforming the Screen 1950–1959* (Los Angeles: University of California Press, 2003), p. 127; Maltby, 'Post-classical Historiographies and Consolidated Entertainment', p. 28.

9. Douglas Gomery, 'Toward a New Media Economics' in David Bordwell and Noel Carroll, *Post-Theory: Reconstructing Film Studies* (Madison: University of Wisconsin Press, 1996), p. 407.

10. Balio, 'Introduction to Part One', pp. 34–5.

11. James L. Baughman, 'The Weakest Chain and the Strongest Link: The American Broadcasting Company and the Motion Picture Industry, 1952–60', in Balio, *Hollywood in the Age of Television*, pp. 97–103.

12. Christopher Anderson, *Hollywood TV: The Studio System in the Fifties* (Austin: University of Texas Press, 1994), p. 7.

13. Anderson, *Hollywood TV*, pp. 167–9; Baughman, 'The Weakest Chain and the Strongest Link', pp. 101–5.

14. Anderson, *Hollywood TV*, p. 169.

15. Baughman, 'The Weakest Chain and the Strongest Link', pp. 107–8.

16. Ibid., pp. 8–9.

17. Anderson, *Hollywood TV*, pp. 167–8.

18. Ibid., pp. 162–3.

19. Balio points to a survey published by *Television Magazine* in September 1963 which reported that 'the percentage of prime-time programming from Hollywood had risen to nearly 70 percent'. In Balio, *Hollywood in the Age of Television*, p. 37.

20. Roger Hagedorn, 'Doubtless to Be Continued: A Brief History of Serial Narrative', in Robert C. Allen (ed.), *To Be Continued: Soap Operas around the World* (London: Routledge, 1995).

21. As Balio has noted, from the mid-1950s onwards, 'the networks repudiated the program hierarchies of influential TV critics who championed dramatic anthology series based on a theatrical model in favor of continuing-character series based on a motion picture model' (Balio, *Hollywood in the Age of Television*, p. 33).

22. Ibid., p. 23.

23. For more on the reduction in output from the studios, see Gary R. Edgerton, *American Film Exhibition and an Analysis of the Industry's Market Structure, 1963–1980* (London: Garland Publishing, 1983).

24. It is also worth noting that roadshowing was not new, having been utilised by studios previously in the late 1920s and early 30s. See Sheldon Hall, 'Tall Revenue Features: The Genealogy of the Modern Blockbuster', in Steve Neale (ed.), *Genre and Contemporary Hollywood* (London: BFI Publishing, 2002), p. 12; Sheldon Hall and Steve Neale, *Epics, Spectacles and Blockbusters: A Hollywood History* (Detroit, MI: Wayne State University Press, 2010), pp. 89–94.

25. Justin Wyatt, 'From Roadshowing to Saturation Release: Majors, Independents, and Marketing/Distribution Innovations', in Jon Lewis (ed.), *The New American Cinema* (London: Duke University Press, 1998), p. 65.

26. Hall, 'Tall Revenue Features'; Steve Neale, 'Hollywood Blockbusters: Historical Dimensions', in Julian Stringer (ed.), *Movie Blockbusters* (London: Routledge, 2003), pp. 47–60; Krämer, *The New Hollywood*; Hall and Neale, *Epics, Spectacles and Blockbusters*.

27. Krämer, *The New Hollywood*, p. 92.

28. Ibid., pp. 111–14.

29. For a snapshot of the effects of the recession, see David J. Londoner, 'The Changing Economics of Entertainment', in Tino Balio (ed.), *The American Film Industry* (London: University of Wisconsin Press, 1985), pp. 603–11. For more about roadshowing, see Hall and Neale, *Epics, Spectacles and Blockbusters*, pp. 159–68.

30. For *Mr. Roberts*, see Memo from Arthur S. Katz to J. L. Warner, 4 March 1963, Production Files, Warner Bros. Archive, USC. For *Peyton Place*, see Agreement between author Grace Metalious and Twentieth Century-Fox, 27 September 1956, Fox Legal Files, UCLA Performing Arts Library. For *The Fly*, see Agreement between George Langelaan and Regal Films, 17 August 1957, Fox Legal Files, UCLA.

31. David Pirie, 'The Deal', in *Anatomy of the Movies* (New York: Macmillan, 1981), p. 45.

32. Thomas Schatz, *Boom and Bust: American Cinema in the 1940s* (Los Angeles: University of California Press, 1997).

33. Between 1950 and 1974, in fact, Wayne featured in all but one of the polls of top ten money-making stars published by Quigley's (1958 being the lone exception). See *The International Motion Picture Almanac*, http://www.quigleypublishing.com/MPalmanac/Top10/Top10_lists.html.

34. Ibid., p. 186.

35. Letter from Hazen and Wallis to Paramount's Bernard Donnenfeld, 8 February 1968, Hal B. Wallis Papers, Margaret Herrick Library.

36. As confirmed in a telegram from Hal Wallis and Joseph Hazen to Marvin Josephson Associates, 23 January 1968, Hal B. Wallis Papers.

37. Nathan to Wallis, 30 July 1970, Hal B. Wallis Papers.

38. Alan Weiss had submitted a brief treatment for a sequel in autumn of 1970, but this was apparently unsatisfactory, as it appears James Poe (screenwriter of *They Shoot Horses, Don't They?* [1969]) was subsequently contracted to write, but failed to deliver, a longer treatment. Various writers were subsequently involved, with Weiss returning to write a full treatment in autumn 1971, which became an unused screenplay.

39. Letter from Wallis to Charles Portis, 22 April 1974, Hal B. Wallis Papers. Wallis reports in his autobiography that 'Most of her ideas were bright and right', and the available script files indicate that many of her voluminous comments were taken on board. See *Starmaker: The Autobiography of Hal Wallis* (New York: Macmillan, 1980), pp. 178–9; Hal B. Wallis Papers and Katharine Hepburn Papers, Margaret Herrick Library.

40. The switch from Paramount to Universal is due to Wallis, whose exclusive commitment to the former expired shortly after the release of *True Grit*, leaving him free to set up Hal B. Wallis Productions at Universal.

41. Mark Thomas McGee, *Fast and Furious: The Story of American International Pictures* (New York: McFarland & Company, 1995), pp. 16–29.

42. Thomas Doherty, *Teenagers and Teenpics: The Juvenilization of American Movies in the 1950s* (Philadelphia, PA: Temple University Press, 2002), p. 30.

43. For more on these, see ibid., pp. 54–65 and 93–114; Timothy Shary, *Teen Movies: American Youth on Screen* (London: Wallflower, 2005), pp. 18–26; Alan Betrock, *The I Was a Teenage Juvenile Delinquent Rock 'n' Roll Horror Beach Party Movie Book* (New York: St. Martin's Press, 1986).

44. 'Film Company Seeks a New Locale for Its Teen-Age Movies', *New York Times*, 6 November 1965.

45. Peter Bart, 'Hollywood Beach Bonanza', *New York Times*, 13 December 1964.

46. 'Hollywood's Morality Code Undergoing First Major Revisions in 35 Years', proclaimed the *New York Times* on 7 April 1965, but it would be more than three years before these revisions took on a standardised form. See also Paul Monaco, *The Sixties: 1960–1969* (New York: Charles Scribner's Sons, 2001), pp. 56–66.

47. David A. Cook, *Lost Illusions: American Cinema in the Shadow of Watergate and Vietnam, 1970–1979* (New York: Charles Scribner's Sons, 2000), p. 259.

48. *Shaft* producer Joel Freeman admitted as much in interview, when he observed of *Cotton Comes to Harlem* that 'I have heard that 70 per cent of that money has come from the black audience, which

is extremely substantial and very important. Essentially, *Shaft* is being made for that audience'
(*Reel* vol. 3 [1971], p. 12).

49. Preview screening data from the Joel Freeman Papers, Margaret Herrick Library. Some 88 per cent
of respondents rated the film 'Good' or 'Excellent', with several respondents requesting sequels:
'They should have more movies about John Shaft like the James Bond 007 type things'; 'This film
should be ideal for a series of "Shaft" sequels'; and 'Please make a sequel immediately.'

50. See *New York Times*, 30 May 1971; treatment by Lewis and Silliphant, MGM Script Files, Margaret
Herrick Library.

51. Balio, 'Introduction to Part Two', in *Hollywood in the Age of Television*, pp. 259–60. See also, Cook, *Lost
Illusions*, pp. 9–12.

52. For a full account of Laughlin's approach to four-walling, see Justin Wyatt, 'From Roadshowing to
Saturation Release', pp. 73–7.

53. With rentals in excess of $32.5 million. See 'The Rise, Fall and Second Coming of Four-Walling',
Variety, 8 January 1975, p. 22; and Cook, *Lost Illusions*, p. 40. As explained by Frederick Wasser, quoting
MPAA research, 'From 1970 to 1972, MPAA members together spent $4 million per year on
network television advertising, about 2 percent of their total movie advertising budget.' See Wasser,
Veni, Vidi, Video: The Hollywood Empire and the VCR (Austin: University of Texas Press, 2001), p. 45.

54. Wyatt, 'From Roadshowing to Saturation Release', p. 77.

55. Dade Hayes and Jonathan Bing, *Open Wide: How Hollywood Box Office Became a National Obsession*
(New York: Miramax Books, 2004), pp. 274–9.

56. See, for example, Gomery, 'The Hollywood Blockbuster', pp. 72–5.

57. Hayes and Bing, *Open Wide*, pp. 274–9.

58. Unusually for a studio-funded film, *Dr. No*'s UK premiere had taken place back in October 1962.

59. Richard Maibaum, 'James Bond's 39 Bumps', *New York Times*, 13 December 1964.

60. The figures quoted here are from *Box Office Mojo*, http://www.boxofficemojo.com/franchises/chart/
?id=jamesbond.htm.

61. Krim quoted in Tino Balio, 'New Producers for Old: United Artists and the Shift to Independent
Production' in Balio, *Hollywood in the Age of Television*, p. 171.

62. *The Magnificent Seven* inspired two sequels, but with lengthy gaps between each – *Return of the
Seven* (1966) and *Magnificent Seven Ride* (1972). *The Pink Panther* was in fact followed within
months by *A Shot in the Dark* (1964), but the speed of its production was due to the fact that Blake
Edwards and William Peter Blatty were able to quickly repurpose a screenplay they were already
working on to incorporate the character of Inspector Clouseau, played again by Peter Sellers. There
followed a four-year gap before *Inspector Clouseau* (1968) appeared, in this case starring Alan Arkin
as Clouseau, and it was not until 1975 that the character (once again played by Sellers) returned in
The Return of the Pink Panther.

63. See, for example, Letter from P. D. Knecht of Warner Bros. to Frank Ferguson of Fox, explaining
Warner no longer had a stake in the project, 30 September 1966, Arthur P. Jacobs Collection,
Loyola Marymount University.

64. Army Archerd, 'Just for Variety', *Variety*, 27 March 1968, p. 2.

65. This is borne out by the budget information for *Beneath the Planet of the Apes* in the Arthur P.
Jacobs Collection, which lists no additional fee for story rights for Boulle, only story and screenplay
costs.

66. 'A sequel would just be further adventures among the monkeys', was, he later claimed in his autobiography, Heston's initial response. See Charlton Heston, *In The Arena: The Autobiography* (London: HarperCollins, 1995), p. 397.

67. Letter from Jacobs to Paul Dehn, 29 December 1969, Arthur P. Jacobs Collection.

68. Letter from Dehn to Jacobs, 31 December 1970, Arthur P. Jacobs Collection.

69. Memos from Jack Hirshberg to Selwyn Rausch, 21 February 1969 and 14 March 1969, Arthur P. Jacobs Collection.

70. This one-page timeline accompanies a twenty-two-page treatment for *Conquest*, dated 21 March 1971, Arthur P. Jacobs Collection.

Chapter 4

1. 'Warner Bros Sets Succession Plan', *Variety*, 22 September 2010, http://www.variety.com/article/VR1118024498.html.

2. Arthur DeVany, *Hollywood Economics: How Extreme Uncertainty Shapes the Film Industry* (London: Routledge, 2004), p. 6.

3. The use of the term 'ancillary' is increasingly inappropriate, given the large proportion of a film's total revenue derived from these outlets.

4. Thomas Schatz, 'The New Hollywood' in Jim Collins, Hilary Radner and Ava Preacher Collins (eds), *Film Theory Goes to the Movies* (London: Routledge, 1993), p. 20.

5. Edward Jay Epstein, *The Big Picture* (New York: Random House, 2005), pp. 93–105. For an overview on the specific holdings and respective forms of horizontal and vertical integration practised by these companies, see Eileen R. Meehan, 'Media Empires: Corporate Structures and Lines of Control', *Jump Cut* no. 52 (Summer 2010), http://www.ejumpcut.org/currentissue/MeehanCorporate/text.html.

6. Susan Royal, 'Steven Spielberg in His Adventures on Earth', American Premiere, July 1982, in Lester D. Friedman and Brent Notbohm (eds), *Steven Spielberg Interviews* (Jackson: University of Mississippi Press, 2000), pp. 103–4.

7. A *New York Times* article estimated that 'the number of film renters today certainly runs into the hundreds of thousands', although actual figures were unavailable. See Jane Scovell Appleton, 'Harpo, Garbo and Gable for Rent', *New York Times*, 10 November 1974.

8. Bruce A. Austin, 'Home Video: The Second-run "Theater" of the 1990s', in Tino Balio (ed.), *Hollywood in the Age of Television* (London: Unwin Hyman, 1990), pp. 319–49. I have not dwelt on the development of HBO here, because, although hugely important in terms of a broader historical overview, it had little direct or immediate impact on the development of the sequel form at that time – unlike the development of home video.

9. See, for example, Frederick Wasser, 'Ancillary Markets – Video and DVD: Hollywood Retools', in Paul MacDonald and Janet Wasko (eds), *The Contemporary Hollywood Film Industry* (Oxford: Blackwell Publishing, 2008), pp. 120–1; Austin, 'Home Video', pp. 326–8; Douglas Gomery, *Shared Pleasures: A History of Movie Presentation in the United States* (London: BFI Publishing, 1992), pp. 278–81; Stephen Prince, *A New Pot of Gold: Hollywood under the Electronic Rainbow, 1980–1989* (Berkeley: University of California Press, 2000), pp. 99–103.

10. Wasser, 'Ancillary Markets', p. 122.

11. See James Lardner, *Fast Forward: Hollywood, the Japanese, and the Onslaught of the VCR* (New York: W. W. Norton, 1987), pp. 206–17.

12. Epstein, *The Big Picture*, pp. 51–2.

13. For a full timeline of these in-house developments, see Frederick Wasser, *Veni, Vidi, Video: The Hollywood Empire and the VCR* (Austin: University of Texas Press, 2001), Table 3.3, p. 96.

14. Hans Fantel, 'Does Visionary Business Call for a Corporate Sage?', *New York Times*, 17 June 1990, http://www.nytimes.com/1990/06/17/arts/video-does-visionary-business-call-for-a-corporate-sage.html.

15. Nielsen figures on percentage of VCR ownership from Paul B. Lindstrom, 'Home Video: The Consumer Impact', in Mark R. Levy (ed.), *The VCR Age: Home Video and Mass Communication* (London: Sage, 1989); MPAA figures on prerecorded videocassette sales quoted in Prince, *A New Pot of Gold*, p. 95.

16. See Gomery, *Shared Pleasures*, pp. 103–15, for a detailed account of Cineplex Odeon's positive influence on the exhibition industry.

17. Quoted in 'General Cinema Outlook', *Variety*, 5 November 1980, p. 36. Release figures quoted in Joel Finler, *The Hollywood Story* (London: Wallflower, 2003), p. 367.

18. Wasser, *Veni, Vidi, Video*, p. 94.

19. Justin Wyatt, 'The Formation of the "Major Independent": Miramax, New Line and the New Hollywood', in Steve Neale and Murray Smith (eds), *Contemporary Hollywood Cinema* (London: Routledge, 1998), pp. 74–6.

20. David Sanjek, 'Home Alone: The Phenomenon of Direct-to-video', *Cineaste* vol. 21 no. 1 (1995), pp. 98–100.

21. In her insightful study of the erotic thriller, Linda Ruth Williams has remarked on the 'narrative amnesia' which marks most DTV sequels in that genre, with actors often reappearing as different characters. I would suggest that it is too much to infer, as Williams does, that this is also necessarily true of the 'DTV genre' as a whole – although it is certainly more prevalent in the DTV arena than elsewhere, the erotic thriller is at the far end of the spectrum, whereas in other genres (particularly horror) a modicum of continuity is usually in evidence. See Linda Ruth Williams, *The Erotic Thriller in Contemporary Cinema* (Edinburgh: Edinburgh University Press, 2005), pp. 364–7.

22. Quoted in Wasser, *Veni, Vidi, Video*, p. 123.

23. Ibid., pp. 122–3; Prince, *A New Pot of Gold*, pp. 150–1.

24. Vajna quoted in 'Vajna and Kassar Planning Series of Biennial "First Blood" Pictures', *Variety*, 7 November 1984, p. 26.

25. Prince, *A New Pot of Gold*, p. 147.

26. See 'Growth of an Indie', *Variety*, 18–24 September 1995, p. 56; Keith Collins, 'A Brief History', *Variety*, 22 August 2004, http://www.variety.com/article/VR1117909431.html; Justin Wyatt, 'The Formation of the "Major Independent"', pp. 76–7.

27. This figure is quoted by Bob Shaye in Frederick S. Clarke, 'Nightmare on Elm Street: The Phenomenon', *Cinefantastique* vol. 18 no. 5 (July 1988), pp. 6–7.

28. Interview with the author, 10 June 2009.

29. 'Pickups Sought by New Line to Boost Sked', *Variety*, 6 March 1985, pp. 6, 322.

30. Clarke, 'Nightmare on Elm Street', p. 7.

31. Wyatt, 'The Formation of the "Major Independent"', p. 77.

32. Wasser, *Veni, Vidi, Video*, p. 121.

33. Ibid., p. 122.

34. Justin Wyatt, 'Independents, Packaging, and Inflationary Pressures in 1980s Hollywood', in Prince, *A New Pot of Gold* p. 145; 'Vajna & Kassar Planning Series of Biennial "First Blood" Pictures', p. 26.

35. Wasser, 'Ancillary Markets, pp. 127–8; Epstein, *The Big Picture*, pp. 211–15. 'Relatively', because Fox, Paramount and Disney initially held out from releasing their titles on the new format. It was only a matter of months before they relented, however, with Lieberfarb reportedly winning over Fox, the last of the holdouts, by convincing Time Warner to carry Fox News on its cable networks. See Daniel Frankel, 'DVD Timeline', *Variety*, 23 April 2007, http://www.variety.com/article/VR1117963613.html.

36. Held back in part by the format war, video took nearly eight years to reach 10 per cent penetration of TV-owning households in the US; DVD, on the other hand, passed that tipping point in under three years, establishing itself as a presence in more than 46 million homes (43.1 per cent of all TV-owning households) by 2003 (Epstein, *The Big Picture*, p. 216).

37. Such is the case with Tom Schatz's otherwise authoritative 'The Studio System', where he suggests that, by the early 2000s, there were effectively three production categories: $100 million blockbusters produced by the majors; $40 million arthouse and niche-market fare produced by their indie subsidiaries; and films budgeted at less than $10 million produced by genuinely independent producer-distributors. Schatz in MacDonald and Wasko, *The Contemporary Hollywood Film Industry*, p. 31.

38. As Stephen Prince has noted, the home video-strategy was not, as is often assumed, an innovation of Michael Eisner, who became Disney's chairman and CEO in 1984. See Prince, *A New Pot of Gold*, p. 75.

39. Paramount's pricing strategy resulted in more than 100,000 units of *Wrath of Khan* being sold – a record at that time. Rentals were considerably less profitable for the studios, because they received only an initial flat fee from rental dealers, rather than a percentage of revenue per 'turn'. A turn is industry parlance for a single rental transaction. Rental dealers were legally allowed to cut studios out of rental revenues on the basis of the 'First Sale' doctrine in the 1976 Copyright Act, which contends that copyright owners do not have control over the physical embodiments (such as books or videos) of that copyrighted material. For more on 'First Sale', see Gomery, *Shared Pleasures*, pp. 284–7; Wasser, *Veni, Vidi, Video*, pp. 101–3; Prince, *A New Pot of Gold*, p. 104.

40. Douglas Gomery, 'Disney's Business History: A Reinterpretation', in Eric Smoodin (ed.), *Disney Discourse: Producing the Magic Kingdom* (London: Routledge, 1994) p. 74.

41. Ron Grover, *The Disney Touch: Disney, ABC and the Quest for the World's Greatest Media Empire* (rev. edn) (London: Irwin, 1997), pp. 132–3; Janet Wasko, *Understanding Disney* (Cambridge: Polity Press, 2001). p. 45.

42. Adam Sandler, 'Disney Devises Vid Sequel to "Aladdin"', *Variety*, 10 February 1994, http://www.variety.com/article/VR118257.html.

43. Kenneth M. Chanko, 'Who Says a Movie Sequel Can't Be Made for Home Video?', *New York Times*, 19 June 1994, http://www.nytimes.com/1994/06/19/movies/film-who-says-a-movie-sequel-can-t-be-made-for-home-video.html.

44. And, as Universal home-video chief Louis Feola notes, they 'no doubt benefited from Disney's marketing muscle in the retail pipeline promoting the concept of made-for-video movies'. See Feola, 'Made for Video Movies', in Jason E. Squire (ed.), *The Movie Business Book: International 3rd*

Edition (Maidenhead: McGraw Hill, Open University Press, 2006), pp. 437–44. See also Adam Sandler, 'U Cartoon Arm Moves Focus to Kidvid Titles', *Variety*, 13 July 1993, http://www.variety.com/ article/VR108676.html. For more on the dominance of family-friendly fare in the sell-through market, see Al Stewart, 'Tale of the Tapes Is Based on Vid Sales', *Variety*, 7 February 1993, http://www.variety.com/article/VR103764.html.

45. For reporting on the phenomenon of repeat viewing among children and young adults, see Emily Yoffe, 'Play It Again, Mom (Again and Again)', *New York Times*, 13 July 2003, http://www.nytimes.com/ 2003/07/13/movies/film-play-it-again-mom-again-and-again.html). For an academic approach to this pattern of behaviour in relation to film as an art and a business, see Robert C. Allen, 'Home Alone Together: Hollywood and the "Family" Film', in Melvyn Stokes and Richard Maltby (eds), *Identifying Hollywood's Audiences* (London: BFI Publishing, 1999), pp. 109–31; Barbara Klinger, *Beyond the Multiplex* (London: University of California Press, 2006), pp. 135–90.

46. Chanko, 'Who Says a Movie Sequel Can't Be Made for Home Video?'.

47. Sallie Hoffmeister, 'Appeal of Direct-to-video Grows among Film Studios', *New York Times*, 8 November 1994, http://www.nytimes.com/1994/11/08/business/appeal-of-direct-to-video-grows-among-film-studios.html. In terms of sales growth, rental sales increased by just under 7 per cent in 1993, whereas retail sales increased by just under 24 per cent in the same period, based on calculations made from MPAA figures quoted in Paul McDonald, *Video and DVD Industries* (London: BFI Publishing, 2007), p. 124.

48. See Michael Mallory, 'A Whole New World for Walt Disney', *Variety*, 23 March 1997, http://www.variety.com/vstory/VR1117342397.html; Hoffmeister, 'Appeal of Direct-to-video Grows among Film Studios'.

49. Edward Jay Epstein, *The Rise of the Home Entertainment Economy*, http://www.edwardjayepstein. com/mpa2004.html.

50. McDonald, *Video and DVD Industries*, pp. 150–2.

51. Scott Hettrick, 'Disney Ramps up Vid Preem Sequel Slate', *Variety*, 18 September 2001, http://www.variety.com/article/VR1117852843.html; Scott Hettrick, 'Disney Toons up DVD Unit', *Variety*, 10 June 2003, http://www.variety.com/article/VR1117887693.html.

52. Adam Sandler, 'Feola Tops U Family Unit', *Variety*, 3 February 1998, http://www.variety.com/article/ VR1117467391.html.

53. Scott Hettrick, 'Fox Ups DVD Pic Preems' *Variety*, 17 February 2004, http://www.variety.com/ article/VR1117916453.html; 'Par Hits Home with Original DVD Preems,' *Variety*, 15 October 2005, http://www.variety.com/article/VR1117931047.html; 'Lion Taming Disc Biz', *Variety*, 26 August 2004, http://www.variety.com/article/VR1117909669.html.

54. Brooke Barnes, 'Direct-to-DVD Releases Shed Their Loser Label', *New York Times*, 28 January 2008.

55. Ultimately followed by a subsequent return to the big screen in *American Reunion* (2012).

56. The six major studios, MGM and Lionsgate have accounted for 85–95 per cent of US home-video revenues in every year between 2000 and 2009. US home-entertainment industry statistics for the past decade derived from *Video Business*, a trade publication which merged with *Variety* in the early 2000s. Statistics accessible at http://www.variety.com/article/VR6301486.html.

57. Quoted in Daniel Frankel, 'Home Is Where the Franchise Is', *Variety*, 9 October 2006, http://www.variety.com/article/VR1117951580.html; Variety Staff Writers, 'Home Entertainment Leader Report', *Variety*, 7 January 2009, http://www.variety.com/article/VR1117998130.html.

58. Frankel, 'Home Is Where the Franchise Is'.

59. A few examples include Edward Neumeier, writer of all three *Starship Troopers* films (1997–), promoted to director duty on the third instalment; Charles Grosvenor, who directed no less than nine of the thirteen *The Land before Time* films (1988–); and the tireless Eugene Levy, who has reprised his role as Mr Levenstein in all eight (at the time of writing) *American Pie* episodes.

60. Both quoted in Alex Godfrey, 'Sequel Opportunity Offenders', *Guardian Guide*, 31 July 2010, pp. 6–9.

61. Dade Hayes, 'Sequels More than Equal', *Variety*, 4 September 2001, http://www.variety.com/article/VR1117852205.html.

62. *Austin Powers: The Spy Who Shagged Me* (1999) took $54 million in its opening weekend and $206 million in total at the North American box office, versus its predecessor's $53 million US total; *Pirates of the Caribbean: Dead Man's Chest* (2006) grossed $423 million versus *Pirates of the Caribbean: The Curse of the Black Pearl*'s (2003) $305 million; *Transporter 2* (2005) grossed $43 million versus *The Transporter*'s (2002) $25 million; *Harold and Kumar Escape from Guantanmo Bay* (2008) grossed $38 million, versus *Harold and Kumar Go to White Castle*'s (2004) $18 million; and *Saw II* (2005) grossed $87 million, versus *Saw*'s $55 million. All figures from http://www.boxoffice-mojo.com/franchises/. See also Ben Fritz, 'Vid Auds Deliver "Transporter"', *Variety*, 11 September 2005, http://www.variety.com/article/VR1117928903.html.

63. A double pack containing the first two movies, a triple pack containing all three in both 'rated' and 'unrated' versions.

64. Janet Wasko, *How Hollywood Works* (London: Sage, 2003), pp. 161–5; Epstein, *The Big Picture*, pp. 225–8.

65. Jill Goldsmith, 'Discs Driving Pix-toy Tie-in', *Variety*, 9 June 2004, http://www.variety.com/article/VR1117906224.html.

66. Barnes, 'Direct-to-DVD Releases Shed Their Loser Label'.

67. It is something of an irony that, in their quest to maximise the potential of their intellectual property, the studios became involved, directly or indirectly, in producing more physical products (discs, tapes, toys and so on) than ever before.

68. Peter Bart, 'Are All Films Created Sequel?', *Variety*, 28 July 2002, http://www.variety.com/article/VR1117870320.html.

69. Aljean Harmetz, 'Price Is Replaced as Chief of Columbia Pictures', *New York Times*, 8 October 1983, http://www.nytimes.com/1983/10/08/arts/price-is-replaced-as-chief-of-columbia-pictures.html.

70. Bart, 'Are All Films Created Sequel?'

71. Cook, *Lost Illusions*, p. 51.

72. See ibid., pp. 47–51; Tom Shone, *Blockbuster: How the Jaws and Jedi Generation Turned Hollywood into a Boom Town* (London: Simon & Schuster, 2004), pp. 65–6; Michael Pye and Linda Myles, *The Movie Brats: How the Film Generation Took over Hollywood* (London: Faber and Faber, 1979), pp. 113–39.

73. Shone, *Blockbuster*, p. 66.

74. Barry M. Freiman, 'One-on-one Interview with Producer Ilya Salkind', *Superman.com*, February 2006, http://www.supermanhomepage.com/movies/movies.php?topic=interview-salkind; Harlan Kennedy, 'Super Salkinds', *Film Comment* vol. 29 no. 3 (May–June 1983), pp. 49–55; Susan Heller Anderson, 'It's a Bird! It's a Plane! It's a Movie!', *New York Times*, 26 June 1977.

75. See Wasser, *Veni, Vidi, Video*, p. 106; Sheldon Hall and Steve Neale, *Epics, Spectacles and Blockbusters: A Hollywood History* (Detroit, MI: Wayne State University Press, 2010), p. 222.

76. See Epstein, *The Big Picture*, pp. 42–3, for an overview. For a more detailed account of the machinations of the deal, led by Steve Ross, see Connie Bruck, *Master of the Game: How Steve Ross Rode the Light Fantastic from Undertaker to Creator of the Largest Media Conglomerate in the World* (New York: Simon & Schuster, 1994), pp. 44–62.

77. Carol Olten, 'It's a Bird! It's a Plane! No, It's Super Bucks!', *San Diego Union*, 6 August 1978, p. E1; Aljean Harmetz, 'The Marketing of Superman and His Paraphernalia', *New York Times*, 21 June 1981, http://www.nytimes.com/1981/06/21/movies/the-marketing-of-superman-and-his-paraphernalia.html.

78. Brown, 'The Years without Ross', *Premiere*, January 1996, p. 36.

79. Prince, *A New Pot of Gold*, pp. 64–70.

80. Jerome Christensen, 'The Time Warner Conspiracy: *JFK*, *Batman*, and the Manager Theory of Hollywood Film', *Critical Inquiry* no. 28 (Spring 2002). For more on *Batman*'s status in relation to the new conglomerate era, see Eileen Meehan, 'Holy Commodity Fetish Batman!: The Political Economy of a Commercial Intertext', in Roberta E. Pearson and William Uricchio (eds), *The Many Lives of Batman* (London: Routledge, 1991); Jon Lewis, 'Money Matters: Hollywood in the Corporate Era', in Lewis (ed.) *The New American Cinema* (Durham, NC: Duke University Press, 1998).

81. Shone, *Blockbuster*, pp. 186–7.

82. Hayes and Bing, *Open Wide*, p. 281.

83. For more on the narrowing window for exhibition see Charles Acland, 'Theatrical Exhibition: Accelerated Cinema', in MacDonald and Wasko, *The Contemporary Hollywood Film Industry*, pp. 83–105.

84. Burton was undoubtedly also selected with traditional commercial considerations in mind, as Warner did not officially hire the director until *Beetlejuice* (1988) proved itself at the box office. See Will Brooker, *Batman Unmasked* (London: Continuum, 2000), p. 292.

85. For Keaton's take on events see Fred Schruers, 'Bat Mitzvah', *Premiere* vol. 5 no. 11 (July 1992), pp. 56–64. For reporting on his salary increase, see 'Batman 3!', *Entertainment Weekly*, 1 October 1993, http://www.ew.com/ew/article/0,,308195,00.html.

86. See Alan Jones, 'Batman in Production', *Cinefantastique* (November 1989), pp. 75–88; Mark Salisbury, *Burton on Burton* (London: Faber and Faber, 1995), p. 102.

87. Paul Grainge, *Brand Hollywood* (London: Routledge, 2008), pp. 130–4.

88. Dana Harris, 'Potter Planted', *Variety*, 28 March 2000, http://www.variety.com/article/VR1117779988.html.

89. Quoted in Grainge, *Brand Hollywood*, p. 140.

90. The notion of which will be discussed further in Chapter 7.

91. See http://www.boxofficemojo.com/franchises/chart/?id=harrypotter.htm.

92. Following the commercial failure of two of their 'serious' films (*Duplicity* [2008] and *State of Play* [2009]), for example, Universal chairman Marc Shmuger remarked that his current priority was marrying talent 'with properties that can become worldwide events and be sequelized'. Quoted in Marc Graser, 'Universal Has Franchise Fever', *Variety*, 24 April 2009, http://www.variety.com/article/VR1118002848.html.

93. A distribution arm of Disney, established in the early 1980s as an outlet for less family-orientated fare.

94. Claudia Eller, 'Steel Set to Ankle Disney', *Variety*, 20 December 1992, http://www.variety.com/article/VR102254.html.

95. Claudia Eller, 'Bill Duke Gets in on the "Act"', *Variety*, 2 February 1993, http://www.variety.com/article/VR103609.html.

96. Anne Thompson and Tatiana Siegel, 'Dreamworks Nabs Rights to "Activity"', *Variety*, 30 January 2008. http://www.variety.com/article/VR1117979902.html; Dave McNary, 'Extracurricular "Activity" for Film', *Variety*, 27 October 2009, http://www.variety.com/article/VR1118010479.html.

97. Dave McNary, 'Paramount to Produce More Micro-budget Films', *Variety*, 10 December 2009, http://www.variety.com/article/VR1118012597.

98. Pamela McClintock, '"Paranormal 2" to Face off with "Saw VII 3D"', *Variety*, 30 March 2010, http://www.variety.com/article/VR1118017086.

99. Diane Garrett and Tatiana Siegel, 'Warner Weds Phillips Film', *Variety*, 4 October 2007, http://www.variety.com/article/VR1117973450; Nicki Finke, 'How *The Hangover* Got Made', *LA Weekly*, 12–18 June 2010, p. 17.

100. Legendary is an independent production company that entered into a deal with Warner Bros. to co-finance and co-produce forty films with the studio starting in 2005. See Marc Graser, 'Legendary Pictures Eyes New Credit Line', *Variety*, 15 April 2011, http://variety.com/2011/film/news/legendary-pictures-eyes-new-credit-line-1118035532/.

101. Michael Fleming, 'Hangover Helmer Still on a High', *Variety*, 9 July 2009, http://www.variety.com/article/VR1118005838.

102. Michael Fleming, 'WB Gets Tipsy with "Hangover" Sequel', *Variety*, 5 April 2009, http://www.variety.com/article/VR1118002135.

103. Stephen Farber, 'They Made Him Two Offers He Couldn't Refuse', *New York Times*, 22 December 1974; Peter Cowie, *The Godfather Book* (London: Faber and Faber, 1997), pp. 75–7.

104. Aljean Harmetz, 'Bonus Deal for Stallone', *New York Times*, 11 May 1982, http://www.nytimes.com/1982/05/11/movies/bonus-deal-for-stallone.html; Aljean Harmetz, 'Hollywood Battles Killer Budgets', *New York Times*, 31 May 1987, http://www.nytimes.com/1987/05/31/business/hollywood-battles-killer-budgets.html.

105. Epstein, *The Big Picture*, p. 18; See also Geraldine Fabrikant, 'The Hole in Hollywood's Pocket', *New York Times*, 10 December 1990, http://www.nytimes.com/1990/12/10/business/the-hole-in-hollywood-s-pocket.html.

106. Leonard Klady, 'A Script to Die for', *Variety*, 9 May 1993, http://www.variety.com/article/VR106678; Jonathan Bing, 'Actors Savor Star Bucks', *Variety*, 1 April 2002, http://www.variety.com/article/VR1117864688.

107. Ibid.; Claudia Eller, 'Whoopi Singing All the Way to the Bank on Sister Sequel', *Variety*, 30 November 1992, http://www.variety.com/article/VR101682.html; 'Mail Sends Ryan $10 M', *Variety*, 17 November 1997, http://www.variety.com/article/VR11662167.

108. Claudia Eller, 'Culkin's Dad Sacks Mark', *Variety*, 2 December 1992, http://www.variety.com/article/VR101748; Larry Rohter, 'How a 9-Year-Old Boy Rode a Dark Horse to Success', *New York Times*, 10 December 1990, http://www.nytimes.com/1990/12/10/movies/how-a-9-year-old-boy-rode-a-dark-horse-to-success.html.

109. 'Bill Shatner Returning for Star Trek IV', *Variety*, 30 January 1985, p. 18.

110. Author's interview with Wes Craven, 9 June, 2009; Author's interview with Joe Dante, 30 June 2010.

111. For more on this, see Prince, *A New Pot of Gold*, p. 172.

112. Michael Fleming, '"Daredevil" Dedication Pays Dividends', *Variety*, 6 February 2003, http://www.variety.com/article/VR1117880146.html; Pamela McClintock, 'Warners' Men in Tights', *Variety*, 22 February 2006, http://www.variety.com/article/VR1117938709.html; Michael Fleming, 'Aussie Has Bulk for "Hulk"', *Variety*, 14 October 2001, http://www.variety.com/article/VR1117854264.html; Anne Thompson, 'Favreau Keeps "Iron Man" Light', *Variety*, 25 April 2008, http://www.variety.com/article/VR1117984627.html; Pamela McClintock, 'Transformers Dominates Box Office', *Variety*, 8 July 2007, http://www.variety.com/article/VR1117968186.html.

113. Exceptions to this include Steve Martin, who simultaneously committed to both *The Pink Panther* (2006) remake and a sequel, and Morgan Freeman, who had a contractual clause to reprise his role of Alex Cross in *Along Came a Spider* (2001), prequel to *Kiss the Girls* (1997). Both were established stars, but in both cases it was clear from the source material (the original MGM comedy series and a series of detective novels by James Patterson, respectively) that the intention was to create more than one film. See Dana Harris, 'Clouseau on Caper for MGM', *Variety*, 16 November 2003, http://www.variety.com/article/VR1117895779; Michael Fleming, 'Par Picks "Girls" Sequel', *Variety*, 11 November 1998, http://www.variety.com/article/VR1117488416.

114. Michael Fleming, 'Samuel Jackson Joins "Iron" Cast', *Variety*, 25 February 2009, http://www.variety.com/article/VR1118000573; Marc Graser, 'Lean-minded Marvel Offers Stars Tentpole Potential', *Variety*, 29 March 2010, pp. 6, 25.

115. Michael Fleming, 'Scooby 2 Unleashed', *Variety*, 19 June 2002, http://www.variety.com/article/VR1117868779; Michael Fleming, 'All Ingredients in Place for "Pie 3"', *Variety*, 7 August 2002, http://www.variety.com/article/VR1117870927; Meredith Amdur, 'Good News for Rupe', *Variety*, 12 February 2003, http://www.variety.com/article/VR1117880458; Michael Fleming, 'New Man for the "Job"', *Variety*, 19 July 2004, http://www.variety.com/article/VR1117907994); Michael Fleming, 'New Line Orders More "Hairspray"', *Variety*, 23 July 2008, http://www.variety.com/article/VR1117989390.

116. This was one of the explanations given for the inflated production budget of $200 million for the sequel versus $120 million for the original. See Michael Fleming, 'Maguire Spins "Spider-Man"', *Variety*, 30 July 2000, http://variety.com/2000/film/news/maguire-spins-spider-man-1117784384/; Claude Brodesser, 'Spider-Man Players Caught in Sequel Web', *Variety*, 4 April 2002, http://www.variety.com/article/VR1117864968; Dana Harris, 'A Web of Spidey Intrigue', *Variety*, 17 March 2003, http://www.variety.com/article/VR1117882569; Claude Brodesser and Dana Harris, 'Tobey's Tangled Rep Web', *Variety*, 13 April 2003, http://www.variety.com/article/VR1117884592; Nicole Laporte, 'Spidey Spins Web for Third Time', *Variety*, 2 March 2004, http://www.variety.com/article/VR1117901100.

117. Mark Silverman, 'Par Inks "BevHills Cop" Producers to New Deal over a Year Early', *Variety*, 3 April 1985, p. 4; Prince, *A New Pot of Gold*, p. 172.

118. 'Turner Wants More $$ for Jewel; Fox Sues', *Variety*, 6 February 1985, p. 3; Michael Fleming, 'Diesel Heads to CAA', *Variety*, 2 April 2006, http://www.variety.com/article/VR1117940837.

119. Rick Altman, *Film/Genre* (London: BFI Publishing, 1999), p. 117.

120. Lawrence Cohn, 'Horror, Sci-fi Pix Earn 37 Per Cent of Rentals', *Variety*, 19 November 1980, pp. 5, 32.

121. In particular, see Robert E. Kapsis, 'Hollywood Genres and the Production of Culture Perspective', *Current Research in Film* vol. 5 (1991), pp. 68–85; Prince, *A New Pot of Gold*, pp. 298–9; Andrew

Tudor, 'From Paranoia to Postmodernism? The Horror Movie in Late Modern Society', in Steve Neale (ed.), *Genre and Contemporary Hollywood* (London: BFI Publishing, 2002), pp. 105–7.

122. For more about the structure of this cycle, see Richard Nowell, *Blood Money: A History of the First Teen Slasher Cycle* (London: Continuum, 2011).

123. 'Police Academy II', *Variety*, 9 January 1985, pp. 6, 30.

124. Of course not every such sequel can be directly traced to a cycle in this way, but even if their conceit or execution seem relatively original – as with *The Blair Witch Project* (1999) and *Final Destination* (2000) – this does not mean that the commercial rationale for their existence was any less opportunistic.

125. Edward Jay Epstein, 'The Midas Formula', *Slate*, 31 May 2005, http://www.slate.com/id/2119701/.

126. Peter Caranicas, 'Studios Hit with Home Video Slump', *Variety*, 1 May 2010, http://www.variety.com/article/VR1118018573.html; Marc Graser, 'CES: Hollywood Homevid Biz Stable in 2012', *Variety*, 8 January 2013, http://variety.com/2013/digital/news/ces-hollywood-homevid-biz-stable-in-2012-1118064338/.

Chapter 5

1. Kristin Thompson, *Storytelling in Film and Television* (London: Harvard University Press, 2003), p. 76.

2. This project actually began in one of the final chapters of *The Classical Hollywood Cinema* itself, with Bordwell and Staiger asserting that, despite the influence of art cinema on certain New Hollywood directors, 'the classical style remains the dominant model for feature filmmaking'. See David Bordwell, Janet Staiger and Kristin Thompson, *The Classical Hollywood Cinema: Film Style and Mode of Production* (London: Routledge, 1985) p. 370.

3. Kristin Thompson, *Storytelling in the New Hollywood: Understanding Classical Narrative Technique* (London: Harvard University Press, 1999), p. 12.

4. The notion of 'high concept' was originally elaborated by Justin Wyatt and latterly modified by Richard Maltby. See Justin Wyatt, *High Concept* (Austin: University of Texas Press, 1994); Richard Maltby '"Nobody Knows Everything": Post-classical Historiographies and Consolidated Entertainment', in Steve Neale and Murray Smith (eds), *Contemporary Hollywood Cinema* (London: Routledge, 1998), pp. 21–44. See also Timothy Corrigan, *A Cinema without Walls: Movies and Culture after Vietnam* (New York: Rutgers University Press, 1991); Thomas Schatz, 'The New Hollywood', in Jim Collins, Hilary Radner and Ava Preacher Collins (eds), *Film Theory Goes to the Movies* (New York: Routledge, 1993), pp. 8–36.

5. David Bordwell, *The Way Hollywood Tells It: Story and Style in Modern Movies* (Berkeley: University of California Press, 2006), p. 5.

6. Schatz, 'The New Hollywood', p. 22.

7. Ibid.

8. Ibid., p. 33.

9. Wyatt, *High Concept*, p. 8.

10. Bordwell, *The Way Hollywood Tells It*, p. 9. This is a point made previously by both Murray Smith and Warren Buckland. See Smith, 'Theses on the Philosophy of Hollywood History', pp. 3–20; and Buckland, 'A Close Encounter with *Raiders of the Lost Ark*: Notes on Narrative Aspects of the New Hollywood Blockbuster', pp. 166–78; both in Neale and Smith, *Contemporary Hollywood Cinema*.

11. Thompson, *Storytelling in the New Hollywood*, p. 344.

12. Sheila Roberts, 'Sylvester Stallone Interview, Rambo', *Movies Online,* http://www.moviesonline.ca/ movienews_13893.html.

13. Bordwell *et al., The Classical Hollywood Cinema,* p. 35.

14. Ibid., p. 47.

15. Ibid.

16. Ibid., p. 82.

17. Ibid., p. 371.

18. Thompson, *Storytelling in the New Hollywood,* p. 12.

19. Ibid., p. 29.

20. Bordwell *et al., The Classical Hollywood Cinema,* p. 36.

21. Ibid.

22. Ibid., p. 18.

23. David Bordwell, *Narration in the Fiction Film* (London: Methuen, 1985), p. 159.

24. Bordwell *et al., The Classical Hollywood Cinema,* p. 12.

25. Bordwell, *Narration in the Fiction Film,* p. 50.

26. Ibid.

27. Ibid., p. 53.

28. Ibid., p. 49.

29. Ibid.

30. Barry King describes the spectator as 'more the subject of information processing than a concrete individual', while Andrew Britton asserts that the viewer activity described 'amounts to little more than the learning and decipherment of "schemata"'. See King, 'The Story Continues … ', *Screen* vol. 28 no. 3 (Summer 1987), p. 64; Britton, 'The Philosophy of the Pigeonhole: Wisconsin Formalism and "The Classical Style"', *CineAction!* (Winter 1988/9), p. 51.

31. As per Bordwell's forthright response to King: Bordwell, 'Adventures in the Highlands of Theory', *Screen* vol. 29 no. 1 (Winter 1988), pp. 72–97.

32. Bordwell *et al., The Classical Hollywood Cinema,* p. 19.

33. Ibid., p. 20.

34. Bordwell, *Narration in the Fiction Film,* pp. 36, 164, 42.

35. It is noteworthy that generic motivation gets but one fleeting mention in Thompson's *Storytelling in the New Hollywood* (and this again using the now rather tired example of the song-and-dance number in the musical) and none whatsoever in Bordwell's *The Way Hollywood Tells It.* See *Storytelling in the New Hollywood,* p. 13; *The Way Hollywood Tells It,* p. 52.

36. Geoff King, *New Hollywood Cinema: An Introduction* (London: I. B. Tauris, 2002), p. 219.

37. Richard Maltby's analysis of *Casablanca* is a useful demonstration of this. See '"A Brief Romantic Interlude": Dick and Jane Go to 3½ Seconds of the Classical Hollywood Cinema', in David Bordwell and Noel Carroll, *Post-Theory: Reconstructing Film Studies* (Madison: University of Wisconsin Press, 1996), pp. 434–59.

38. A boxset containing the orginal trilogy sold 100,000 units in the UK in the first five months of 2008, with around 200,000 units of various Rambo formats sold in the US during the same period – and this is only one example of the multifarious types of exploitation which can occur upon the arrival of a new sequel to an existing series. Box-office figures taken from www.boxofficemojo.com and www.iboe.com. DVD/Blu-ray figures taken from the UK Charts Company, https://ukcharts.co.uk.

39. See, for example, Victor Erlich, *Russian Formalism: History-Doctrine* (London: Yale University Press, 1965), pp. 241–3.

40. Bordwell et al., *The Classical Hollywood Cinema*, pp. 16–17.

41. Ibid., p. 16.

42. Thompson, *Storytelling in Film and Television*, p. 76.

43. Ibid., p. 105.

44. Fleming, 'Maguire Spins "Spider-Man"', *Variety*, 30 July 2000, http://variety.com/2000/film/news/maguire-spins-spider-man-1117784384/.

45. Henry Jenkins, *Convergence Culture: Where Old and New Media Collide* (New York: New York University Press, 2006).

46. Ibid., p. 94.

47. Ibid., pp. 95, 97.

48. Some aspects of Jenkins's argument are a little unclear. Early on, for example, he suggests that 'Each franchise entry needs to be self-contained so you don't need to have seen the film to enjoy the game, and vice versa', but in proffering *The Matrix* as an example, and counterposing its narrative gaps to the redundancy of the classical Hollywood cinema, he seems to suggest otherwise. See ibid., p. 106.

49. Kristin Thompson, *The Frodo Franchise: The Lord of the Rings and Modern Hollywood* (London: University of California Press, 2007), p. 73.

Chapter 6

1. The most convincing critique of the classical paradigm is that its narratological emphasis, while providing an accurate description of the way Hollywood movies tell stories, fails to acknowledge the multifarious pleasures those movies offer, only some of which are the direct result of narrative construction. Dirk Eitzen, for example, proposes that 'what the classical Hollywood cinema is fundamentally about is not the production of a certain kind of narrative but, rather, the production of certain kinds of emotion', while Richard Maltby, putting forth a 'consumerist' account of Hollywood, argues that 'narrative functions as part of the provision of pleasure in cinema, not as the point of it'. Both of these accounts overcompensate somewhat, demoting narrative to such a minor role that they effectively deny that an audience might take any pleasure in its construction, but their observations are apposite to the workings of the Hollywood sequel because they furnish an indication of the broad spectrum of motivations that might lead an audience to come back for more. See: Dirk Eitzen, 'Comedy and Classicism', in Richard Allen and Murray Smith (eds), *Film Theory and Philosophy* (Oxford: Clarendon Press, 1997), pp. 394–411; Richard Maltby, *Hollywood Cinema* (Oxford: Blackwell, 1995), p. 324.

2. David Bordwell, Janet Staiger and Kristin Thompson, *The Classical Hollywood Cinema: Film Style and Mode of Production to 1960* (London: Routledge, 1985), p. 19.

3. Gérard Genette, *Palimpsests* (Lincoln: University of Nebraska Press, 1982), p. 162.

4. Robert Stam, 'From Text to Intertext,' in Robert Stam and Toby Miller (eds), *Film Theory: An Introduction* (London: Blackwell, 1999), p. 209.

5. Mikhail Iampolski, *The Memory of Tiresias* (London: University of California Press, 1998); Barbara Klinger, 'Digressions at the Cinema: Reception and Mass Culture', *Cinema Journal* vol. 28 no. 4

(Summer 1989), pp. 3–19; Umberto Eco, *Travels in Hyperreality* (London: Picador, 1987); Tom
Gunning, 'The Intertextuality of Early Cinema', in Robert Stam and Alessandra Raengo (eds),
A Companion to Literature and Film (London: Blackwell, 2004), pp. 127–41.

6. Ibid., p. 248.

7. Ibid., p. 31.

8. See Jim Collins, 'Genericity in the Nineties: Eclectic Irony and the New Sincerity', in Jim Collins,
Hilary Radner and Ava Preacher Collins (eds), *Film Theory Goes to the Movies* (London: Routledge,
1993), pp. 242–63; Fredric Jameson, 'Postmodernism and Consumer Society', in Hal Foster (ed.), *The
Anti-aesthetic: Essays on Postmodern Culture* (Washington, DC: Bay Press, 1983), pp. 111–25;
Umberto Eco, 'Casablanca: Cult Movies and Intertextual Collage', in Eco, *Travels*, pp. 197–210.

9. Noel Carroll, *Interpreting the Moving Image* (Cambridge: Cambridge University Press, 1998), p. 241.

10. Ibid., p. 245.

11. Ibid., pp. 10–14.

12. Furthermore, the vast majority of viewers will probably be aware (via paratextual markers such
as the film's title) that what they are watching is a sequel, and will therefore be able to make
sense of McClane's comment as a reference to earlier events – even if they have not seen the
first film.

13. Richard Dyer, *Stars* (London: BFI Publishing, 1979).

14. Christine Geraghty, 'Re-examining Stardom: Questions of Texts, Bodies and Performance', in
Christine Gledhill and Linda Williams (eds), *Reinventing Film Studies* (London: Arnold, 2000), p. 185.

15. Alan Lovell and Peter Krämer (eds), *Screen Acting* (London: Routledge, 1999); Christine Geraghty,
'Performing as a Lady and a Dame: Reflections on Acting and Genre', in Thomas Austin and Martin
Barker (eds), *Contemporary Hollywood Stardom* (London: Arnold, 2003).

16. Jackie Stacey, *Star Gazing* (London: Routledge, 1994); Martin Barker and Kate Brooks, *Knowing
Audiences* (Luton: University of Luton Press, 1998); Rachel Moseley, *Growing up with Audrey Hepburn*
(Manchester: Manchester University Press, 2002).

17. Alan Lovell, 'I Went in Search of Deborah Kerr, Jodie Foster and Julianne Moore but Got Waylaid
…', in Austin and Barker, *Contemporary Hollywood Stardom*, p. 261.

18. One interesting exception to this is Peter Krämer's account of Sandra Bullock's varying career
fortunes. See Peter Krämer, 'The Rise and Fall of Sandra Bullock: Notes on Starmaking and Female
Stardom in Contemporary Hollywood', in Andy Willis (ed.), *Film Stars: Hollywood and Beyond*
(Manchester: Manchester University Press, 2004), pp. 89–112.

19. Jenny Cooney, 'Harder than the Rest', *Empire*, September 1991, p. 80.

20. Terence Rafferty, *New Yorker*, http://www.newyorker.com/arts/reviews/film/terminator_2_
judgment_day_cameron.

21. Cooney, 'Harder than the Rest', p. 79.

22. *The Net* grossed more than $50 million in North America, making it a solid success, while *While You
Were Sleeping* was a hit, generating more than $80 million and becoming the fifteenth highest-
grosser of the year. Figures from *Box Office Mojo*, http://www.boxofficemojo.com/people/
chart/?view=Actor&id=sandrabullock.htm.

23. Krämer, 'The Rise and Fall of Sandra Bullock', p. 104.

24. Emanuel Levy, *Variety*, 9 June 1997, http://www.variety.com/review/VE1117341118.html?
categoryid=31&cs=1&query=speed+2+keanu.

25. Bergman interviewed in Charlotte Chandler, *Ingrid: A Personal Biography* (London: Simon & Schuster, 2007), p. 111.

26. For example, Catherine Constable, 'Becoming the Monster's Mother: Morphologies of Identity in the *Alien* Series', in Annette Kuhn (ed.), *Alien Zone II* (London: Verso, 1999), pp. 173–202; Patricia Melzer, 'Technoscience's Stepdaughter: The Feminist *Cyborg* in Alien Resurrection', in *Alien Constructions* (Austin: University of Texas Press, 2006) pp. 108–48; Mary Ann Doane, 'Technophilia: Technology, Representation and the Feminine', in Sean Redmond (ed.), *Liquid Metal: The Science Fiction Film Reader* (London: Wallflower, 2004), pp. 182–91; Christine Cornea, *Science Fiction Cinema: Between Fantasy and Reality* (Edinburgh: Edinburgh University Press, 2007), pp. 146–54; Patricia Linton, 'Aliens, (M)Others, Cyborgs: The Emerging Ideology of Hybridity', in Deborah Cartmell, I.Q. Hunter, Heidi Kaye and Imelda Whelehan (eds), *Alien Identities* (London: Pluto Press, 1999), pp. 172–87; and Carol J. Clover *Men, Women and Chainsaws: Gender in the Modern Horror Film* (London: BFI Publishing, 1992). I suspect in part this is because much of the above builds from Barbara Creed's famous essay, 'Alien and the Monstrous-Feminine', in Annette Kuhn (ed.), *Alien Zone* (London: Verso, 1990), which addresses the first film only and therefore develops no larger discussion of Ripley's development as a character.

27. Danny Peary, 'Playing Ripley in *Alien*', excerpted in Peary (ed.), *Omni's Screen Flights/Screen Fantasies* (New York: Dolphin, 1984), p. 160.

28. Randy and Jean-Marc Lofficier, 'Interview with James Cameron and Gale Ann Hurd', originally published in *L'Écran Fantastique* no. 73, October 1986, taken from Lee Goldberg, Lofficier *et al.*, *Science Fiction Filmmaking in the 1980s: Interviews* (London: McFarland & Company, 1995), pp. 8–9.

29. Geraghty, 'Re-examining Stardom, p. 192.

30. Marcia Pally, 'Sigourney Takes Control', *Film Comment* vol. 22 no. 6 (November–December 1986), pp. 20–1.

31. See Garth Pearce, 'Return to the Forbidden Planet', *Empire*, November 1992, p. 64; Stephen Rebello, 'Ripley's Game', *Movieline*, September 1997, p. 59.

32. Richard deCordova, *Picture Personalities: The Emergence of the Star System in America* (Urbana: University of Illinois Press, 1990).

33. For example, see Hannah McGill, 'The Rise and Fall of Star Power', *Sight and Sound* vol. 20 no. 2 (February 2010), p. 43.

34. William Uricchio and Roberta Pearson, 'I'm Not Fooled by That Cheap Disguise', in *The Many Lives of Batman* (London: BFI Publishing, 1991), p. 185.

35. Dyer is the exception here, in that he touches on these issues when discussing the apparent mismatch between the already known character of Lorelei Lee and Marilyn Monroe's contradictory 'star image' in *Gentleman Prefer Blondes*, in contrast to the 'perfect fit' between Clark Gable's persona and the character of Rhett Butler in *Gone with the Wind* – but even here the emphasis is on well-established stars, ignoring the possibility that a character might on occasion be equally or better known and of greater commercial importance than the star. See Dyer, *Stars*, pp. 142–9.

36. Mark Salisbury, *Burton on Burton*, rev. edn (London: Faber and Faber, 2000), p. 71.

37. As discussed in 'Dark Star', *Observer*, 5 June 2005, http://www.guardian.co.uk/film/2005/jun/05/features.magazine.

38. I write 'need to know' as opposed to simply 'know'.

39. Andrew Britton, 'Stars and Genre', in Gledhill, *Reinventing Film Sudies*, p. 198.

Chapter 7

1. Internal memo from Harry Kurnitz to Everett Riskinn, headed 'Notes on the Draft of The Thin Man's Rival', 7 May 1942, MGM/Turner Script Files, USC Cinematic Arts Library.

2. See, for example, Henry Jenkins, '"Just Men in Tights": Rewriting Silver Age Comics in an Era of Multiplicity', in Mark Jancovich and Lincoln Geraghty (eds), *The Shifting Definitions of Genre: Essays on Labelling Films, Television Shows and Media* (London: McFarland, 2008), p. 231. See also Steve Neale, *Genre and Hollywood* (London: Routledge, 2000); Barry Langford, *Film Genre: Hollywood and Beyond* (Edinburgh: Edinburgh University Press, 2005), p. 7.

3. Langford, *Film Genre*, p. 1.

4. For an account of this historical turn, see Christine Gledhill, 'Rethinking Genre', in Christine Gledhill and Linda Williams (eds), *Rethinking Film Studies* (London: Arnold, 2000), p. 239. Rick Altman, Richard Maltby, Steve Neale, Lawrence Alloway, Barbara Klinger and Tino Balio have all argued the case for paying close attention to cyclicism. See Richard Maltby, *Hollywood Cinema: An Introduction* (Oxford: Blackwell, 1995), pp. 107–43; Neale, *Genre and Hollywood*, pp. 231–42; Barbara Klinger, '"Local" Genres: The Hollywood Adult Film in the 1950s', in Jacky Bratton, Jim Cook and Christine Gledhill (eds), *Melodrama: Stage, Picture, Screen* (London: BFI Publishing, 1994), pp. 134–46; Tino Balio, *Grand Design: Hollywood as a Modern Business Enterprise, 1930–1939* (Berkeley: University of California Press, 1995), pp. 73–109; Altman, *Film/Genre* (London: BFI Publishing, 1999), pp. 59–62.

5. An early exception to this rule, during what we might call the first wave of genre theory revisionism, were the evolutionary models posited by Thomas Schatz, Jane Feuer, Brian Taves and John Calweti, all of which attempted to chart the process of generic change and transformation. Schatz, for example, identified four developmental stages – experimental, classic, refinement and baroque – and proposed that each genre progresses 'from straightforward storytelling to self-conscious formalism'. As Rick Altman has pointed out, evolutionary models such as this 'paradoxically stress generic predictability more than variation', suggesting a standardised trajectory for genres which bears little resemblance to the 'unexpected mutations' characterising biological evolution. See Thomas Schatz, *Hollywood Genres: Formula, Filmmaking and the Studio System* (New York: Random House, 1981); Altman, *Film/Genre*, pp. 21–2.

6. Barry Grant, *Film Genre* (London: Wallflower, 2007), p. 36.

7. Altman, *Film/Genre*, p. 38.

8. Ibid., p. 43.

9. Balio, *Grand Design*, pp. 179–312.

10. Richard Nowell, *Blood Money: A History of the First Teen Slasher Film Cycle* (London: Continuum, 2011), pp. 44–6.

11. Nowell, *Blood Money*, p. 46.

12. Ibid., pp. 45–51.

13. Altman, *Film/Genre*, p. 117.

14. Roger Ebert, *Chicago-Sun Times*, 1 July 1969, http://rogerebert.suntimes.com/apps/pbcs.dll/article?AID=/19690701/REVIEWS/907010301/1023.

15. See, for example, David Thomson's suggestion that '*Alien* is far more atmospheric and less active than *Aliens*'; and *Empire Online*'s assertion that *Aliens*' strength as a sequel lies in it 'entirely changing

genre, from haunted-house-in-space to balls-to-the-wall action'. Thomson, *The Alien Quartet* (London: Bloomsbury, 1998), p. 96; '50 Greatest Sequels', *Empire*, undated article http://www.empireonline.com/50greatestsequels.

16. Umberto Eco, 'The Myth of Superman', in *The Role of the Reader* (London: Indiana University Press, 1979), pp. 114–24.

17. Ibid., p. 124.

18. These are the arrival of a new character, including a baby; the departure (or death) of an existing character; the relocation of existing characters to another setting and/or set of circumstances; the emergence of a new, completely unrelated case/mission/quest to be solved or undertaken; the return of an old nemesis or problem; or, in a variation of the latter form, a repeat encounter between characters who were dramatically at odds in the previous film.

19. See, for example, Andrew Tudor, 'From Paranoia to Postmodernism? The Horror Movie in Late Modern Society', in Steve Neale (ed.), *Genre and Contemporary Hollywood* (London: BFI Publishing, 2002), pp. 105–16; Paul Wells, *The Horror Genre* (London: Wallflower, 2000); Isabel Cristina Pinedo, *Recreational Terror: Women and the Pleasures of Horror Film Viewing* (New York: State University of New York Press, 1997); Carolyn Jess-Cooke, *Film Sequels* (Edinburgh: Edinburgh University Press, 2009), pp. 52–71.

20. Closer comparison with the first film reveals one particularly glaring, presumably intentional, 'continuity error': on one wall of this new version of Sidney's bedroom hangs a sizeable poster for the rock band Creed. Not only was this poster not a feature of the original decoration (the only poster we see in *Scream* advertises the band The Indigo Girls), but Creed were in fact still unknown at the time of *Scream*'s release, releasing their first album in 1997.

21. Christopher Richards, *The Idea of the Sequel: A Theoretically Orientated Study of Literary Sequels with Special Emphasis on Three Examples from the First Half of the Eighteenth Century,* Unpublished Thesis, University of Leeds, 1989, p. 303.

22. *Rambo: First Blood Part II* grossed more than $150 million in North America and $30 million worldwide, figures which respectively triple and double the totals of the original and which, even allowing for a considerable increase in production budget, suggest that the sequel was at least as profitable as *First Blood. See* Box Office Mojo, http://www.boxofficemojo.com/franchises/chart/?id=rambo.htm.

23. 'Belles on Their Toes: Memorandum on First Draft', 3 April 1951, p. 1, Twentieth Century-Fox Collection, USC Cinematic Arts Library.

24. With domestic rentals of $1.85 million, it was the thirteenth largest Fox release of 1951. See Aubrey Solomon, *Twentieth Century-Fox: A Corporate and Financial History* (London: Scarecrow Press, 1988), p. 224.

25. 'Belles on Their Toes, p. 2.

26. Eco, 'The Myth of Superman', p. 120.

27. Interestingly, with *Skyfall* (2012), the Bond series has again reverted to a more standalone approach, avoiding direct references to the events of the previous two films.

28. As defined by Kristin Thompson in *Storytelling in Film and Television* (London: Harvard University Press, 2003), p. 97.

29. In relation to television, we might note also that the boom in the reality genre since 2000 has created a situation in which aspects of the traditional game-show format have taken on a serialised

form more common to soap opera, as demonstrated by *The Apprentice*, *Big Brother*, *The X-Factor* and so on.

30. On television, see Jason Mittell, 'Narrative Complexity in Contemporary American Television', *Velvet Light Trap* no. 58 (Fall 2006), pp. 29–40; Graeme Turner, 'Genre Hybridity and Mutations', in Glen Creeber (ed.), *The Television Genre Book* (London: BFI Publishing, 2001), p. 6; and Glen Creeber, *Serial Television* (London: BFI Publishing, 2004), pp. 8–10; Sarah Kozloff, 'Narrative Theory and Television', in Robert C. Allen (ed.), *Channels of Discourse Reassembled: Television and Contemporary Criticism* (London: Routledge, 1992), pp. 90–2; Gaby Albrath, Marion Gymnich and Carola Surkamp, 'Introduction: Towards a Narratology of TV Series' in Albrath and Gymnich (eds), *Narrative Strategies in Television Series* (Basingstoke: Palgrave Macmillan, 2005), pp. 1–37. On comics, see Henry Jenkins, '"Just Men in Tights": Rewriting Silver Age Comics in an Era of Multiplicity', in Mark Jancovich and Christine Geraghty (eds), *The Shifting Definitions of Genre: Essays on Labelling Films, Television Shows and Media* (London: McFarland & Company, 2008), p. 234. On video games, see Dan Ackerman, 'What Videogame Sequels Get Wrong', CNET, 21 January 2010, http://news.cnet.com/8301-17938_105-10438325-1.html; Geoff King and Tanya Krzywinska, *Tomb Raiders and Space Invaders: Videogame Forms and Contexts* (London: I. B. Tauris: 2006), pp. 39–54.

31. It is on this basis that the sequel has, since the late 1990s, increasingly come to be conceptualised as a 'brand extension' among academics working in the fields of marketing and economics. See Thorston Hennig-Thurau, Mark B. Houston and Torsten Heitjans, 'Conceptualizing and Measuring the Monetary Value of Brand Extensions: The Case of Motion Pictures', *Journal of Marketing* vol. 73 no. 6 (November 2009), pp. 167–83. Other examples include Joshua Eliashberg, 'Demand and Supply Dynamics for Sequentially Released Products in International Markets: The Case of Motion Pictures', *Marketing Science* vol. 22 (Summer 2003), pp. 329–54; Sanjay Sood and Xavier Dreze, 'Brand Extensions of Experiential Goods: Movie Sequel Evaluations', *Journal of Consumer Research* vol. 33 (December 2006), pp. 352–60; Justin Anderson, 'How Sequels Seduce: Consumers' Affective Expectations for Entertainment Experiences' (PhD dissertation 2007, University of Southern California, Los Angeles).

Conclusion

1. *Romance of Tarzan* review, *WIDS Daily*, 16 October 1918, p. 4.
2. '"Series and Serial" in One New Kalem Plan', *Motion Picture News*, 7 July 1917. Kalem was to be bought later that same year by Vitagraph.
3. In response to a question from the author about the differences between multi-part storytelling in film and television, asked at the 'Joss Whedon: A Life in Pictures' event at the British Film and Television Academy, 14 June 2013.
4. Jason Mittell, 'Narrative Complexity in Contemporary American Television', *Velvet Light Trap* no. 58 (Fall 2006), p. 31.

Select bibliography

Allen, Richard and Smith, Murray, *Film Theory and Philosophy* (Oxford: Clarendon Press, 1997).

Altman, Rick, *Film/Genre* (London: BFI Publishing, 1999).

Anderson, Christopher, *Hollywood TV: The Studio System in the Fifties* (Austin: University of Texas Press, 1994).

Austin, Bruce A., 'Home Video: The Second-run "Theater" of the 1990s', in Tino Balio (ed.), *Hollywood in the Age of Television* (London: Unwin Hyman, 1990), pp. 319–49.

Balio, Tino, *United Artists: The Company Built by the Stars* (Madison: University of Wisconsin Press, 1976).

—— *United Artists: The Company That Changed the Film Industry* (Madison: University of Wisconsin Press, 1987).

—— (ed.), *Hollywood in the Age of Television* (Boston, MA: Unwin Hyman, 1990).

—— *Grand Design: Hollywood as a Modern Business Enterprise, 1930–1939* (Berkeley: University of California Press, 1995).

Barker, Martin and Austin, Thomas (eds), *Contemporary Hollywood Stardom* (Arnold: London, 2003).

Bing, Jonathan, and Hayes, Dade, *Open Wide: How Hollywood Box Office Became a National Obsession* (New York: Miramax Books, 2004).

Bordwell, David, *Narration in the Fiction Film* (London: Methuen, 1985).

—— and Carroll, Noel, *Post-Theory: Reconstructing Film Studies* (Madison: University of Wisconsin Press, 1996).

—— *The Way Hollywood Tells It* (Berkeley: University of California Press, 2006).

——, Staiger, Janet and Thompson, Kristin, *The Classical Hollywood Cinema: Film Style and Mode of Production to 1960* (London: Routledge, 1985).

—— 'Historical Poetics of Cinema', in Barton Palmer (ed.), *The Cinematic Text: Methods and Approaches* (Atlanta: Georgia State University Press, 1988), pp. 369–98.

Bowser, Eileen, *The Transformation of Cinema 1907–1915* (New York: Charles Scribner's Sons, 1990).

Britton, Andrew, 'The Philosophy of the Pigeonhole: Wisconsin Formalism and "The Classical Style"', *CineAction!* (Winter 88/89), pp. 47–63.

Brewster, Ben, 'Periodization of Early Cinema', in Charlie Keil and Shelley Stamp (eds), *American Cinema's Transitional Era: Audiences, Institutions, Practices* (Berkeley: University of California Press, 2004), pp. 66–75.

Budra, Paul and Schellenberg, Betty (eds), *Part Two: Reflections on the Sequel* (London: University of Toronto Press, 1998).

Cook, David A., *Lost Illusions: American Cinema in the Shadow of Watergate and Vietnam, 1970–1979* (New York: Charles Scribner's Sons, 2000).

Cowie, Elizabeth, 'Storytelling: Classical Hollywood Cinema and Classical Narrative', in Neale and Smith, *Contemporary Hollywood Cinema*, pp. 178–90.

deCordova, Richard, *Picture Personalities: The Emergence of the Star System in America* (Urbana: University of Ilinois Press, 1990).

Dominick, Joseph R., 'Film Economics and Film Content: 1964–1983', *Current Research in Film* vol. 3 (1987), pp. 137–53.

Dyer, Richard, *Stars* (London: BFI Publishing, 1979).

Eco, Umberto, 'The Myth of Superman', in *The Role of the Reader* (London: Indiana University Press, 1979), pp. 114–24.

—— 'Innovation and Repetition: Between Modern and Post-modern Aesthetics', *Daedalus* vol. 114 no. 4 (Fall 1985), pp. 161–84.

Eitzen, Dirk, 'Comedy and Classicism', in Allen and Smith, *Film Theory and Philosophy* (Oxford: Clarendon Press, 1997), pp. 394–411.

Epstein, Edward Jay, 'The Midas Formula', *Slate*, 31 May 2005, http://www.slate.com/id/2119701/.

—— *The Big Picture* (New York: Random House, 2005).

Genette, Gérard, *Palimpsests: Literature in the Second Degree* (Lincoln: University of Nebraska Press, 1982).

Glancy, H. Mark, 'MGM Film Grosses, 1924–1948: The Eddie Mannix Ledger', *Historical Journal of Film, Radio and Television* vol. 12 no. 2 (1992), pp. 127–44.

—— 'Warner Bros Film Grosses, 1921–51: The William Schaefer Ledger', *Historical Journal of Film, Radio and Television* vol. 15 no.1 (1995), Appendix 1, pp. 55–73.

Gledhill, Christine, 'Rethinking Genre', in Christine Gledhill and Linda Williams (eds), *Rethinking Film Studies* (London: Arnold, 2000), pp. 221–43.

Gomery, Douglas, *Shared Pleasures: A History of Movie Presentation in the United States* (London: BFI Publishing, 1992).

—— *The Hollywood Studio System: A History* (London: BFI Publishing, 2005).

Grainge, Paul, *Brand Hollywood* (London: Routledge, 2008).

Gunning, Tom, 'Cinema of Attractions', in Thomas Elsaesser (ed.), *Early Cinema: Space, Frame, Narrative* (London: BFI Publishing, 1990), pp. 56–62.

—— 'The Intertextuality of Early Cinema', in Robert Stam and Alessandra Raengo (eds), *A Companion to Literature and Film* (London: Blackwell, 2004), pp. 127–41.

Hagedorn, Roger, 'Technology and Economic Exploitation: The Serial as a Form of Narrative Presentation', *Wide Angle* vol. 10 no. 4 (1988), pp. 4–12.

—— 'Doubtless to Be Continued: A Brief History of Serial Narrative', in Robert C. Allen (ed.), *To Be Continued: Soap Operas around the World* (London: Routledge, 1995), pp. 27–48.

Hall, Sheldon, 'Tall Revenue Features: The Genealogy of the Modern Blockbuster', in Steve Neale (ed.), *Genre and Contemporary Hollywood* (London: BFI Publishing, 2002), pp. 11–26.

—— and Neale, Steve, *Epics, Spectacles and Blockbusters: A Hollywood History* (Detroit, MI: Wayne State University Press, 2010).

Jenkins, Henry, 'Historical Poetics', in Joanne Hollows and Mark Jancovich (eds), *Approaches to Popular Film* (Manchester University Press: Manchester 1995), pp. 99–122.

—— *Convergence Culture: Where Old and New Media Collide* (New York: New York University Press, 2006).

—— '"Just Men in Tights": Rewriting Silver Age Comics in an Era of Multiplicity', in Mark Jancovich and Christine Geraghty (eds), *The Shifting Definitions of Genre: Essays on Labelling Films, Television Shows and Media* (London: McFarland & Company, 2008), pp. 230–43.

Jess-Cooke Carolyn, *Film Sequels: Theory and Practice from Hollywood to Bollywood* (Edinburgh: Edinburgh University Press, 2009).

Klinger, Barbara, 'Digressions at the Cinema: Reception and Mass Culture', *Cinema Journal* vol. 28 no. 4 (Summer 1989), pp. 3–19.

—— *Beyond the Multiplex* (Berkeley: University of California Press, 2006).

Koszarski, Richard, *An Evening's Entertainment: The Age of the Silent Feature Picture 1915–1928* (New York: Charles Scribner's Sons, 1990).

Krämer, Peter, *The New Hollywood: From Bonnie and Clyde to Star Wars* (London: Wallflower, 2005).

Lambert, Josh, '"Wait for the Next Pictures": Intertextuality and Cliffhanger Continuity in Early Cinema and Comic Strips', *Cinema Journal* vol. 48 no. 2 (Winter 2009), pp. 3–25.

Lev, Peter, *Transforming the Screen 1950–1959* (London: University of California Press, 2003).

Lewis, Jon, 'Money Matters: Hollywood in the Corporate Era', in *The New American Cinema* (Durham, NC: Duke University Press, 1998), pp. 87–121.

Londoner, David J., 'The Changing Economics of Entertainment', in Tino Balio (ed.), *The American Film Industry* (Madison: University of Wisconsin Press, 1985), pp. 603–11.

Maltby, Richard, *Hollywood Cinema: An Introduction* (Oxford: Blackwell, 1995).

—— '"A Brief Romantic Interlude": Dick and Jane Go to 3½ Seconds of the Classical Hollywood Cinema', in Bordwell and Carroll, *Post-Theory*, pp. 434–59.

McDonald, Paul and Wasko, Janet (eds), *The Contemporary Hollywood Film Industry* (Oxford: Blackwell, 2008), pp. 120–32.

McDonald, Paul, *Video and DVD Industries* (London: BFI Publishing, 2007).

Meehan, Eileen, 'Holy Commodity Fetish Batman! The Political Economy of a Commercial Intertext', in Roberta E. Pearson and William Uricchio (eds), *The Many Lives of Batman* (London: Routledge, 1991), pp. 47–65.

Mittell, Jason, 'Narrative Complexity in Contemporary American Television', *Velvet Light Trap* vol. 58 (Fall 2006), pp. 29–40.

Monaco, Paul, *The Sixties: 1960–1969* (New York: Charles Scribner's Sons, 2001).

Murray, Simone, 'Brand Loyalties: Rethinking Content within Global Corporate Media', *Media, Culture & Society* vol. 27 no. 3 (May 2005), pp. 415–35.

Musser, Charles, *The Emergence of Cinema: The American Screen to 1907* (New York: Charles Scribner's Sons, 1990).

—— 'Moving Towards Fictional Narratives: Story Films Become the Dominant Product, 1903–1904', in Lee Grieveson and Peter Krämer (eds), *The Silent Cinema Reader* (London: Routledge, 2004), pp. 87–102.

Neale, Steve, *Genre and Hollywood* (London: Routledge, 2000).

—— and Smith, Murray (eds), *Contemporary Hollywood Cinema* (London: Routledge, 1998), pp. 74–90.

Nowell, Richard, *Blood Money: A History of the First Teen Slasher Film Cycle* (London: Continuum, 2011).

Pirie, David, 'The Deal', in *Anatomy of the Movies* (New York: Macmillan, 1981), pp. 40–61.

Prince, Stephen, *A New Pot of Gold: Hollywood under the Electronic Rainbow, 1980–1989* (Berkeley: University of California Press, 2000).

Richards, Christopher, *The Idea of the Sequel: A Theoretically Orientated Study of Literary Sequels with Special Emphasis on Three Examples from the First Half of the Eighteenth Century*, Unpublished Thesis, University of Leeds, 1989.

Schatz, Thomas, *The Genius of the System: Hollywood Filmmaking in the Studio Era* (New York: Pantheon, 1988).

—— 'The New Hollywood', in J. Collins, H. Radner and A. P. Collins (eds), *Film Theory Goes to the Movies* (New York: Routledge, 1993), pp. 8–36.

—— *Boom and Bust: American Cinema in the 1940s* (Berkeley: University of California Press, 1999).

Simonet, Thomas, 'Conglomerates and Content: Remakes, Sequels, and Series in the New Hollywood', *Current Research in Film: Audiences, Economics, and Law* vol. 3 (1987), pp. 154–62.

Singer, Ben, *Melodrama and Modernity: Early Sensational Cinema and Its Contexts* (New York: Columbia University Press, 2001).

Slide, Anthony, *Early American Cinema* (rev. edn) (New York: A. S. Barnes, 1994).

Stacey, Jackie, *Star Gazing* (London: Routledge, 1994).

Thompson, Kristin, *Storytelling in the New Hollywood: Understanding Classical Narrative Technique* (London: Harvard University Press, 1999).

—— *Storytelling in Film and Television* (London: Harvard University Press, 2003).

Verevis, Constantine and Jess-Cooke, Carolyn (eds), *Second Takes: Critical Approaches to the Film Sequel* (Albany: State University of New York Press, 2010).

Wasko, Janet, *How Hollywood Works* (London: Sage, 2003).

Wasser, Frederick, *Veni, Vidi, Video: The Hollywood Empire and the VCR* (Austin: University of Texas Press, 2001).

Wyatt, Justin, *High Concept: Movies and Marketing in Hollywood* (Austin: University of Texas Press, 1994).

—— 'From Roadshowing to Saturation Release: Majors, Independents, and Marketing/Distribution Innovations', in Jon Lewis (ed.), *The New American Cinema* (Durham, NC: Duke University Press, 1998), pp. 64–87.

Index

Note: Page numbers in **bold** indicate detailed analysis. Those in *italic* refer to illustrations. *n* = endnote; *t* = table.

List of Illustrations

Don Q Son of Zorro, Elton Corporation; *The Son of the Sheik*, Feature Productions; *Tarzan Finds a Son!*, Metro-Goldwyn-Mayer; *Shadow of the Thin Man*, Loew's Incorporated/Metro-Goldwyn-Mayer; *The Bells of St. Mary's*, © Rainbow Productions; *Rooster Cogburn*, © Universal Pictures; *Shaft's Big Score!,* Metro-Goldwyn-Mayer/Shaft Productions; *Harry Potter and the Prisoner of Azkaban*, © P of A Productions Limited; *Gremlins 2: The New Batch*, Amblin Entertainment/Warner Bros.; *First Blood*, Carolco Pictures/Anabasis; *Rambo*, © Equity Pictures Medienfonds GmbH & Co. KG IV; *Die Hard 2*, Twentieth Century-Fox Film Corporation; *Terminator 2: Judgment Day*, © Carolco Pictures Inc./© Carolco International; *Aliens*, © Twentieth Century-Fox Film Corporation; *Scream 3*, Konrad Pictures; *Quantum of Solace*, © Danjaq LLC/© Columbia Pictures Industries Inc.